Mandates and Democracy

Sometimes politicians run for office promising one set of policies and then, if they win, they switch to very different ones. Latin American presidents in recent years have frequently run promising to avoid pro-market reforms and harsh economic adjustment, then win and transform immediately into enthusiastic market reformers. Does it matter when politicians ignore the promises they made and the preferences of their constituents? If politicians want to be reelected or see their party reelected at the end of their term, why would they impose unpopular policies? Susan Stokes explores questions of mandates, promises, and democratic theory in light of the Latin American experience. She develops a model of policy switches and tests it with statistical and qualitative data from Latin American elections over the last two decades. She concludes that politicians may change course because they believe that unpopular policies are best for constituents and hence also will best serve their own political ambitions. Nevertheless, even though good representatives will sometimes switch policies, abrupt changes of course tend to erode the quality of democracy.

Susan C. Stokes is Professor of Political Science at the University of Chicago and Director of the Chicago Center on Democracy. Professor Stokes is co-editor of *Democracy, Accountability, and Representation* (1999) and editor of *Public Support for Market Reforms in New Democracies* (2001). She is the author of *Cultures in Conflict: Social Movements and the State in Peru* (1995) and of many articles on democratic theory, political economy, and Latin American politics.

Cambridge Studies in Comparative Politics

General Editor
Margaret Levi   *University of Washington, Seattle*

Associate Editors
Robert H. Bates   *Harvard University*
Peter Hall   *Harvard University*
Stephen Hanson   *University of Washington, Seattle*
Peter Lange   *Duke University*
Helen Milner   *Columbia University*
Frances Rosenbluth   *Yale University*
Susan Stokes   *University of Chicago*
Sidney Tarrow   *Cornell University*

Other Books in the Series

Stefano Bartolini, *The Political Mobilization of the European Left, 1860–1980: The Class Cleavage*
Carles Boix, *Political Parties, Growth and Equality: Conservative and Social Democratic Economic Strategies in the World Economy*
Catherine Boone, *Merchant Capital and the Roots of State Power in Senegal, 1930–1985*
Michael Bratton and Nicolas van de Walle, *Democratic Experiments in Africa: Regime Transitions in Comparative Perspective*
Valerie Bunce, *Leaving Socialism and Leaving the State: The End of Yugoslavia, the Soviet Union and Czechoslovakia*
Ruth Berins Collier, *Paths Toward Democracy: The Working Class and Elites in Western Europe and South America*
Donatella della Porta, *Social Movements, Political Violence, and the State*
Gerald Easter, *Reconstructing the State: Personal Networks and Elite Identity*
Roberto Franzosi, *The Puzzle of Strikes: Class and State Strategies in Postwar Italy*
Geoffrey Garrett, *Partisan Politics in the Global Economy*
Miriam Golden, *Heroic Defeats: The Politics of Job Loss*
Frances Hagopian, *Traditional Politics and Regime Change in Brazil*
J. Rogers Hollingsworth and Robert Boyer, eds., *Contemporary Capitalism: The Embeddedness of Institutions*
Ellen Immergut, *Health Politics: Interests and Institutions in Western Europe*
Torben Iversen, *Contested Economic Institutions*

List continues on page following the Index.

Mandates and Democracy

NEOLIBERALISM BY SURPRISE IN LATIN AMERICA

SUSAN C. STOKES

University of Chicago

CAMBRIDGE
UNIVERSITY PRESS

PUBLISHED BY THE PRESS SYNDICATE OF THE UNIVERSITY OF CAMBRIDGE
The Pitt Building, Trumpington Street, Cambridge, United Kingdom

CAMBRIDGE UNIVERSITY PRESS
The Edinburgh Building, Cambridge CB2 2RU, UK
40 West 20th Street, New York, NY 10011-4211, USA
10 Stamford Road, Oakleigh, VIC 3166, Australia
Ruiz de Alarcón 13, 28014 Madrid, Spain
Dock House, The Waterfront, Cape Town 8001, South Africa

http://www.cambridge.org

First published 2001

Printed in the United States of America

Typeface Janson Text 10/13 pt.   *System* QuarkXPress [BTS]

A catalog record for this book is available from the British Library.

Library of Congress Cataloging in Publication Data
Stokes, Susan Carol.
   Mandates and democracy : neoliberalism by surprise in Latin America /
Susan C. Stokes.
      p.   cm. – (Cambridge studies in comparative politics)
   Includes bibliographical references and index.
   ISBN 0-521-80118-4 – ISBN 0-521-80511-2 (pb.)
   1. Democracy – Latin America.   2. Latin America – Politics and government –
1980–   3. Latin America – Economic conditions – 1982–   4. Latin America –
Economic policy.   I. Title. II. Series.
JL966 .S76   2001
320'.6'098 – dc21   00-065153

ISBN 0 521 80118 4 hardback
ISBN 0 521 80511 2 paperback

This book is dedicated to the memory of my father, Donald E. Stokes, who opened many paths in the study of democracy, and to the memory of Luis Castro Leyva, who struggled to defend it.

Contents

Preface   *page* xi

1   ELECTIONS, MANDATES, AND REPRESENTATION   1
2   ELECTIONS AND ECONOMIC POLICY IN LATIN
    AMERICA   25
3   EXPLAINING POLICY SWITCHES   60
4   ARE PARTIES WHAT'S WRONG WITH DEMOCRACY
    IN LATIN AMERICA?   102
5   NEOLIBERALISM WITHOUT MANDATES: CITIZENS
    RESPOND   122
6   MANDATES AND DEMOCRATIC THEORY   154
7   SUMMARY, PREDICTIONS, UNSETTLED
    QUESTIONS   185

References   197
Author Index   211
Subject Index   215

Preface

In a conversation with a friend in a South American city, I mentioned my interest in the phenomenon of politicians sometimes promising things in campaigns and then, in office, changing course, as did the president of her country when he first took office. Anger flashed across her face, as she blurted out, "It was completely authoritarian what he did, changing like that. It was antidemocratic."

A month later, in the same city, I presented some preliminary research findings at a scholarly seminar. The audience was social scientists and historians of varying political leanings. In their writings, some present had excoriated the government's economic liberalization program and others extolled it. As I read quotes from their president's speeches in the previous presidential campaign, their reaction was not anger of the sort my friend had expressed but irony. Laughter broke out as I read the then-candidate's pronouncements, his promises not to raise prices – as he later did – and privatize industry – as he later would do – and to protect local business against foreign competition – which he later failed to do.

Why was ironic laughter, not anger, the response of this sophisticated audience, who seemed almost to have forgotten the discarded statist identity of the candidate-cum-president? To be sure, many had condemned the change of policies at the time they were announced. But as time passed and the election receded, the political debate was not over consistency and candidates who mislead but over the policies themselves. Were they in the public's interest? Would they promote growth? Price stability? A fair share for the poor?

These varying reactions suggest distinct perspectives on the importance to democracy of consistency between what politicians say when they seek office and what they do once they have attained it. Is democracy tarnished

– perhaps even destroyed – when candidates hide their true policy intentions in campaigns, in effect depriving citizens of a choice over which policies the future government will carry out? If so, my friend's lingering anger seems justified. Or do politicians sometimes have good reasons to hide their intentions? And do citizens' chances to cast judgment on policies at the end of the term compensate for their limited ability to make future-oriented choices? If so, the ironic laughter of my colleagues, caught up as they were in the current actions of the government rather than with what was said in the past, seems appropriate.

This book is an effort to think through the import for democracy of mandates and their violation. I study this question through the lens of economic policy in Latin America. Like Eastern Europe and parts of Asia and Africa, Latin America in the last decades of the twentieth century faced two major challenges: to strengthen and deepen democracy and to stabilize and reorient economic life. Both challenges will persist well into the new century. They are profoundly related. Economic reorientation must be carried out by elected governments, which have to worry about whether the economic changes occurring on their watch will help them or hurt them in the next election. And the manner of economic reorientation may enhance or undermine democratic governance.

My debt to friends, colleagues, and family is large. Adam Przeworski was deeply influential in my formulation of the problem. I profited greatly from conversations with him and with Bernard Manin. The Chicago Center on Democracy was an exciting place to share ideas, and I am grateful to colleagues there for their criticisms and encouragement, in particular (in addition to Przeworski and Manin) to Bob Barros, José Antonio Cheibub, Jon Elster, James Fearon, and Steven Holmes. In Peru, the Instituto de Estudios Peruanos provided a hospitable and stimulating environment; I thank Julio Cotler, Carlos Iván Degregori, and Lucía Romero, among others. In Argentina, Carlos Acuña welcomed me to Centro de Estudios de Estado y Sociedad and kindly offered guidance. In Venezuela, Luis Castro Leyva was the kindest and most empathetic of hosts; he is missed.

Matthew Cleary, Marta Fraile, Pieter Van Houten, José María Maravall, and Andrew Rehfeld commented on chapters, for which I thank them. Several kind souls read and commented on the whole manuscript: Delia Boylan, James Fearon, Mark Hansen, Gretchen Helmke, David Laitin, Steve Pincus, Sybil Stokes, Lisa Wedeen, and Pete Wolfe. I am grateful to

John Carey and an anonymous reviewer for Cambridge University Press for excellent comments and suggestions. Many thanks also to Lewis Bateman, Helen Greenberg, and Helen Wheeler at Cambridge University Press.

This project could not have been carried out without research assistance from a talented set of young scholars. They are John Baughman, Eduardo Guerrero, Alejandro López, María Elena Martínez, Leonardo Pérez Esquivel, Guillermo Trejo, Carlos Vargas, and Patricio Navia.

I gratefully acknowledge financial support from the Social Science Research Council–MacArthur Foundation Program in International Peace and Security, the National Science Foundation (Grant SBR-9617796), and the Social Science Division of the University of Chicago.

The love of my husband, Steve Pincus, and of my son, Sam, are always deeply sustaining.

1

Elections, Mandates, and Representation

Neoliberalism by Surprise

Latin American governments undertook a revolutionary reorientation of their economies in the final decades of the twentieth century, from statist to market-oriented models. They demolished tariff barriers, privatized hundreds of state-owned enterprises, deregulated product, capital, and labor markets, and slashed state employment. What distinguished these from earlier drives toward economic liberalization is that they were carried out by governments that had to win elections before coming to office and knew they would face new elections at the end of their term.

The marriage of economic liberalization and democracy, first considered doomed, has endured. It has not always been smooth. Not all governments promoting liberalization have survived to the next election. Venezuela's Carlos Andrés Pérez (1989–1993) was shaken by two coup attempts by military officers angry about reforms and was later impeached on corruption charges. Austerity measures under President Abdalá Bucaram (1996) in Ecuador set off street protests and were the backdrop to his impeachment less than seven months after he assumed office. Liberalization and its aftermath set off riots and strikes from the Dominican Republic to Argentina. Yet on the whole, what stands out is the endurance of democratic governments. During these revolutionary decades, only two coups d'etat brought down elected governments.[1]

---

[1] The coups were in Peru in 1992 and in Ecuador in 2000. In the Peruvian case the phrase is perhaps not apt, because the Peruvian coup of 1992 was orchestrated by the president against congress.

It would be a mistake, however, to infer that the elected governments that liberalized their economies were simply enacting the people's will. The timing, priorities, magnitude, content, style, and sequencing of economic reform programs are controversial, their distributional impact is potentially powerful, and their public support is mixed. And although this was the era of economic liberalization and democracy, it was not always the era of economic liberalization via democracy. In many countries the neoliberal economic revolution was not approved ex ante by popular mandate. Carlos Menem of Argentina hinted at a moratorium on payments of the foreign debt and, once in office, sent his former right-wing opponent, who had advocated full repayment, to Washington as his chief debt negotiator. Alberto Fujimori of Peru pounded away in his campaign on the theme of "*el anti-shock*" – no surprise price increases – only to institute the largest price adjustment in recent memory 10 days after taking office. And Carlos Andrés Pérez of Venezuela promised an across-the-board wage increase and, once in office, assembled leaders of the private sector to reassure them that no increase was in store. These are just three of a dozen examples that could be mentioned, and they suggest that nowhere was inconsistency more evident than in economic policy.

Figure 1.1 gives a sense of the frequency of divergence of campaign promises on economic policy and the direction of divergence. The horizontal axis locates campaign *messages* of presidential candidates along a continuum, from what I call, following Elster (1995), *efficiency-oriented policies* of market competition to *security-oriented policies* of state intervention. The vertical axis locates early government *policies* along this same continuum. If campaign messages reliably predicted policy, all cases would fall on the 45-degree line. The Latin American cases cluster around this line and in the off-diagonal southeastern region of the figure, indicating a strong thrust toward security-to-efficiency violations of mandate.

The phenomenon of policy switches is broader than Latin America and broader than economic policy. Governments in the advanced industrial democracies usually follow through on campaign pledges; when they don't, they run the risk of stirring controversy. When George Bush in 1990 reneged on his histrionically made "read my lips, no new taxes" pledge, his own partisans were outraged; some claim that his reversal contributed to his failure to win reelection in 1992. A West German social-liberal coalition government reneged in 1976 on a campaign commitment to increase old-age pensions. Governments in New Zealand and Australia in the 1980s

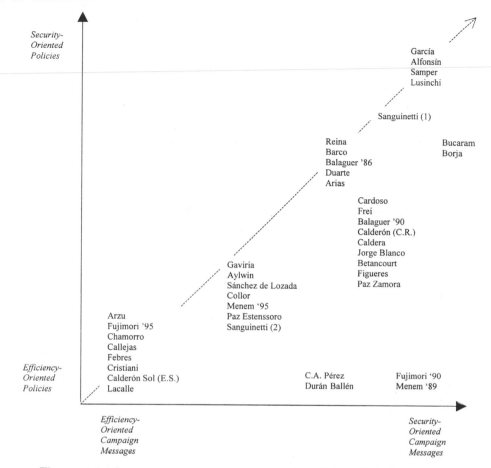

Figure 1.1 Campaign messages and economic policies of Latin American presidents, 1982–1996.

reversed their campaign economic pledges. The mother of a Cambridge, England, schoolgirl whose daughter's scholarship at a private school was phased out took the Blair government to court, citing the Labour Party's campaign pledge to protect the scholarships of current students. The judge in the case agreed with the government that, from a legal standpoint, "pre-election pledges are irrelevant" and that the secretary of state for education was "not bound by himself or others in opposition" and was "also entitled to change policy." But the judge chastised the government:

3

It is a sorry state of affairs when [the Secretary] has to explain away his own letter as mistaken and unclear and a statement by the Prime Minister as an incorrect representation of policy, taken out of context. (Cited in *The Independent*, July 13, 1999)

Similarly, when Latin American governments pursued policies bearing little resemblance to their campaign pronouncements, they opened up a debate about mandates and democracy. By *mandates* I mean the expectations politicians create in campaigns about the actions they will take if they win. On one side of this debate, policy switches were just one more indication that something was seriously amiss in Latin America's democracies. The ideal of representative democracy, in which citizens choose leaders who are then constrained by the institutions of government and by the people's will, was caricatured by senators and deputies isolated from constituents, by courts subservient to the government of the day, and by presidents who ruled not in collaboration with parliaments but by decree, and not by pursuing the policies the people wanted but just the opposite ones. Some observers came to suspect that these were not democracies at all but some other kind of regime. "New Democracies, Which Democracies?" lamented the title of an essay by a Brazilian political scientist (Weffort, 1992); the mood elsewhere on the continent was equally grim.

Observing the violation of mandates, some scholars were driven to the view not, like Weffort's, that democracy in Latin America was an empty set, but that the internal logic of these systems differed fundamentally from that of the *representative* democracies of the advanced industrial world. Because they were fundamentally different they deserved a different name, and Guillermo O'Donnell (1994) gave them one: *delegative democracies*. In representative democracies politicians represent citizens, but in delegative democracies the people elect leaders who then do as they please.[2] "The president is taken to be the embodiment of the nation and the main custodian and definer of its interests. The policies of his government need bear no resemblance to the promises of his campaign – has not the president been authorized to govern as he (or she) thinks best?" (O'Donnell 1994:59–60).

---

[2] The term *delegation* is subject to some confusion. O'Donnell (1994) uses the term to denote politicians who are unconstrained by citizens or political institutions. The more traditional usage, as explained by Pitkin (1967), denotes representatives who are closely guided by the represented, such as delegates who are sent with a specific message or mission by those on whose behalf they are acting.

O'Donnell draws a link between mandates and representation. If the president governs "as he thinks best," voters must be delegating all power to him and negating any place for their views or preferences in the making of policy. If the policies of his government bear no resemblance to the promises of his campaign, he must not be representing.

But other writers have been less troubled by the violation of mandates and unwilling to declare democratic representation stillborn in Latin America. In a thoughtful essay on representation and Latin American politics, Carlota Jackisch enumerates reasons why a government's actions might not conform to the opinions of citizens:

The impossibility that the electors should know the facts implicit in problems, the natural propensity for each individual to feel that the needs which are closest to him should be the highest priorities for the government, and in general the [citizens'] inability to visualize the conjunction of problems and to be aware of the impossibility of maximizing all values simultaneously, all of this argues in favor of a greater independence of those who have to make decisions in the field of politics. (1998:16; author's translation)

Jorge Domínguez (1998), in turn, finds that the damage done to democracy when politicians renege on campaign promises is mitigated by the electorate's ability to make ex post judgments. "Democracy malfunctions when politicians lie, but democracy is self-correcting: It allows the voters to render judgments iteratively" (1998:78–79). And, in his view, policy switchers have frequently passed the accountability test: "Voters later had opportunities to pass judgment on the liars and the relative merits of the programs eventually adopted. In the Dominican Republic and Venezuela, they punished the liar's party in the next presidential elections. In both Argentina and Peru, however, voters approved a change in the constitution to permit the incumbent president's immediate reelection, and then reelected him" (78).

Whereas O'Donnell stresses the fulfillment of mandates as a condition of democratic representation, Domínguez stresses accountability. On one side is the claim that when governments violate mandates, they necessarily fail to represent their constituents. On the other is the claim that the violation of mandates matters little as long as governments can be held accountable.

The argument I will develop in this book is that neither claim is right, although both contain some truth. Governments that want nothing more than to promote the welfare of their constituents may sometimes not only renege on campaign pronouncements, they may in fact dissimulate in campaigns and then switch to unpopular policies. But the fact that representative politicians may violate mandates should not induce complacence about the import of mandates to democracy. First, holding governments accountable is a tricky business, not always easy for voters to manage. Because it is tricky, bad governments as well as good may be tempted to violate mandates. Second, the violation of mandates may indicate that voters are ill informed about the choices they and their country face. Ultimately they cannot make good choices unless they are well informed, and governments that mislead them about these choices may perpetuate misperceptions.

The controversy over whether mandates matter is not new to democratic theory. European and American theorists of representative government in the eighteenth century developed skepticism about the role of citizen opinion as a guide to government policy, skepticism widely associated with the writings of Edmund Burke but shared by other thinkers as well. In Chapter 6, I critically examine the grounds for this skepticism, which relies heavily on ideas of the superior judgment of politicians in comparison to their constituents. This idea of superior judgment coexists uneasily with these thinkers' commitment to the *election* of government by voters.

In the remainder of this chapter, I show that mandate violations present an uncomfortable fact for democratic theory. From the perspective of spatial models of party competition the violation of mandates is puzzling. In these models, candidates who wish to win elections should campaign on popular policies; governments that wish to win reelection should govern with popular policies. The bulk of empirical research supports the prediction that politicians generally pursue policies that they pronounced in campaigns. Yet politicians do sometimes renege on important campaign promises, as the preceding examples suggest and as this book will amply show. In turn, what I call *rent-seeking* models of democracy assume that campaign pronouncements place no constraints, legal or political, on governments. Campaigns are therefore not predictive of governments' policies. Yet this view coexists uneasily with strong evidence that campaigns generally are predictive of policy. We need a deeper understanding of campaign pronouncements and their power to predict policy, and of the conditions under which this power wanes. In achieving such an understanding, we will gain a better grasp not only of mandates, but also of the broader dynamics of democracy.

The discussion that follows will also bring to light limitations of normative democratic theory with regard to mandates and their violation. The prevailing views can be summarized as follows. Either the democratic ideal is one of representatives who are responsive to constituents and hence bound by campaign positions, and democracy achieves this ideal. Or the democratic ideal is one of representatives who act independently of constituents' opinions and are hence unconstrained by campaign statements, and democracy achieves *this* ideal. Or the democratic ideal is one of responsive governments, but in actual practice constituents fail to induce governments to be responsive or to fulfill their promises. I argue, instead, that mandate violations and representation may not be as clearly at odds as these views suggest.

Spatial Models of Democracy and the Puzzle of Mandate Violations

Let us begin with some simple assumptions about politicians and voters. Politicians want to win office, which means that the incumbent party wishes to win reelection and the opposition wishes to win election. Each voter wants the government to act in his or her interest. When deciding whether to vote for the incumbent government or a party of the opposition, voters listen to campaign pronouncements and vote for the candidate whose positions are closest to their own. The party occupying the position closest to the one preferred by a majority of voters wins.

Hence, imagine an election at time t, in which we will assume, for convenience, that there is no incumbent. Parties A and B compete. Party A's policy pronouncements are more in line with a majority of voters' preferences, and A wins. A knows that the policies it campaigned on were popular with voters; that is why it won. Because this party, now in government, wishes to win again at the election that will take place at time $t + 1$, it follows through on its campaign pronouncements. It has no reason not to and, by the assumptions of the model, every reason to do so: this is the surest route to reelection.

Under some modifications that make the model more realistic, parties should still use campaigns to signal their intentions and then follow through on these intentions when they win. Even if voters choose whom to vote for by first evaluating the *performance* of the incumbent (as opposed to its proposals in the reelection campaign), and do so before they listen to the proposals of challengers, Anthony Downs (1957), to whom

7

the model is due, claimed that campaign proposals – both of incumbents and of challengers – will still be predictive of the actions of governments and hence credible to voters.

Downs called the fulfillment of mandates *reliability*; "the absence of reliability means that voters cannot predict the behavior of parties from what the parties say they will do" (105). Reliability, he noted, is desirable. If parties were unreliable, voters would ignore their statements and pay attention only to their actions or the outcomes that they could observe during a government's term in office. But because the opposition may have been out of power for some time, voters will have no rational way to judge it. Therefore rational voting demands reliable parties. But what incentives do parties have to be reliable?

The answer, according to Downs, is that voters prefer reliable parties to unreliable ones. "They would rather vote for a party that can be relied upon to carry out its imperfect proposals than one whose behavior cannot be predicted at all" (107). Why might voters have such a preference for reliability? Downs suggested that reliability makes human relations predictable and hence comes to be valued per se (108). Hence the party that shows itself over time to be reliable will increase its share of the vote, and competition for votes will drive opposition parties to be reliable. And the incumbent party, even though judged more on performance than on pronouncements, may find itself out of office in the future. It therefore also has an interest in building a reputation for reliability by making campaign pronouncements that turn out to be predictive (see also Banks, 1990; Hinich and Munger, 1994).

Evidence that campaigns in the real world are predictive of the policies of governments supports the theory-derived conclusion that politicians in democracies have incentives to reveal their true intentions in campaigns and then follow through on these intentions. Research reveals, with perhaps surprising regularity, that campaign manifestos, slogans, ads, and speeches usually predict well what governments do in office. A number of studies of the advanced industrial democracies explore whether preelection party programs and politicians' campaign announcements accurately predict government policy. Fishel (1985) and Krukones (1984) examine campaign announcements made by presidential candidates in the United States and arrive at estimates of high congruence between announced positions and the policies of the administrations that the successful candidates go on to lead (see also Keeler, 1993; Mayhew, 1974). The Comparative Manifestos Project, a research project comparing the programs and performance of governments in 10 advanced industrial democracies in the post–World War II period, was an effort to answer the question "do party programs predict policy?" Specifically, do changes in party programs over time predict changing government priorities, and do differences between the programs of competing parties predict policy differences when the party in power changes? (see Budge, Robertson, and Hearl, 1987; Klingemann, Hofferbert, and Budge, 1994). Party manifestos predicted policy better in some countries than in others, but in general, governments did what their party manifestos promised. (For a methodological critique, see King and Laver, 1993.)

In addition to their power and simplicity, the attraction of spatial models of party competition lies in their normatively appealing implications. The reliability of parties is one such implication. Another is the *responsiveness* of governments to constituents. By responsiveness I mean the tendency of governments to pursue policies that a majority of voters prefers. If we agree provisionally that the fulfillment of citizens' wishes is an appropriate objective of elected governments, the model is normatively satisfying. As Brian Barry (1977) notes, the drive for power acts on politicians as the profit motive acts on entrepreneurs, keeping the one responsive to citizens and the others responsive to consumers.

From the vantage point of spatial models, governments that ignore their mandates therefore do not merely present a puzzle – what possible strategic considerations might induce such behavior? – they also set off normative alarms. If governments that we would consider "good" (responsive) pursue policies consistent with campaign messages, then inconsistent governments are probably "bad." O'Donnell's proposition, not Domínguez's, would seem to be supported.

Rent-Seeking and the Impossibility of Mandates

Spatial models, then, tend to underpredict policy switches. Rent-seeking models may predict such switches but connect them exclusively with failures of representation. Recall that in the spatial model sketched earlier, politicians are not selflessly public-spirited, but driven by the desire to win and retain office. They pay attention to constituents' opinions because doing so helps their chances of reelection. But what if holding office is more valuable to them when they can use it to do things that constituents would not want them to do? They may wish to shirk, applying themselves with less than full energy to the people's business (Austen-Smith and

Banks, 1989; Banks and Sundaram, 1993; Ferejohn, 1986). They may wish to steal public monies (Stigler, 1975; Tullock, 1988). They may wish to indulge their own ideological principles and pursue unpopular policies (Alesina and Speer, 1988; Banks, 1990; Calvert, 1985; Wittman, 1977). Or they may make concessions to special interests in exchange for campaign contributions (Becker, 1958; Stigler, 1975). I will call governments that pursue these kinds of objectives, at constituents' expense, *rent-seekers* (see Manin, Przeworski, and Stokes, 1999).

Theorists of democracy who emphasize the rent-seeking propensities of politicians tend to view campaign pronouncements as noncredible and therefore the electoral campaign as an unimportant phenomenon.[3] Ferejohn criticized the Downsian paradigm, which he calls the *pure theory of elections*, noting that "little attention is paid to the possibility that, once in office, the politician's preferences may diverge from those of his constituents and that he may therefore choose policies at variance from his platform" (1986:5). Why might rent-seeking governments send misleading signals in campaigns? To get elected, parties would pronounce themselves to be in favor of popular policies. To extract rents, the government might then switch to unpopular policies – say, ones that a special interest favored or ones that the president thought, against public opinion, were best. But doing so would undermine the governing party's credibility in future elections. Why should voters believe future pronouncements if past ones turned out to be misleading?

If voters infer from this experience that no parties' campaign pronouncements are credible, then making false promises won't work the next time around as a strategy to get elected and we no longer have an explanation of policy switches. Alesina (1988) and Alesina and Speer (1988) formally describe an equilibrium of this sort. Individual officeholders have policy preferences at odds with those of the median voter and are indifferent to reelection, and their parties, which have an interest in future electoral victories, lack any means to force them to pursue popular policies.[4] Under these conditions, whatever candidates say, voters always expect them to act according to their own, and not voters', preferences.

---

[3] For exceptions, see Harrington (1993a, 1993b; see Chapter 3) and Canes-Wrone, Herron, and Shotts (1999).

[4] According to Alesina and Speer (1988), officeholders are indifferent to reelection because they are at the end of their careers. These authors also vary their model to consider when parties are able to induce officeholders to pursue the preferences of the median voter.

Candidates therefore announce their real intentions in campaigns, which are at odds with voters' preferred policies. Politicians are reliable but unresponsive.

What happens when rent-seekers are reelectable? They should not, after all, be indifferent to reelection. Their continuing ability to extract rents depends on their continuing hold on office. If voters know whether and at what level officeholders are shirking, stealing, or indulging their idiosyncratic preferences, the threat of nonreelection can induce office-holders to reduce the rents they extract, particularly if voters can agree to a common response (Ferejohn, 1986; Grossman and Noh, 1990). Office-holders would forego rents up to the point at which they are indifferent between reelection and rent extraction in the current term. But this modicum of control over rent-seekers or would-be rent-seekers depends on voters' ability to monitor officeholders, an ability that may be impeded by institutional arrangements and by the cost of information-gathering (Arnold, 1993; Powell, 1990; Stigler, 1975). Even in a world in which voters know a lot about officeholders' actions, we are far from Downs's prediction of responsive policies.

Policy *switches*, as opposed to universally incredible campaign appeals, should happen, according to the rent-seeking models under consideration, when at least some parties make their intentions known in campaigns, others hide them, and voters can't be sure who's revealing and who's dis-simulating. This heterogeneity in campaign strategies might happen if the candidate pool included different types of politicians, some of them in the Downsian mold, who "act solely to attain the income, prestige, and power which come from being in office" (1957:28), others in the rent-seeking mold, with other objectives that they are willing to trade off against holding on to office.[5] Even if voters can extract some information from campaigns useful for discerning one type of candidate from the other, they will sometimes choose badly and elect parties whose pronouncements in favor of popular policies are mere postures. These parties will revert once in office to the actions they or their sponsors really intended. In sum, in rent-seeking models of democracy it is unrepresentative politicians who violate mandates.

---

[5] The difference may also be institutional. Officeholders in a system in which government is closely monitored, say by the press or interest associations (see Arnold, 1993), may simply have no opportunity to extract rents, and hence act like Downsian office-seekers, whereas officeholders in an unmonitored system with the same objective function will have more opportunity to extract rents.

Taking Mandates Seriously

Empirical research, which points in general to the consistency of campaign messages and government policy, warns us against abstract models that can't make sense of this consistency. But I argue in this section that there may be good theoretical reasons as well for considering the signals politicians send in campaigns as informative, if not perfectly predictive – and hence good reasons to consider policy switches as an important (if atypical) phenomenon in need of an explanation.

As we have seen, the trend in contemporary democratic theory has been to downplay the importance of campaign messages and therefore of mandates. Some writers infer from the fact that politicians may have self-interested reasons for not following through on campaign pronouncements (Ferejohn, 1986), or from the fact that mandates are not legally binding in any democratic system (Manin, 1997), that therefore campaign messages reveal little about candidates' real intentions and the policies they will enact. The notion of mandates becomes meaningless. But these inferences are hasty. I show in the following discussion that if voters have good reasons to believe that some parties, at least, will follow through on their pronouncements, then they have good reasons to pay attention to campaigns, even if sometimes they will misfire.

Consider the following situation in which voter i faces a choice between two candidates, one, candidate A, touting policy a, the other, candidate B, supporting policy b. The voter prefers a over b. She knows that, if elected, A will be under pressure to violate his mandate and enact b. Yet if A is still more likely to enact policy a than is B, campaign messages should be incorporated into her decision how to vote.

Recent Latin American politics offers a case in point. Argentine voters who inferred the future course of policy under a Peronist government from Carlos Menem's 1989 campaign were profoundly surprised, as were Peruvians who inferred future policy from Alberto Fujimori's 1990 campaign. The same would have been true of voters in various other countries in the region where presidential candidates ran touting expansionist policies and metamorphosed into neoliberals soon after taking office. Dramatic changes of policy took place after 12 of the 42 elections[6] (see Chapter

---

[6] This figure excludes two elections, one in Honduras in 1985 and the other in the Dominican Republic in 1994, where I was unable to find data on either campaigns or early policy.

Table 1.1. *Presidential Elections and Policy Switches in Latin America's Democracies, 1982–1995*

Country	Year	Country	Year
Argentina	1983	**Ecuador**	1984
	1989 s		**1988 s**
	1995		**1992 s**
Bolivia	1985	El Salvador	1984
	1989 s		1989
	1993		1994
Brazil	1989	Guatemala	1985 v
	1994		1990 v
Chile	1989		1995
	1993	Honduras	1985
Colombia	**1982 s**		1989
	1986		1993
	1990	Nicaragua	1984
	1994		1990
Costa Rica	1982 v	**Peru**	1985
	1986		**1990 s**
	1990 s		1995
	1994 s	Uruguay	1984
Dominican Rep.	**1982 s**		1989
	1986		1994
	1990 s	**Venezuela**	1983
	1994 v		**1988 s**
			1993 s

Notes: s denotes an election followed by a policy switch. v denotes an election after a vague campaign, one in which candidates make no policy proposals.

2 and Table 1.2). And in an additional three cases, campaigns were too vague for voters to infer much of anything about the future course of policy. Hence in 15 elections, the winners' campaign was vague or misleading. In the remaining 27 elections, winners offered an accurate picture of the policies to come.

Latin American campaigns were informative if candidates who would later pursue neoliberal or efficiency-oriented policies were even slightly more likely to announce these policies in campaigns than were candidates who would pursue security-oriented economic policies. A simple application of Bayes's rule illustrates the point. Let {S,E} stand for security or efficiency policies, respectively, that candidates would pursue once in office, and let {"S","E"} stand for the campaign messages of security and efficiency. Let Pr(E) be the prior probability a voter ascribes to any given candidate that he or she will pursue efficiency policies. If this prior probability is based on the proportion of governments pursuing such policies, then Pr(E) = 29/39 = 0.74 (omitting from the sample vague campaigns). If the voter pays attention to campaign messages, then the posterior probability that a candidate will pursue E, having announced "E," is Pr(E|"E") = 1.0 (calculated from data in Tables 1.1 and 1.2). Because 1.0 > 0.74, Pr(E|"E") > Pr(E), the campaign is informative.

Table 1.2. *Campaign Pronouncements and Early Policy in Latin America, 1982–1995*

| Country | Year | Policy Orientation | | Switch? |
		Campaign	Government	
Argentina	1983	Security	Security	No
	1989	Security	Efficiency	Yes
	1995	Efficiency	Efficiency	No
Bolivia	1985	Efficiency	Efficiency	No
	1989	Security	Efficiency	Yes
	1993	Efficiency	Efficiency	No
Brazil	1989	Efficiency	Efficiency	No
	1994	Efficiency	Efficiency	No
Chile	1989	Efficiency	Efficiency	No
	1993	Efficiency	Efficiency	No
Colombia	1982	Security	Efficiency	Yes
	1986	Security	Security	No
	1990	Efficiency	Efficiency	No
	1994	Security	Security	No
Costa Rica	1982	Vague	Efficiency	No
	1986	Security	Security	No
	1990	Security	Efficiency	Yes
	1994	Security	Efficiency	Yes
Dom. Rep.	1982	Security	Efficiency	Yes
	1986	Security	Security	No
	1990	Security	Efficiency	Yes
	1994	Vague	dk	No

| Country | Year | Policy Orientation | | Switch? |
		Campaign	Government	
Ecuador	1984	Efficiency	Efficiency	No
	1988	Security	Efficiency	Yes
	1992	Security	Efficiency	Yes
El Salvador	1984	Security	Security	No
	1989	Efficiency	Efficiency	No
	1994	Efficiency	Efficiency	No
Guatemala	1985	Vague	Efficiency	No
	1990	Vague	Efficiency	No
	1995	Efficiency	Efficiency	No
Honduras	1985	dk	Efficiency	dk
	1989	Efficiency	Efficiency	No
	1993	Security	Security	No
Nicaragua	1990	Efficiency	Efficiency	No
Peru	1985	Security	Security	No
	1990	Security	Efficiency	Yes
	1995	Efficiency	Efficiency	No
Uruguay	1984	Security	Security	No
	1989	Efficiency	Efficiency	No
	1994	Efficiency	Efficiency	No
Venezuela	1983	Security	Security	No
	1988	Security	Efficiency	Yes
	1993	Security	Efficiency	Yes

Note: dk, don't know.

The corresponding prior probability of a candidate's imposing economic security-oriented policies is $Pr(S) = 0.26$, whereas (by Bayes's rule) the posterior probability $Pr(S \mid \text{"S"}) = 0.45$; here again campaign messages are informative.

Thus, even in this informationally impoverished environment, voters who cared about the contours of the next government's economic policies could pick up some clues from campaigns. Voters who feared efficiency-oriented programs were well advised to listen hard for messages indicating a candidate's intention to implement such programs and vote for someone else. Voters who wanted security-oriented policies were well advised to support candidates pronouncing themselves in favor of such policies, even if 12 of the 22 candidates who made such pronouncements later reneged.

Policy intentions are not the only thing campaigns teach us. Since the time of the pioneering work of the Michigan School in the 1960s, and of Murray Edelman (1964), scholars of American politics have depicted voters as motivated by socialization, affect, and identity. These motivations may be purely expressive: there must be moments when voters use elections to express solidarity, rage, or loyalty, without regard for the future. But people also vote on identity and affect instrumentally to achieve a better future. They also try to learn from campaigns about the qualities of the people and parties they are being asked to chose among. Indeed, in addition to communicating policy intentions, another function of campaigns is to impart clues about the qualities of possible future officeholders. Voters who pay attention and select candidates with an eye toward their future behavior can enhance the representativeness of the governments they elect (see Enelow, Endersby, and Munger, 1995; Fearon, 1999).

To illustrate, consider the situation of a voter who knows that politicians are of two types, the *ideologue* and the *power-seeker*, but doesn't know before the campaign how particular candidates sort into these types. He knows that some types of candidates are more likely than others to deviate from their campaign proposals if they win. Four candidates compete; for simplicity we will assume that none is an incumbent. The voter thinks of himself as falling on the left of a left–right ideological dimension. Party labels allow him to locate the candidates on this same dimension. Without any additional information about candidates, the expected utility for the voter i of a term under candidate j is

$$E(u_{i,j}) = p_{Lj}(v_{iL}) + (1 - p_{Lj})(v_{iR})$$

where $p_{(Lj)}$ is the probability of a government under j enacting policies consistent with a left orientation, v_{iL} is the value to i of these policies (or of the outcomes attendant on them), $1 - p_{Lj}$ is the probability of j enacting rightist policies, and v_{iR} is the value to i of rightist policies.

Candidates A and C are known to belong to the Left Party, candidates B and D to the Right Party. Voter i derives utility 10 from the policies a leftist will enact and -10 from the policies of a rightist. He knows that ideological candidates will remain faithful to their announced orientation with a probability of 1.0. Power-seekers will fulfill mandates with a probability of 0.7 and will switch to the opposite orientation with a probability of 0.3. Power-seekers are more likely to stick with their campaign-announced policies than to switch because they believe that these policies will benefit voters and hence improve their reelection chances.

How might campaigns reveal information about the underlying characteristics or *types* of candidates to the attentive public? They display candidates modifying positions in response to poll results or sticking with unpopular views and trying to convince voters that these views are right; they display some politicians as pragmatic and others as driven by conviction; and they give all kinds of clues about the hold of parties over politicians, the internal dynamics of parties, the kinds of constituencies politicians court, and the general competence of people running for office.

Assume for simplicity that the campaign reveals to our hypothetical voter the respective types of each candidate with full certainty, with the following results:

	Left	*Right*
Ideological	*A*	*B*
Power-seeker	*C*	*D*

Because our voter derives utility of 10 from a Left government and −10 from a Right government, the following expected utilities can be assigned to a future government led by each candidate:

	Left	*Right*
Principled	*A* $10(1.0) - 10(0)$ $= 10$	*B* $-10(1.0) + 10(0)$ $= -10$
Power-seeker	*C* $10(0.7) - 10(0.3)$ $= 4$	*D* $-10(0.7) + 10(0.3)$ $= -4$

In this example, the campaign informs the voter that he should vote for *A* over *C*; what's more, he now knows that he should fear a term under the ideological rightist (*B*) more than the power-seeking rightist (*D*), information that may become useful to him should candidates *B* and *D* face each other in a primary or a run-off. To the extent that voters garner information about the reliability of politicians, and hence the probability that they will do what they claim, campaigns permit voters to make better choices. Information revealing other sorts of characteristics about

17

politicians, such as their competence and integrity, will similarly improve voters' choices.

In sum, if all politicians lie in campaigns, voters are unlikely to pay attention to campaign pronouncements, which are reduced to "mere rhetoric." Yet if some politicians dissimulate and others reveal their intentions, voters will pick up clues about future policy from campaigns, as well as other useful information, and hence will rationally pay attention to them.

The thrust of this excursion into models of political economy is to resolve our strategic puzzle – if governments want to win reelection, why would they change course after their campaigns and impose unpopular policies? – by positing bad governments that will occasionally come to power and violate mandates. In what sense are the theoretical policy switchers we have been considering bad? First, they undermine reliability, which, as we have seen, may be of considerable value in social relations and in many normative systems is an inherent good. Second, they are unresponsive, meaning that their policies are out of line with those preferred by a majority of citizens. Majoritarian responsiveness is not usually considered an unalloyed good, but it is generally seen as preferable to alternatives, such as responsiveness to special interests or to no societal interests (see Dahl, 1989). Third, they violate notions of representation, which I define as actions by a government to maximize the welfare of constituents, given the government's beliefs about the impact of its actions on constituents' welfare (see Pitkin, 1967, for a critical discussion and Chapter 6 of this study). The conception of rent-seeking, which, so far in this discussion, lies behind the violation of mandates, is orthogonal to representation. Thus far O'Donnell's intuition, that policy switches indicate the absence of democratic representation in Latin America, seems to be on the mark.

Representation by Dissimulation?

Yet perhaps this is too narrow a standpoint from which to consider mandates and too narrow a standpoint from which to consider the normative qualities of elected governments. Governments that belie their mandates and change course are by definition *unresponsive*: they are acting against current public opinion. But perhaps they are acting in what they believe to be the best interests of constituents, notwithstanding current opinion. Perhaps they are attempting to *represent* their constituents.

18

Consider the following example. A politician runs for office promising expansion of production and employment, security-oriented economic policies. She wins, but learns once in office that she was misinformed about the state of the economy. Perhaps the fiscal deficit was larger than the outgoing government admitted, and given a large deficit, efficiency-oriented measures are required: fiscal austerity and liberalization, measures that will create unemployment, at least over the short term. No new election takes place and no new signal is sent, but the good representative knows that under tight fiscal constraints efficiency is called for, and policies change.

Or perhaps conditions change after the election, again in such a way that efficiency-oriented policies are in the best interest of citizens. Perhaps the world prices of leading exports fall or foreign lending dries up for reasons that have nothing to do with the domestic government's actions. If the changed conditions render the policies announced in the campaign inappropriate, the good representative will violate mandates and change course. She will violate the mandate *in order to be* a good representative.

Under both scenarios, the O'Donnell thesis, that violations of mandates indicate unrepresentative governments, is false.

Finally, consider a politician who runs for president convinced that efficiency-oriented policies will greatly improve the health of the economy. A few tough years are in store, but before his term has expired, growth will resume. He also believes, however, that most voters disagree and will not give him their support if he reveals his true intentions. What are his options? He could act as a passive mirror of the majorities' preferences, increasing his election chances by running on a security-oriented platform and pursuing measures consistent with his platform once in office. The option is unattractive: he believes that these measures are flawed and that voters will not be satisfied with the state of the economy by the end of his term. He wishes to be elected and then reelected; even if he faces term limits, he wants to go down in history as a success. A second option is therefore more attractive: dissimulate in the campaign, switch once in office, and trust that citizens will judge his term as successful ex post even if they would have rejected his policies ex ante.

The candidate facing this dilemma has a third option. He might use campaign messages to impart his information and beliefs to voters, hoping to persuade them that their policy instincts are wrong and that the currently unpopular course will actually turn out for the best. If voters don't come around before this election, perhaps they will two or three elections

19

from now. But if voters' skepticism derives from the association of un-popular policies with rent-seeking politicians, they may write off the honest candidate as a self-deluded ideologue or spokesman for some special interest. To make the point more concrete, consider the politician who believes that opening a previously protected economy to international trade is in the interest of the vast majority of consumers, including his party's working-class constituents. But trade liberalization was the tradi-tional banner of the export bourgeoisie, a sector believed to be indifferent to the welfare of domestic workers – indeed, to have an interest in keeping workers' wages low. In this case he doesn't expect mere words to persuade voters, but he believes that the tangible fruits of liberalization will persuade them that this initially unpopular route was in fact the right one.

The scenario just described salvages a kind of representation in the face of unreliable and dissimulating politicians. But in other ways it does not fit a picture of democracy that is particularly reassuring. Even when politi-cians have good reasons to lie and switch, our intuition is that their actions, though perhaps justifiable, do not improve the quality of democracy. The model of the violation of mandates just discussed involves politicians who believe that citizens' beliefs about the effect of policies on their own future welfare are inaccurate. The politicians may be right, in which case their actions are an effort to represent constituents; but the picture of con-stituents is not reassuring in that they don't fully understand the real choices they face and cannot glean sufficient information from the politi-cal process to fill in the gaps in their understanding. Alternatively, the politicians may be wrong about the effect of policy on citizens' welfare, in which case they are not only paternalistic but incompetent. The O'Don-nell proposition, that violation of mandates signals unrepresentative governments, may be incorrect in a narrow sense. But his intuition that something is amiss in democracies in which politicians violate mandates may nevertheless be right.

Summary

When many Latin American governments quickly abandoned the eco-nomic policies they recently campaigned in favor of, observers feared that these governments were failing to carry out the democratic function of representation. Theories of democracy tended to predict that governments would signal their true policy intentions in campaigns and attempt to carry these intentions out in office. And theories that predicted the violation of mandates linked this violation to governments that were acting against the interests of constituents. Yet we saw that politicians who want to represent may under some conditions hide their intentions and then switch policies in office. These conditions include when, once in office, governments learn that the conditions under which they will have to operate are different than expected in ways that render the old policies inappropriate, and when candidates believe that the policies voters dislike are in fact best for voters, but that their appropriateness will only become evident to voters after they have been implemented.

A Look at What Follows

This book is an effort to explain the sometimes surprising electoral politics of economic policy making and neoliberal reforms in post-debt-crisis Latin America. It is also an effort to explore the implications of Latin American electoral politics and economic change for the quality of democracy in the region and for democratic theory more broadly. When politicians violate their campaign promises, are they responding to special interests or powerful outsiders? Do they anticipate that citizens, informed by the results of policies that they initially fear, will recognize these as in their own interests? Or do they simply hope citizens will forget before the next election? Perhaps term limits and other institutions make them indifferent to citizens' preferences altogether. What are the implications of coalitional politics for economic policy and for the predictiveness of campaigns? Do citizens expect politicians to appeal to them in campaigns and then, once in office, rule as the politician sees fit? Do citizens consider policy proposals at all in deciding how to vote? And do they display inconsistent ex ante versus ex post postures toward pro-market reforms and other economic measures – do their policy preferences change in light of outcomes?

Chapter 2, "Elections and Economic Policy in Latin America," describes party strategy, campaign appeals, and economic policy in several Latin American countries, some in which governments pursued the economic policies they had advocated in the campaign and others in which they switched, not infrequently to policies they had earlier ridiculed. I intend in this chapter to give some understanding of the economic policy debates that surfaced in electoral campaigns and the ways in which these debates informed, or failed to inform, policy making. Against the view that globalization and the debt crisis permitted only one rational response – deep and rapid liberalization – this chapter gives a flavor of the variety of methods proposed for dealing with the crisis.

Chapter 3, "Explaining Policy Switches," makes use of cross-national economic, electoral, and institutional data, along with interviews with and writings of key actors, to develop an explanation of policy switches, one that emphasizes conflicts between elite and mass beliefs about the appropriateness of alternative policies. I evaluate competing propositions. The first one is that politicians who violated their mandates were attempting to represent their constituents, if only to promote their or their parties' future electoral prospects. The second one is that politicians who violated their mandates did so to secure rents, benefits that they enjoy at citizens' expense.

The policy changes I analyze in this chapter are ones that happen straightaway, at the beginning of a new government's term. In putting together a database on policy consistency (described in the next chapter), I coded governments as violating mandates only when they changed course during the first six months of the president's term. This time frame may seem arbitrary; policies change and evolve constantly during governmental terms. The reason for this restriction is theoretical. I am interested in understanding the conditions that induce candidates and parties to reveal their intentions in campaigns and then the conditions that encourage them to follow through on these intentions. As Ferejohn (1995) has noted, studies of campaign-to-policy consistency confound governments that change policies because conditions change with governments that never intended to follow through on campaign pronouncements.[7] By looking at switches that happen early, I am better able to isolate policy switches by governments that failed to reveal their policy intentions in campaigns.

Chapter 4, "Are Parties What's Wrong with Democracy in Latin America?," is a critical appraisal of the claim that weak parties lie at the heart of what is wrong with Latin American democracy. Scholars who make this claim ignore the long line of democratic theorists who viewed parties with skepticism. Two and a half centuries before the recent wave of transitions, when the United States was a new democracy, its institu-

---

[7] Ferejohn's criticism is least apt with regard to the Comparative Manifestos Project, which examined how well changes in party manifestos predicted changes in government budgetary priorities in the first two years of the government's term.

tional engineers tried to write political parties out of the new system. Recent formal theory reinforces some of their skepticism. I present some evidence that parties in Latin America that were relatively strong induced governments to reveal their policy intentions in campaigns, and once in office to follow through on these intentions, whereas policy switches were more likely under relatively weak parties. Yet the deeper normative question – did parties therefore induce governments to represent constituent interests? – depends on one's theory of parties, and we are a long way from having settled this debate.

In Chapter 5, "Neoliberalism without Mandates: Citizens Respond,"[8] I pose the question "Why did voters sometimes not punish politicians for implementing policies that voters initially opposed?" I use survey and electoral data to explore the response of citizens in Latin America to neoliberalism by surprise. In some countries, governments that adopted unmandated policies at the beginning of their terms were greeted with hostility, strikes, even violence, and were readily turned out of office, some even before they had served out their terms. In others, governments that changed just as abruptly enjoyed substantial popularity and, as Domínguez (1998) notes, were rewarded with reelection at the end of the term. Did people change their minds about neoliberalism once they saw its results? When policy-switching governments were reelected, did they draw support from the same constituents and on the same policy dimensions? Or were their ex post judgments driven by other outcomes?

Chapter 6, "Mandates and Democratic Theory," returns to the conceptual and normative questions raised in Chapter 1 in light of the prior analysis of policy change. I review the long-defended principle that representatives should act according to their best judgment, unconstrained by the opinions of constituents. This claim rests on some ideas about the contrasting knowledge and capabilities of citizens and politicians. I outline reasons why constituent opinion and campaign messages should constrain governments, even though good policy-making sometimes requires that governments ignore current public opinion.

Chapter 7, "Summary, Predictions, Unsettled Questions," in addition to summarizing what we have learned about the causes and significance of violations of mandate, signals some further problems. The model of policy switches that I propose in the book fits the Latin American cases well. But

---

[8] This chapter draws heavily on a paper co-authored with John Baughman; see Stokes and Baughman (1999).

it begs questions about where politicians' beliefs come from, how their competitive discourse influences voters' beliefs, and why politicians' beliefs are frequently wrong. A full theory of democracy must grapple with these questions.

2

Elections and Economic Policy in Latin America

The last two decades of the twentieth century were the era of new democracies and new market economies. But democracy was not always the road to the market. It was not if by democracy we have in mind government by popular will. Nowhere did the tension between the people's will and market transformation rise to the surface more frequently than in Latin America. Some politicians, it is true, won elections after campaigning in favor of efficiency-oriented policies – reducing the size of the state, privatizing state-owned enterprises, and opening trade – and once in office actively pursued this agenda. Other politicians won after campaigning in favor of security-oriented policies – job creation, industrial policy, and a gradualist approach to inflation stabilization – and once in office carried out *these* policies. Still a third set of politicians won after making only the vaguest of campaign pronouncements, ones from which even the most attentive voters would garner little about the policies the candidate would pursue in office. Finally, a sizable minority of Latin American presidents ran for office pronouncing themselves in favor of security-oriented policies, only to switch to an efficiency-oriented agenda once in office.

The reaction of citizens to liberalization, preannounced or not, also varied. Some governments that embarked on pro-market reforms went down to defeat, whether by impeachment or at the ballot box. Public opinion deemed others a success. Paradoxically, two politicians who had campaigned most strenuously in favor of security-oriented policies and switched to radical efficiency programs were by the end of their first term among the most popular on the continent, rewrote their constitutions so that they could run for reelection at the end of the term, ran, and won.

A full account of the electoral politics of economic policy making would answer the following questions: Why do some politicians campaign promising efficiency-oriented reforms, others security policies? What determines who wins? Why do politicians sometimes send signals to voters about their policy intentions that turn out to be accurate predictions, and why do they sometimes send signals that are not remotely predictive of the policy course they embark on once elected? And what determines people's responses, both to policies per se and to the consistency or lack thereof of the government?

As a first step toward answering these questions, this chapter provides sketches of the varying electoral contexts of economic policy making in Latin America since the onset of the debt crisis in the 1980s. These sketches begin to suggest some answers to the questions. We shall see that certain economic conditions increase the probability of electoral victory of candidates espousing alternatively security- or efficiency-oriented programs. Although we would expect politicians to adjust their campaign proposals accordingly, they do not always do so, and we shall begin to get a sense of some reasons why. Questions of credibility, of the advantages of pursuing policies preferred by markets, and of the competitiveness of races all come into play in shaping the policy signals that candidates send to voters.

The discussion is structured around the four campaign-to-policy trajectories laid out earlier. I first discuss politicians who came to office pronouncing themselves neoliberals and pursued a neoliberal program from the outset; my research identifies 17 in all. Next, I turn to politicians (10) who offered security-oriented policies to voters in the campaign and followed through on these pronouncements once in office. I then offer evidence of politicians who came to office without having offered any discernible policy proposals (four). Finally, I discuss a fourth kind of politician, one central to my theoretical concerns. This is the politician who pronounced himself[1] in favor of security-oriented policies in the campaign and then shifted, usually immediately but always within months of the inauguration, to an efficiency-oriented program.[2] My research identified

---

[1] Latin America had one woman president in this period, Violeta Chamorro of Nicaragua (1990–1996), who promised efficiency-oriented policies and stuck with her promises early on.

[2] Some welfare-oriented politicians gravitated toward an efficiency-oriented program after several years had elapsed. For example, Peru's Alan García (1985–1990) shifted from expansionist policies to austerity in 1988. I do not consider these as cases of policy shift, saving

Table 2.1. *Early Government Policy, by Consistency with Campaign Pronouncements*

	Early government policies	
	Efficiency-Oriented	Security-Oriented
Consistent with campaign	17 (59%)	10 (100%)
Switch from campaign	12 (41%)	0 (0)
TOTAL	29 (100%)	10 (100%)

Vague or no information: 5

12 new presidents who violated their promises about economic policy (see Table 2.1).

Consistent Efficiency-Oriented Politicians

A cursory examination of some of the governments that promised efficiency policies, won, and carried these policies out (or tried to) underscores the importance of crisis economic conditions in persuading voters to support neoliberalism. Indeed, the large literature on the politics of economic reforms frequently repeats the view that economic crisis makes otherwise unpopular reforms palatable (Alesina and Drazen, 1991; Dornbusch and Edwards, 1991; Edwards, 1995; Geddes, 1994; Grindle and Thomas, 1991; Haggard and Kaufman, 1992, 1995; Nelson 1990, 1992; Tommasi and Velasco, 1996; for a review see Tommasi and Velasco, 1995). On this formulation, an inherited set of ill-advised policies, unfavorable shifts in the terms of trade, rising world interests rates, and ultimately the drying up of foreign sources of finance produced fiscal crises, inflation, currency instability, and falling output, which in turn forced governments toward reforms. In a general assessment of democracy and markets in the region,

the category for politicians who renege on campaign pronouncements early. As explained in Chapter 1, my theoretical interest is in the conditions that induced politicians to reveal their intentions in campaigns and then to act on those intentions in office. When governments later changed course, this was in response to changed conditions; in García's case, to an inflation and balance-of-payments crisis – partly exogenous, partly the perverse result of García's policies – that the candidate and his advisors appear not to have anticipated early.

Domínguez writes, "the great Latin American depression of the 1980s ... forced many to reassess their basic assumptions about the statist, import-substitution policy framework that had prevailed for decades" (1998:72).

Refitted to take into account the electoral context, the hypothesis is that adverse economic conditions induce voters to elect neoliberal governments, which then pursue efficiency-oriented programs.

To test this hypothesis, I analyze the impact of economic conditions on electoral outcomes in 44 Latin American presidential elections. The data are from the Latin American Campaign and Policy (LACAP) database, a cross-national statistical database I constructed. The LACAP database includes observations for all competitive presidential elections in Latin America between 1982 and 1995. I culled information from published sources (newspapers, transcripts of campaign speeches, and party manifestos) concerning the economic policy positions of the major presidential candidates. This information permitted a coding of the winning candidates' campaigns, according to the expectations of future policy that they would have created among attentive voters. All campaigns were coded as either efficiency-oriented, security-oriented, or too vague to create any expectations as to the direction of future policy. Published information, the secondary literature, and in some countries interviews with government officials allowed me to code each government as pursuing an initial set of economic policies that were security- or efficiency-oriented. The combination of the two codings, of campaigns and then of early policy, allowed me to classify each government as acting consistently with its campaign or as switching policies once in power (vague campaigners were treated separately). The LACAP database also incorporated information about economic conditions and about political outcomes and institutions.

Treating economic policy as though it were dichotomous, either efficiency- or security-oriented, obviously fails to capture a more complex reality. In the real world these policies are matters of degree; governments often employ admixtures, for example of employment programs along with austerity; they may liberalize trade but hesitate to privatize state firms; and so on. Yet the difficulty of quantifying the degrees of security or efficiency counsels against continuous codings and in favor of reducing positions to a dichotomous choice. And political discourse tends to frame complex proposals in terms of simple choices, often between statist and pro-market orientations.

Table 2.2. *Probit Model of Security-Oriented Candidate, 38 Observations*

Variable	Coefficient	Std. Error	z-Stat.	Prob$|z| \geq x$
Constant	0.43	0.53	0.81	0.47
GDP[a]	−0.21	0.09	−2.23	0.03
Inflation[b]	−0.4E−4	0.2E−4	−2.00	0.05
Transition[c]	0.08	0.03	2.58	0.01
Margin[d]	−0.07	0.04	−2.00	0.05

Maximum likelihood estimates
  Log-likelihood   −15.11
  Restricted (slopes = 0) log-l.   −25.86
  Chi-squared (4)   21.50
  Significance level   0.0003
  Pseudo-R^2 = 0.42

Frequencies of actual and predicted outcomes

Predicted outcome has maximum probability.

Actual	Predicted 0	1	TOTAL
0	12	4	16
1	3	19	22
TOTAL	15	23	38

[a] Average annual percentage change in GDP in the two years before the year of the election. Source: *International Financial Statistics*, IMF.
[b] Average inflation rate in the two quarters leading up to the election. Source: *International Financial Statistics*, IMF.
[c] Number of years since the return to democracy.
[d] Difference in vote share going to the winner and the second-place candidate.

As evidence in favor of the hypothesis that economic crisis in an undifferentiated sense produced neoliberal policies, we would expect bad economic conditions to precede the election of efficiency-oriented candidates, good conditions to precede the election of security-oriented candidates. To test this hypothesis, I estimate a probit model in which the dependent variable is the probability of a security-oriented candidate being elected. The independent variables include the average inflation rate in the four quarters leading up to the election (Inflation) and the average percentage change in the gross domestic product in the two years leading up to the election (GDP).[3]

---

[3] The model also estimates the impact of the difference in the share of the vote going to the two top candidates on the probability of election of an efficiency-oriented politician

Voters elected security-oriented candidates when inflation fell, as predicted. But, contrary to the hypothesis implicit in the studies cited earlier, people didn't turn to neoliberal reformers as a way out of recession. Under conditions of slow growth they turned instead to security-oriented candidates. Voters behaved as though they lived under the Phillips curve and had to trade off inflation and unemployment. They turned to neoliberal reformers as an antidote to inflation and to expansionists as an antidote to slow growth. Note that not in all cases did people face a Phillips curve trade-off between inflation and output or unemployment. During bouts of hyperinflation, such as in Bolivia in the early 1980s and in Nicaragua, Peru, and Argentina in the late 1980s, output also fell. But under conditions of stagnation and relatively low inflation, security-oriented policies were the preferred instrument for economic improvement. And under conditions of growth with higher inflation, efficiency policies were seen as an instrument for fighting inflation. Hence, the view that crisis induces efficiency policies is not wrong, but it is insufficiently specified.

Fernando Collor of Brazil (1989–1993) exemplifies a neoliberal candidate who won under conditions of growth and inflation. When Collor defeated his opponent, Luiz Ignacio "Lula" da Silva, the Brazilian economy was expanding at an annual rate of 3%, impressive by regional standards in this period. But inflation averaged 240%. Ernesto Lacalle of Uruguay (1989–1994) was another efficiency-oriented politician who came to power under conditions of relatively strong growth with high inflation. In the 1989 presidential campaign, Lacalle of the Blanco Party (more conservative than the Colorados) declared that a "free exchange rate, open economy, free and unrestricted flow of capital stocks and returns are aspects that we are going to keep until death and we are deepening them even more" (*El Día*, November 23, 1989). He also called for limits on the right to strike, a reduction in the ratio of state workers among the total workforce to 1 in 10, and a broad privatization of state-owned enterprises. Lacalle won the election with 39% of the popular vote; once in power, the Lacalle government followed through on his campaign pronouncements.

(MARGIN) and the number of years that elapsed between the transition to democracy and the election (TRANS). These effects are discussed later in this chapter and in Chapter 3. International reserves and deficits, and the rate of devaluation or revaluation of the exchange rate in the quarter before the election – not shown – had no impact on election results.

If high inflation favored neoliberal candidates, why didn't candidates converge on a neoliberal program when inflation was high? Sometimes they did. In Uruguay in 1989, Lacalle's major opponent, Jorge Batle of the Colorados, described himself as a "libertarian radical-liberal" (an unorthodox self-description for a Colorado), inveighed against state intervention, and contended that "where systems of market economies have been applied, the lowest unemployment rates have been achieved" (*Visión*, November 13, 1989).

In some settings, then, the answer to the question "Why did some candidates offer efficiency proposals and win?" turns on economic conditions and the policy preferences these conditions induced in voters. Yet politicians favoring efficiency-oriented policies sometimes won even though voters' ideal point probably lay further in the direction of security-oriented economic policies.[4] One anchor that kept candidates from shifting in pursuit of votes was their own ideology and that of their constituents. Consider again the Brazilian election of 1989. It seems ludicrous to imagine Lula shifting to a campaign posture of neoliberalism. His ideological commitment to redistribution and statist protections was shared by his labor constituents and other allies; a drastic programmatic change would have sheared away these constituents (see Keck, 1992; see also Przeworski and Sprague, 1986). Even if Lula had tried such a feat, it is doubtful that he would have been taken seriously.

Credibility problems were at the heart of the inability of candidates to shift campaign positions, even when they did try. In more general terms, we can see that the problem of credibility of campaign pronouncements forced some politicians to reveal their true policy intentions, reducing the likelihood that they would renege on their pronouncements once in power.

---

[4] Students of U.S. politics have used mass public opinion data, combined with systematic ratings of the policy positions of legislators (such as Americans for Democratic Action ratings) to measure the distance between constituents' ideal points and the roll-call behavior of their representatives. See Achen (1978), Bartels (1991), Jackson and King (1989), Miller and Stokes (1966), Page and Shapiro (1992), Stimson, MacKuen, and Erickson (1995). My study makes extensive use of public opinion data from several countries to get at the response of public opinion to government policy (see Chapter 5). But because of data limitations, I have not undertaken anything like the systematic assessment of the relative positions of voters and politicians of the American studies. Statements here concerning these positions draw from some polls, from a more qualitative assessment of campaign pronouncements and government policies, and from the opinions of country experts.

Credibility as an inducement to the revelation of true intentions is apparent in two cases considered here. In one, Chile, the eventual loser's lack of credibility when he tried to refashion himself helps explain how his opponent could win even though he espoused a less redistributive program than most voters wanted. In the other, Nicaragua, the eventual loser anticipated losing credibility if he tried to shift to more popular campaign positions.

The Pinochet regime in Chile had in the 1970s undertaken the first Latin American neoliberal revolution, opening the economy to foreign trade, privatizing nearly 500 firms, and liberalizing capital and labor markets. The great achievements of the Pinochet model were price stability and sustained growth rates for much of the 1980s, with the notable exception of a steep recession in 1982–1983. Yet liberalization imposed a heavy price on the Chilean working class: poverty increased from 17% to 45% between 1970 and 1985, and unemployment rose to 20–25% in Greater Santiago (A. Barry, 1997; see also Graham, 1991).

The record of growing poverty and unemployment left Chileans of modest means anxious for policies that would cancel Chile's "social debt," even if that meant countenancing somewhat greater macroeconomic instability. Opinion polls taken between 1986 and 1991 found a majority among the lower income groups opposed to many dimensions of liberalization (see Arriagada and Graham, 1994). *Concertación*, the alliance of Christian Democrats and Socialists who united around the presidential candidacy of Patricio Aylwin, conducted its own polls, which showed a majority of voters more concerned with unemployment, personal indebtedness, and poverty than with inflation (Angell and Pollack, 1990). Hence one might have expected *Concertación* to pursue votes by marking strong differences with the regime and the partisan right, calling for redistributive policies and for dealing with the social debt. But Aylwin pronounced himself in favor of only moderate alterations in the economic model.

Concertación's manifesto stressed the needs of the poor and of workers and called for raising the minimum wage, but "in line with the possibilities of the economy" (cited in Angell and Pollack, 1990:12). It also called for sound macroeconomic management and extolled the virtues of the model crafted by the military regime. On the campaign trail as well, Aylwin was at pains to make clear his intention not to reverse the neoliberal model, and indeed to drive it further. At a forum with members of the private sector, Aylwin declared, "We will maintain a policy of external openness, fomenting exports, and . . . tariffs will be low and uniform" (FBIS, November 27, 1989). In a debate among presidential candidates, he enumerated the economic achievements of the military regime: "the opening of trade, the diversification of exports and their increase, macroeconomic equilibrium, the containment of inflation to reasonable terms" (*El Mercurio*, October 10, 1989).

Why did *Concertación* favor policies eccentric with regard to the preferences of voters, including those of its own constituents? The conversion of leading Socialists and Christian Democrats to many aspects of Pinochet's economic model has been widely commented on (see Silva, 1996). To the extent that *Concertación's* campaign program reflected its leaders' beliefs about the positive welfare effects of continued free market policies, a call to scrap the inherited model was unlikely.

Concertación's leaders also operated under the shadow of the military regime. The probit model estimated in Table 2.2 suggests that, across the range of Latin American presidential elections, security-oriented politicians were favored in the later years after the fall of military regimes. Recall that the variable "Transition," measuring the number of years since the first postmilitary election, was positively and significantly related to the probability of the election of a security candidate. In Chile, with the plebiscite having ended military rule only a year earlier, and the former dictator still serving as commander-in-chief of the armed forces, *Concertación's* strategy was "to avoid a military–business alliance, which would form if private property were threatened in any way" (Arriagada and Graham, 1994:265). According to Alejandro Foxley, an economist who would serve as Aylwin's finance minister, *Concertación's* opposition to Pinochet meant that its main problem was to "maintain investor confidence and avoid an antagonistic relationship with businessmen" (cited in Silva, 1996:311). Fearing a military–business alliance that might favor another coup if the new government's policies strayed far from the received neoliberal model, the Christian Democratic–Socialist coalition wished to convince the private sector that business conditions would not deteriorate on its watch. The effort was a success, and bond and currency markets rallied in the days following the election.

Had Aylwin faced more intense competition from the right – had the right's attempt to shift campaign positions been more credible – he might have edged closer to the redistributive positions many Chileans desired. And had Aylwin shifted policy positions in the campaign, he might have found it difficult to follow through on his pronouncements. As it was,

33

public opinion polls from the beginning of the campaign showed that Aylwin and *Concertación* were well ahead; and the freshness of victory of the "No" vote in the 1988 plebiscite on continued military rule gave Aylwin added confidence. Aylwin acted "as if the election were a foregone conclusion and as if he were president-elect" (Angell and Pollack, 1990:13). And indeed Aylwin won easily, with 55% of the vote to 29% and 15% for his two right-wing opponents.

The Aylwin campaign's policy pronouncements predicted well the Aylwin government's economic and social policies. The administration pursued macroeconomic stability and deregulation and pushed forward with trade liberalization. At the same time, it produced a more progressive tax code, returned some bargaining rights to workers, expanded social expenditures, and put an antipoverty program in place (see Bosworth, Dornbusch, and Labán, 1994; Hojman, 1990; Silva 1996; for a critical view see Petras and Leiva, 1994).

If *Concertación*'s campaign proposals were not in line with those preferred by the median voter, why did the coalition enjoy such an enduring advantage over the right? The answer is that the right's candidate was linked in the public's mind with the former dictatorship and its policies. This link kept the right from leapfrogging leftward over *Concertación* to take advantage of the gap between *Concertación*'s policies and those preferred by most voters. The right tried to leapfrog. The campaign manifesto of Hernán Büchi, presidential candidate of the *Democracia y Progreso* coalition, called for a million new jobs, private health facilities for all, 100,000 new homes each year, and personal debt reduction programs. Yet Büchi had served in the Pinochet government since 1975, most recently as finance minister; voters doubted that he had really changed into a populist. As Angell and Pollack note, "The economic program produced a reaction of incredulity in some sectors, for here was the austere former Finance Minister far outdoing the opposition in his promises" (1990:12).[5]

Thus, Chile presents us with a case in which the winning party believed that efficiency policies were optimal, perhaps because they would induce

---

[5] Other factors also worked against the right. One was disunity, which seems to increase in inverse proportion to a political force's probability of gaining power. Chile's "binomial" electoral system fostered rivalries between candidates from the same lists. Finally, Büchi had to stave off the challenge of another rightist candidate, Francisco Javier Errázuriz. And Büchi seemed to lack conviction in the campaign, at one point quitting because of a lack of "political vocation" (*contradicción vital*; Angell and Pollack, 1990:8).

optimal economic performance but certainly because diverging from these policies would, party leaders thought, threaten democracy. The major losing party tried to take advantage of the gap between the median voters' ideal point and the position of its opponent but was unable to do so because few people believed it when it tried to adopt a more moderate position. Knowing it faced no credible threat, the eventual winner could safely reveal its policy intentions, even though these diverged in significant ways from what a majority of voters wanted.

The Nicaraguan presidential election of 1990 tells us much about politicians' perceptions of the benefits and risks of changing their positions in the campaign. In a close race, a candidate who changes to a popular position may gain enough votes to win. But a risk is that voters may not believe that the candidate intends to carry out her newly adopted policies. Voters may punish the politician whom they see as vacillating or unreliable. Another risk is the alienation of party activists whose preferences may differ from those of voters. A third risk is that even if voters believe the promise to adopt a popular policy, the government might have to renege on the promise and hurt its longer-term electoral prospects.

In Nicaragua in 1990, Violeta Chamorro of the National Opposition Union (UNO) coalition, the candidate who represented efficiency-oriented policies, beat Daniel Ortega of the Sandinista Front for National Liberation (FSLN), the candidate more attuned to economic security. Chamorro initially sent efficiency-oriented signals during the campaign. But as much as Nicaraguans cared about the economy, they cared more about peace, and they understood that peace was a precondition for any hope of economic recovery (Oquist, 1992; see also Conroy, 1990).

Neither the war nor the economy worked to the advantage of the incumbent Sandinistas. By 1985, the Sandinista government had already attempted to correct macroeconomic and external imbalances with a program of austerity and fiscal adjustment. It again imposed orthodox austerity programs in 1988–1989 (see Stahler-Sholk, 1990). But the government spent much of its budget on defense. The government drastically cut nondefense spending, and the deficit fell from 26% of GDP in 1988 to 5% in 1989. The balance of payments, however, remained under pressure in a hostile international financial and trade environment.

Many Nicaraguans blamed the foreign-financed war and trade embargo for the economic fiasco (Oquist, 1992). But without a credible scenario for future improvement, even voters who exonerated the government had little reason to vote for it.[6] The FSLN's campaign slogan, "*Con Nosotros, Todo Será Mejor*" ("With Us, Everything Will Be Better"), had a hollow ring. In a postelection survey, 75% of respondents agreed with the statement "If the Sandinistas had won, the war would never have ended" (Oquist, 1992:31).

Chamorro's ability to end the war, rather than her economic proposals, attracted voters. These proposals were not designed for mass appeal; rather, they reflected the convictions of her economic policy team, led by Francisco Mayorga, and those of the more conservative parties in the alliance, led by Virgilio Godoy's Independent Liberal Party (PLI). Chamorro's program proposed to freeze government spending, eliminate subsidies, privatize most state agencies and enterprises, and break up collective farms into individual parcels. Polling data showed that the privatization and parcelization proposals, particularly the promise to privatize Areas of People's Property, made many voters fear that Chamorro's government would dismantle the most popular social achievements of the revolution (Oquist, 1992). The Sandinistas tried to take advantage of these fears. But the longing for peace trumped economic concerns.

In February 1990, Chamorro defied opinion polls by winning the election, 54% to Ortega's 41%.

For theoretical purposes, it is instructive to consider the Sandinistas' position on the Chamorro promise to end the draft immediately if she won the election. Ortega refused to make the same promise. Why was Ortega unwilling to shift to a position that was so popular? Nationalism and anti-imperialism made the FSLN reluctant to appear to back down against an imperialist aggressor. But many politicians bury their own preferences to get elected, and then either implement policies they disfavor or do after-election about-faces. Why did Ortega persist in making public his true policy intentions?

A critical factor was that most people, including most Sandinistas, believed that Ortega was likely to win. Most public opinion surveys predicted Ortega's victory (for a discussion see Oquist, 1992). This percep-

---

[6] To the extent that the FSLN provided a narrative in which its victory in 1990 might resolve the economic and security crises, it was as follows: because the opposition had participated in this election, the U.S. government would have to recognize the election as fair and the Sandinista government as democratic (in the previous national election, in 1984, opposition forces had withdrawn). But sections of the FSLN's party manifesto devoted to the issue of pacification are significantly silent on strategy vis-à-vis the United States (see FSLN, 1990).

tion made the risks attached to abandoning his position in pursuit of votes more salient than the advantages. In an interview after the election, Ortega explained that "the Sandinistas might not [have been] able to stick to such a commitment" once in office. Ortega believed voters would see his shift on the draft issue "as a cheap campaign trick" and therefore would not vote for him anyway (quoted in Barnes, 1992:103).[7] In short, Ortega doubted that voters would find an FSLN commitment to end the draft credible, worried that the effort might tarnish his reputation, and foresaw that sending this campaign signal might put him in the position of later reneging, and hence damaging himself and his party. The experience of other politicians suggests that had Ortega known toward the end of the campaign that he was about to lose, he might have shifted toward voters' ideal point on the draft, creating the expectation of a policy that he then would have been likely to violate.

Chamorro's campaign pronouncements were borne out by early UNO government policy. She appointed Mayorga Central Bank president. Mayorga imposed an austerity program, including an immediate 50% devaluation of the córdoba, a reduction of corporate taxes, and mass layoffs of state workers following the repeal of job security legislation passed under the Sandinistas. Reacting to the layoffs and to the privatization and parcelization policies, the pro-Sandinista National Workers' Front (FNT) led a series of strikes in May and July. Strikers were encouraged by continued FSLN control of the armed forces.

The strikes forced Mayorga to resign and the government to compromise with the Sandinistas over economic policy. Antonio Lacayo replaced Mayorga as chief economic architect. The government and the Sandinistas agreed to delay layoffs, lengthen the timetable for introduction of a new currency, and initiate state investment programs in selective agricultural sectors. Detractors on both sides decried the concertation agreements as "co-government." Another round of concertation talks and a second Lacayo plan in mid-1991 created enough stability for International Monetary Fund (IMF) standby loans and an Enhanced Structural Adjustment Facility loan in September (Stahler-Sholk, 1995).

---

[7] Analysts have long debated why polls that gave Ortega a large lead were so far off. Some claim that Nicaraguans were too intimidated by pro-Sandinista pollsters to reveal their true intentions. Yet this claim is belied by many respondents' highly critical statements about the government, including those by many who said that they planned to vote for Ortega. A more likely explanation is that the deep ambivalence about the Sandinistas induced indecision until very late. See Greenberg, cited in Barnes (1992).

Chamorro's modification of the neoliberal program six months into her administration is notable because it was a shift away from efficiency-oriented reforms in favor of security policies. Little mystery surrounds Chamorro's policy changes in late 1990. Powerful forces opposed UNO's initial hard-money policies. These forces drew strength from several conditions in this postrevolutionary state: continued strength of the party of the revolution, which remained the single largest party in the legislature; close ties between this party and the major labor confederation, which could carry out paralyzing strikes; and FSLN control over the armed forces. This was an unusual historical legacy in Latin America and one that forced a partial shift away from radical liberalization of the economy.

Consistent Security-Oriented Politicians

Some Latin American politicians, swimming against the current, announced their intention to pursue security-oriented policies in campaigns and as president made good on these announcements. My research identifies 10 such cases: Raúl Alfonsín of Argentina (1983–1989), Virgilio Barco of Colombia (1986–1990), Ernesto Samper of Colombia (1994–1998), Oscar Arias of Costa Rica (1986–1990), Joaquín Balaguer of the Dominican Republic (in his first term in this period, 1986–1990), Napoleón Duarte of El Salvador (1984–1989), Carlos Roberto Reina of Honduras (1993–1997), Alan García of Peru (1985–1990), Julio Sanguinetti of Uruguay in his first term (1984–1989), and Jaime Lusinchi of Venezuela (1983–1988).

We saw that the newness and perceived fragility of Chilean democracy in 1989 pressed the *Concertación* to announce efficiency-oriented policies in the campaign. In Latin America's older democracies, the apparent security of democratic institutions reduced the pressure of markets on presidential candidates. As a result, the older democracies spawned successful security-oriented candidates, such as Barco and Samper of Colombia and Arias of Costa Rica.

Another example is Jaime Lusinchi of Venezuela. At the onset of the debt crisis, Venezuelan democracy appeared unshakable. Civilian politicians had ruled Venezuela since 1958; the country's two major political parties, the social democratic Democratic Action (AD) and the Christian Democratic Committee for Political Organization and Independent Election (COPEI), were well institutionalized (though internally fractious) organizations that regularly competed with one another and monopolized electoral politics (Coppedge, 1994; Kornblith and Levine, 1995; Levine, 1973). Venezuela's oil wealth endowed the country with the highest per capita GDP in the region, although oil's dominance also distorted economic development and the evolution of a modern state (Hausmann, 1995; Karl, 1987, 1997; Martz, 1982).

In 1983, Lusinchi, AD's candidate for the presidency, ran against the incumbent COPEI party's candidate, Rafael Caldera.[8] Lusinchi's campaign slogan was "Bread, land, and jobs." He called for improved public services, wage adjustments through a social pact, and full employment. Lusinchi announced that if elected he would not sign an agreement with the IMF; instead, he would refinance Venezuela's foreign debt "without generating undesirable effects on Venezuelan living standards" (Social Pact, cited in *Visión*, January 1983).

In addition to the apparent unshakabilty of Venezuela's "old" democracy, economic conditions also favored Lusinchi's expansionist and security-oriented rhetoric. After the second oil shock in 1979, growth slowed and unemployment rose. Oil revenues were high in 1981–1982 and inflation was falling, but economic growth continued to be slow (Hausmann, 1995). Recession hit Venezuela in the final years of the term in office of Lusinchi's predecessor, Luís Herrera Campins. In 1983, the economy contracted 5.5%, and inflation was low. Low growth and low inflation made Lusinchi's rhetoric of expansionism appealing to many voters.

Lusinchi beat Caldera easily, 58–34% (the remainder went to minor party candidates). With continued price stability, Lusinchi felt little pressure to abandon his campaign promises once in office. He adopted a multiple exchange rate system, kept interest rates low, and allowed public spending to fluctuate as a function of the oil economy. Lusinchi undertook no qualitative restructuring (see Hausmann, 1990).

Consistent security-oriented politicians were not unknown to the region's newer democracies. A context of economic contraction, falling real wages, and rising unemployment gave greater resonance to the call for expansionist and redistributive policies even in new democracies.

The generals had relinquished power only five years earlier when Alan García became president of Peru. García succeeded Fernando Belaúnde Terry (1980–1985). Departing military leaders bequeathed to Belaúnde a

---

[8] The Venezuelan constitution stated that presidents must wait two terms before running for reelection. The term limit kept the incumbent, Luis Herrera Campins, from running in 1983 but allowed Caldera, who had been president in 1969–1974, to run.

current-account surplus and relatively low inflation. Belaúnde, in turn, left a more troubled legacy at the end of his term: a mounting debt burden and declining terms of trade. In 1983 output fell 12%, and between 1982 and 1985 real wages fell by more than one-third. The Belaúnde government in 1984 quietly stopped making debt service payments to foreign banks.

With the right discredited by poor economic performance, García's main challenger was Alfonso Barrantes of the United Left coalition. The electoral campaign unfolded against a backdrop of growing economic instability and a bloody conflict between Shining Path insurgents and the Peruvian military. García pledged that an APRA government would only allow imports of basic foods and of manufactures that had no domestic competitors. He called for a united Latin American response to the debt crisis and framed united action as a struggle against imperialism. The APRA manifesto, unveiled shortly before the election in April 1985, announced, "the state will have an active and direct role promoting development and employment," and urged the use of fiscal and trade policies to achieve income redistribution (cited in *Oiga*, June 1985). The campaign adopted a Peruvian waltz with lyrics evoking national pride ("I have pride in being Peruvian and I'm happy") as its theme song.

In contrast, Alfonso Barrantes, the United Left candidate, seemed not to care about winning. The IU also lacked money and was riven by conflict. The disarray of the campaign became evident when it failed to air its television ad until the final weeks before the election.[9]

García defeated Barrantes by a 53–25% margin; the two rightist candidates between them mustered a mere 11% of the vote. APRA controlled a majority of seats in the legislature.

García immediately put in place the program outlined in the campaign, a "heterodox" package aimed at inflation stabilization and redistribution of income (see Pastor and Wise, 1992). It featured a large one-time devaluation of the currency followed by an exchange rate freeze, a 50% reduction in interest to lower capital costs, and a reduction in the real price of government-supplied inputs and public services (electricity, water, telephone, and bus fares). To shore up hard-currency holdings and

---

[9] The sense of lost opportunity was all the greater because the ad itself was a powerfully crafted work oriented to young voters. I had several opportunities to interview and observe Barrantes during the 1985 campaign and found him almost unbelievably unfocused on winning.

allow for the imports required for the expansion, García announced that Peru would repay its foreign debt up to the equivalent of 10% of export earnings.

At first, the program produced stellar results: inflation fell from 158% to 63% in 1986, and growth soared to a cumulative 16% in 1986–1987. Then, in 1988, the economy collapsed.

Part of the blame rested on erroneous assumptions about the impact of deficits on prices. García's economic team designed policies that would, given certain assumptions, gradually reduce inflation, enhance real wages, and redistribute income. The critical assumptions were that markups on cost determined domestic prices, that expectations rather than budget deficits drove inflation, and that low output in the export sector constrained exports. Yet García's anti-inflation package eventually failed: inflation reached 2,800% in 1989 and 7,400% in 1990. Also to blame was the unpredictable policy style of García and the political hostility of international finance. Pastor and Wise note that García's "public stance against the IMF and the anti-imperialist rhetoric accompanying it (unlike the quiet nonpayment of the Belaúnde administration) isolated Peru from the international financial community" (1992:98). In August 1986, the IMF declared Peru an ineligible borrower.

To summarize, politicians in Latin America's older democracies faced less pressure to placate business interests and hence felt freer to advocate redistributive and expansionary policies. Even in newer democracies, when economies contracted and jobs were lost, rich electoral rewards went to politicians who gave voice to voters' desire to restore growth. We have also seen that politicians entertained quite different beliefs about what sorts of economic measures would improve welfare: whereas Aylwin and most of Chile's political leadership, socialists included, had come to embrace liberalization and deregulation, in Peru leaders like García, with constituencies similar to those of Chile's *Concertación*, believed that an unorthodox mix of price controls and fiscal expansion could sustain growth and improve the life of the working class.

Vague Campaigns

Facing a grim international financial climate and internal economic woes, a few politicians chose to reveal as little as possible in their campaigns. In general, candidates who were vague anticipated imposing harsh austerity measures and unpopular reforms, but fear of losing voters' support kept them from articulating more clearly their intentions. In this sense, vague politicians were like security-to-efficiency policy switchers. But they also tried not to send precise but misleading signals of their intentions.

Luis Alberto Monge of Costa Rica's National Liberation Party ran a quintessential vague – and successful – campaign in 1982. Costa Rica's foreign debt was nearly 100% of GDP, interest rates were high, the price of imports, in particular oil, was rising, and export prices were stagnant. The public-sector deficit stood at 15% of GDP, unemployment was 10%, and inflation was 82% (see Lizano, 1991). How would Monge begin to resolve the crisis? His answer was, elect me and I will tell you. "We have prepared ourselves assiduously for three years so as to implement first an emergency program the main ideas of which cannot be specified until we are facing the country's real situation" (cited in *Visión*, March 1982).[10] Aside from some hints that he would deregulate the financial sector and privatize state-owned firms, Monge offered Costa Ricans platitudes: "Production – there can be no peace without food; Justice – there can be no happiness with hunger; Ethics – there can be no public faith without government example; Democracy – there can be no progress without freedom" (*Tico Times*, January 1982).

In fact, to stop inflation, Monge's administration quickly cut the public sector deficit from 15% to 6% of GDP by reducing state employment and subsidies. To restore currency stability it instituted a series of small, preannounced devaluations, the *crawling peg* (see Saborío, 1990). It also proposed the privatization of companies of CODESA, the state holding company, and denationalization of banks (see Wilson, 1999).

Costa Rica in 1982 contrasted with other countries that seemed to lend themselves to vague campaigns. Costa Rica is a country of long-enduring and relatively well-institutionalized political parties (see Carey, 1996; Yashar, 1995) where uninterrupted civilian rule has raised expectations about the quality of the political leadership. In other countries, issueless campaigns and secretiveness concerning policy intentions were linked to histories of military intervention, *caudillismo*, and dictatorship. Consider, for example, the declarations by General Hugo Banzer, the former dictator of Bolivia, in the 1989 campaign: "a party platform for government is

[10] Monge's words anticipate a campaign declaration of France's Jacques Chirac in 1995: "My first worry today is to convince the French people to elect me and not to tell them what I will do after that" (Reuters News Service, April 26, 1995).

42

like a battle plan that cannot be known by the enemy because otherwise the fight is lost" (*Informe R*, November 1989).[11] Banzer seemed to confuse a political campaign with a military campaign. Similarly, Joaquín Balaguer, the long-enduring Dominican leader, managed to distract the populace in his 1994 campaign with racially tinged accusations that his opponent practiced voodoo. Like Monge, when pressed during an earlier (1986) campaign to lay out his economic program, Balaguer responded that he needed "the first 100 days of his government to transpire in order to know the exact situation he will have to manage" before defining the policy (*Visión*, August 1986). The plea for time would have been more compelling if Balaguer hadn't been the incumbent president!

Security to Efficiency: Policy Switches

In 12 elections, politicians pronounced themselves in favor of job creation, growth, improvement in real wages, industrial policy, a gradualist approach to inflation stabilization, and limited repayment of the foreign debt, only to impose austerity and liberal reforms when elected. All immediate, drastic policy switches were in the same direction, from economic security to efficiency. Some efficiency-oriented politicians, such as Chamorro, modified their policies over time, in response to strikes, riots, or congressional resistance. But the phenomenon of early switches, occurring before conditions had changed in any obvious way or before overt opposition had a chance to build, was unidirectional.

Not all of the policy switches my research identified were of the same magnitude or drama. To be considered a policy switcher in the sense used here, it was sufficient for a politician to renege swiftly on a policy position that had been salient in the campaign. Rodrigo Borja, the Democratic Left candidate for the Ecuadorian presidency in 1988, pronounced himself against surprise fiscal adjustments, also known as *shocks*: "All changes will be progressive [i.e., incremental] and pre-programmed" (cited in *Latin American Weekly Report – Andean Group*, June 23, 1988). Three weeks after the election, Borja announced a major price adjustment: his government raised the price of gasoline 100% and electricity 30%; it devalued the sucre by 75% and followed with weekly devaluations of 2.5% (the crawling peg). In his speech announcing these measures, Borja blamed the change of

---

[11] In this election, Banzer came in a close second in the popular vote and was not elected president by the Bolivian congress.

course on "the financial bankruptcy, the economic disorder, the administrative corruption, and the fiscal crisis" left by the outgoing government
(cited in *El Comercio* of Quito, August 31, 1988). In most other respects,
his early (and later) policies were in line with campaign signals and with
his identity as a leader of a social democratic party.

During the campaign, people believed Borja's pro-growth and anti-
fiscal-shock protestations because he was a leader of a center-left party of
long standing. It turned out that they should have believed him less. In
other instances, politicians from right-wing parties that were linked in
voters' minds to a market-oriented economic program went out of their
way to express their concern for issues touching the working classes, issues
such as jobs, housing, and health, in their effort to mobilize electoral
support. When such politicians switched in office to more efficiency-
oriented policies, the switch may have been less surprising to voters,
who would have discounted campaign rhetoric in light of the politicians'
identity.

Borja's successor, Sixto Durán Ballén, illustrates just this phenomenon:
a conservative politician who in the campaign shifts toward the center in
search of votes, only to revert in office to his earlier position. In the 1992
campaign, Durán Ballén represented a recently formed alliance of two
conservative parties, the Unified Republican Party (PRE) and the Conservative Party of Ecuador (PCE). In the first round of the election Durán
Ballén placed second after Jaime Nebot, the candidate of the Social Christian Party (PSC). Their strong electoral performances reflected voters' disaffection with economic performance under the Borja government. Each
candidate's strategy before the second round of balloting was to scare
voters with the prospect of harsh austerity under his opponent. Each candidate accused the other of planning a surprise price adjustment. Durán
Ballén claimed to favor an approach to price stabilization "far from the
'shock' and from gradualism." He also announced that his government
would lower the price of medicines, "which is what poor people need
most." It would sponsor a massive program of construction of low-cost
housing, "substantial" educational reforms, and the extension of medical
services and hospitals (cited in Cornejo Menacho, 1992:9–10).

Durán Ballén won the second round of the election in July, and on September 3 his government announced that it would raise the price of gasoline by 125%, double electricity rates, and devalue the sucre by 35.5%.
The government soon introduced a set of structural reforms, the *Nuevo
Rumbo* or New Route, reducing government spending, freezing public-

sector employment, and eliminating or fusing some small public agencies. The New Route offered early retirement to public employees, imposed a one-time tax on businesses, and held in check the money supply (Banco Central de Ecuador, 1992).

The most stunning policy switches were those in which the candidate's history, partisan affiliation, campaign-crafted identity, and policy pronouncements all signaled a commitment to security-oriented policies, policies that were entirely discarded in favor of a sharp neoliberal turn early in the new government. In the remainder of this chapter I describe three such switches: those of Carlos Menem in Argentina and Alberto Fujimori in Peru in their first terms (1989–1995 and 1990–1995, respectively) and Carlos Andrés Pérez in Venezuela (1989–1993).

Argentina

During the early months of 1989, the outgoing Unión Cívica Radical (UCR) government of Raúl Alfonsín struggled against high (though not yet hyper) inflation, recession, and heavy international indebtedness. The ruling party's presidential candidate, Eduardo Angeloz, distanced himself from some of the incumbent's policies. After the failure of a late 1988 emergency economic plan to control inflation, Angeloz called for the resignation of the finance minister, Juan Sourrouille. Still Angeloz called for "deepening" the economic reforms of the Alfonsín government: the government should continue to liberalize trade, privatize state-owned enterprises, and achieve good standing with international financial institutions.

Alvaro Alsogaray, the candidate of the conservative Unión del Centro Democrático (UCD), called for liberalization of trade, the exchange rate, and wages; for speedy privatizations; and for honoring standing agreements with international creditors.

Carlos Menem was the presidential candidate of the Peronist party (Partido Justicialista, PJ). Menem's was a colorful campaign, which emphasized his fondness for soccer, race cars, and fashion models. His economic message was nationalist and expansionist. He called for stabilizing the economy without imposing hardships on workers or the middle class. A book he and his running mate co-authored during the campaign envisioned a "*revolución productiva*" or productive revolution (Menem and Duhalde, 1989). With mildly expansionist policies to exploit unused industrial capacity, Argentina would overcome depressed real wages, high unemployment, and price instability. At the very moment when the incumbent Alfonsín government was imposing austerity measures – called *paquetazos* – Menem on the campaign trail invented the term *salariazo*, a big upward shock to wages. Consistent with the Peronist tradition, Menem championed a development model that included state ownership of heavy industry, utilities, and oil. To deal with inflation, whereas the UCR and the rightist UCD called for price liberalization, the Peronists favored a "social pact" to establish price and wage levels. To deal with the foreign debt, whereas the UCR and UCD called for "the fulfillment of obligations," the Peronists favored "a cessation of payment of debt service" (*Clarín*, April 28, 1989), although they later moderated this position. On the campaign trail Menem insisted he would not pay Argentina's debt "with the hunger of the Argentine people" (cited in Schuler, 1994). He expressed distrust of Argentina's export bourgeoisie, epitomized by the conglomerate Bunge y Born. And Menem warned Britain that blood might again flow in the Malvinas or Falkland Islands.

In the election on May 14, 1989, Menem won 47% of the vote, Angeloz 37%, and Alsogaray 6%.

The Alfonsín government, which was scheduled to stay in office another seven months, announced a new set of economic measures four days after the election, but inflation continued to surge, reaching nearly 100% before month's end. Rioting and looting on May 23 left 14 dead. The crisis led to an agreement between the government and Menem to move the transition forward from December to July.

Menem's cabinet, announced in July, contained surprises. He named Miguel Roig, a former vice-president of Bunge y Born and "an outstanding symbol of *vendepatria* [sellout] capitalism to all Peronists," as his finance minister (Smith, 1991:52). When Roig died of a heart attack 11 days after taking office, Menem turned the selection of a replacement over to Bunge y Born's president, who chose Nestor Rapanelli, another vice-president of the firm. Menem chose Jorge Triaca, a conservative labor figure to be his labor minister. Triaca's appointment and the government's emerging economic policies precipitated a split in the Peronist labor confederation, the Confederación General de Trabajadores (CGT); the Peronist labor leader Saúl Ubaldini founded an antigovernment wing of the CGT (see McGuire, 1997). Other Menem cabinet appointments also surprised Argentines, as did his efforts, beginning in February 1990, to normalize relations with Britain.

Menem's economic team fashioned policies like the ones his opponents in the campaign had advocated. The Bunge y Born plan (as it was known) included a sharp fiscal adjustment and a 170% devaluation of the austral. The government privatized telecommunications, the state airlines, television and radio stations, petrochemicals, and steel and phased out export taxes and import tariffs (see Smith, 1991). Having called for a moratorium and then five-year cessation of payments on the foreign debt, Menem named Alvaro Alsogaray, the presidential candidate from the right-wing UCD, as his chief debt negotiator in Washington.

By August 1989, only three months after the election, Menem no longer spoke the language of the *salariazo*. He introduced his austerity program exhorting Argentines to accept "a tough, costly, and severe adjustment" requiring "major surgery, no anesthesia" (cited in Smith 1991:53).

Inflation persisted under the austerity plans crafted by the Bunge y Born ministers and their successor, Antonio Erman González. Hyperinflation returned in late 1989. Not until Domingo Cavallo became finance minister in February 1991, and put in place the *convertibility plan*, did inflation abate. The convertibility plan guaranteed, by an act of congress, parity of the peso with the U.S. dollar, and barred increases in the money supply not backed by foreign reserves.

Eventually the Menem government achieved price stability as well as structural reforms such as aggressive privatization. But its program also caused workers to lose jobs and real wages to stagnate. The average unemployment rate in 1993 was 12.7%, in 1995 17.5%, and it rose to over 20% in early 1995. Despite the negative effects of austerity, Menem remained popular, for reasons I explore in Chapter 5. This popularity allowed him to rewrite the constitution (with bipartisan support from the rival UCR), modifying presidential term limits so that Menem could run for an immediate second term. In 1995 he ran and won.

Peru

Peru's 1990 presidential campaign unfolded against the backdrop of a terrible economic crisis. In 1989 GNP had fallen by 10.4%, inflation rose to 2,775%, and the external debt stood at over $19 billion (almost $1,000 per capita). This was only the worst year in a prolonged crisis. The crisis and poor governmental performance discredited the incumbent APRA party's candidate.

47

Indeed, 1990 was not a good year for any of Peru's traditional parties. The APRA candidate could not distance himself from the failed incumbent administration of Alan García (1985–1990). As for the other parties likely to inherit the presidency, the United Left coalition under Barrantes had divided in 1989, leaving the two leftist presidential candidates debilitated. Two rightist parties improved their prospects by forming a coalition behind the candidacy of the novelist Mario Vargas Llosa.

Neither Vargas Llosa, the leading candidate at the outset of the campaign, nor Alberto Fujimori, who emerged as Vargas Llosa's main rival, were professional politicians. But Vargas Llosa had a long involvement in national and international politics, and his candidacy had traditional-party backing. In contrast, Fujimori had no ties to traditional political parties. Born to Japanese natives, Fujimori was a mathematician and, in the 1980s, rector of the National Agrarian University. For a brief time during the García administration he hosted a political talk show on the state television channel. In 1990 he stitched together *Cambio '90* (Change '90), more a campaign vehicle than a party, from socially progressive Protestant evangelicals and an association of informal-sector workers. Fujimori's campaign rose from obscurity during the last month before the first round of the elections in April. On March 8, when his name first appeared in public opinion polls (until then he had been an "Other"), he commanded 4% support. His standing rose to 15% on March 25 and to 21% on April 1 (Apoyo, *Informe de Opinion*, March and April 1990). In the first round of the elections on April 8, Fujimori took 25% of the vote, forcing a run-off with Vargas Llosa, who took 28%.

Economic policy dominated the campaign.[12] No candidate disagreed in 1990 that Peru was in the midst of a dire economic crisis, and none argued for a continuation of the status quo. The economic debate between Vargas Llosa and Fujimori evolved along four lines: the causes of and appropriate remedies for internal and external disequilibria, particularly inflation; the acceptable costs of stabilization in lost security and income; the optimal speed of stabilization; and the appropriate role for the state in the economy.

---

[12] Schmidt (1996:331–332) may overstate the unidimensionality of the campaign debate about economic policy. In fact, Fujimori made occasional statements suggesting a greater concern than Vargas Llosa with human rights, and Vargas Llosa was criticized by APRA and left candidates in the campaign for a controversial report he authored in 1982 exonerating the army for a massacre of journalists in the Andean village of Uchuraccay. But Schmidt is right that economic policy was by far the more important issue.

Vargas Llosa proposed to resolve the crisis through what would amount to a neoliberal revolution. He viewed Peru's overgrown state as the main barrier to economic growth and "modernity." The state should restrict itself to health, education, and communications.

On stabilization, Vargas Llosa proposed a "radical attack" on inflation with a drastic reduction of the fiscal deficit. The first weapon of attack was to be a one-time increase in the prices of consumer goods and state services, a fiscal adjustment or shock. The government would raise prices that remained under its control to realistic levels, end subsidies, and impose heavy exise taxes on energy. Vargas Llosa's proposals reflected his and his advisors' opinion that inflation was a monetary phenomenon (see the discussion in Iguíñiz, 1991). They viewed "populist" budget deficits and fast monetary growth as the cause of inflation.

After the fiscal adjustment, Vargas Llosa promised that his government would pursue structural reforms, sharply reducing the size of the government workforce, privatizing industry, and ending "mercantilist" trade protection. These measures, painful in the short term, would increase general security in the future. As a Vargas Llosa campaign slogan put it, "It will cost us . . . but together we will make the Great Change" (*"Nos costurá . . . pero juntos haremos el Gran Cambio"*).

Postmortems of the campaign stressed Vargas Llosa's error in projecting a lack of concern for those who would bear the burdens of adjustment, burdens such as lowered real incomes and unemployment. A Vargas Llosa television ad dramatized the inefficiency of public-sector employees by depicting a monkey, symbolizing the bureaucrat, urinating on a desk. The ad was controversial not only because of its bad taste – stills from it appeared on the covers of even pro–Vargas Llosa magazines, which carried critical stories – but also because of its message of disdain for public employees, who could expect to be fired en masse. The state employed only 10% of the workforce, but the message that Vargas Llosa would accept unemployment as a cost of structural adjustment frightened public- and private-sector workers alike.

This fear was reinforced by Vargas Llosa's call to eliminate job security laws, a message he gave even in hostile forums. His memoirs contain an account of a speech before the General Confederation of Workers of Peru (CGTP), Peru's largest labor confederation, in which he called workers with job security a "tiny minority" and job security laws an "obstacle to growth" (Vargas Llosa, 1993:427). The image he created in the minds of many was of a liberal ideologue willing to sacrifice

49

any modicum of economic security in favor of efficiency-promoting reforms.[13]

Fujimori's campaign rhetoric had a different flavor. His strategy was to appeal to the lower and lower middle classes by advocating stabilization with a minimum of recession and job loss. Fujimori's political nose led him to take on as advisors center-left economists, political independents whose message the candidate sensed as resonating with the preferences of the poor and exploiting their fears.

In the campaign Fujimori attempted to stake out a centrist position on economic issues; he sharpened this position after the general election in April and before run-off election in June by offering more specific proposals. His two prominent economic advisors were Santiago Roca, a professor of business administration at the School of Higher Studies in Administration (ESAN), and Adolfo Figueroa, a neo-Keynesian economist from the Catholic University. The informed public expected either Roca or Figueroa to become economic minister and the other president of the Central Bank under a Fujimori administration. Both served as campaign directors and brought in a set of academics and policy analysts, all independents with a center-left orientation.

What were the economic proposals that Fujimori drew from his advisors? First, opposition to a draconian fiscal adjustment, the "shock." The team argued that if the next government immediately raised the prices of government services, removed subsidies on basic goods, and devalued the currency, inflation would only get worse. The inertial component of inflation meant that such shocks, administered repeatedly in the 1970s and 1980s, only accelerated inflation. So central was this theme that it became known inside the Fujimori campaign as *el anti-shock*.

What's more, they contended, austerity measures would widen the income gap between rich and poor, a politically unacceptable outcome in a country with one of the world's most skewed income distributions (and at the time one of the world's most successful guerrilla movements). And income concentration would lower private investment and retard growth (see Figueroa, 1993). The advice of Fujimori's economists was that the government should bring inflation under control by negotiating price controls and wage indexation with business and labor. Only then should it gradually raise the prices of public-sector goods and services and adjust

---

[13] For the contribution of electoral rules to Vargas Llosa's defeat, see Schmidt (1996).

the exchange rate. If the next government followed this path, it would achieve "stabilization without recession" (*Cambio '90*, 1990).

The Fujimori team also advocated a sequenced approach to debt negotiations. Peru's foreign debt stood at $19 billion in 1990; the country had accumulated arrears of $9 billion, and it was $800 million in arrears to the IMF. Whereas Vargas Llosa proposed immediate negotiations with foreign creditors and international financial institutions, the Fujimori team believed that the next government should bring inflation under control before commencing debt negotiations; this sequence would allow Peru to face foreign creditors in a stronger bargaining position. Finally, Fujimori envisioned a larger role for the state in the economy than did Vargas Llosa. His platform evoked a "debureaucratized" state that would stimulate selected industrial and agricultural sectors. He opposed Vargas Llosa's calls for blanket privatization: major state firms would remain public but be made more efficient. The state would provide incentives to manufacturing sectors composed of small, labor-intensive firms ("microindustry"); these firms would be at the center of Peru's "Social Pact for Development" (*Cambio '90*, 1990).

The Fujimori campaign translated the candidate's proposals for stabilization, debt, and industrial policy from the recondite language of academic economists into positions, slogans, and symbols aimed at the mass public. An APRA television ad that appeared before the general election helped Fujimori get across the message that Vargas Llosa's proposals were risky. It featured footage from the animated film *Pink Floyd: The Wall* that showed monsters devouring people and children crying while the ground opened under their feet. The message, though sponsored by APRA, echoed Fujimori's grim predictions about the consequences of Vargas Llosa's proposed stabilization strategy: lost income and jobs.

Poor voters' fears of the fiscal adjustment and structural reforms, and support from APRA and the left, helped Fujimori defeat Vargas Llosa in the runoff election in June by a margin of 57–35% (8% invalid).[14]

Geographic patterns of support for the candidates, as well as polling data, point to strong class effects on voters' choices. The urban and middle

[14] Schmidt (1996) and Tanaka (1998) present evidence that García secretly supported candidates other than his own APRA's Luis Alva Castro: first Alfonso Barrantes, then Fujimori. Had Alva Castro performed well in the election, he would have been in a position to take party leadership away from García and be the party's candidate again in 1995.

and upper classes supported Vargas Llosa (see Degregori and Grompone, 1991). Slogans like "Together we will make the Great Change" notwithstanding, Vargas Llosa failed to convince working-class voters that his proposed economic reform program was in the interests of all. In a postelection poll, 46% of lower-class respondents who had voted against Vargas Llosa said they opposed him because he "represented the interests of the rich", and another 17% "because of his right-wing ideas" (Apoyo, June 1990).[15] The urban lower classes and middle classes, as well as the peasantry and rural workers, voted for Fujimori.

Against this evidence, some argue that not policy positions but an ethnic divide between white and nonwhite Peruvians explains the outcome of the 1990 election. During the campaign, Peruvian analysts commented on Fujimori's ethnicity (see De Gregori and Grompone, 1991; Klaiber, 1990). According to these analysts, nonwhite Peruvians supported Fujimori because he was a *chinito* and opposed Vargas Llosa because he was of European descent. And, the analysts continued, ethnic solidarity caused non-European Peruvians to accept Fujimori's postelection switch to neoliberalism.

This analysis is not all wrong, but it is not entirely right either. It would be a mistake to think of ethnic identity as driving the voting behavior of most working-class Peruvians. Fujimori's supporters were similar, in class and ethnic terms, to people who had voted in 1980 for Fernando Belaúnde, whose European ancestry was as evident as Vargas Llosa's. Many Peruvians of indigenous, African, and Asian descent voted for Alan García in 1985, rather than for Alfonso Barrantes, who is smaller and darker than García. A mix of ethnic identity along with ideology, partisan sympathies, and policy preferences influenced working-class voters (see Cameron 1994; Dietz, 1985, 1996; Stokes 1995). The crucial point is that ethnic identity and policy orientation were not entirely separate. Fujimori was unknown to Peruvians two months before they elected him president. Any facts about him added appreciably to the stock of information, and his non-European and nonelite background was one valuable fact. Being Japanese-Peruvian helped Fujimori because voters were afraid of the *policies* Vargas Llosa advocated so vigorously, policies that they believed were against their economic interests. Voters had to construct Fujimori's identity out of thin

[15] These were the responses of the two poorest groups of respondents to Apoyo's June poll of 300 Lima residents. Sixteen percent opposed Vargas Llosa because they "didn't trust him or didn't like him" and 5% for "other reasons."

air from the meager facts of his ethnic identity and his calls for jobs, gradualism, and protection of national industry. It was not that Fujimori's ethnic identity rather than his policy pronouncements attracted voter support; the two were tightly interwoven.

Ten days after Fujimori's inauguration, on August 7, the new president ordered the army to roll tanks onto the streets of Lima in preparation for the announcement the next day of a package of dramatic price increases: the shock. The government raised price of gasoline by 3,140%, the price of kerosene, used as cooking fuel by poor consumers, by 6,964%. It removed subsidies for many basic foodstuffs, and their prices soared: bread by 1,567%, cooking oil by 639%, sugar by 552%, and rice by 533%. Medicine prices rose on average by 1,385%. These increases had a devastating short-term effect on the household budgets of poor families. According to Iguíñiz (1991:405–406), the one-time payment of 8 million *intis* that private-sector employers were supposed to give workers to soften the impact of the measures (but that many never received) was the equivalent of 10 days' worth of bread for the average family. Real wages of privatesector workers fell to about half of their preadjustment levels, and those of public-sector workers by even more. Official estimates put the number of people suffering extreme poverty at 7 million before the measures and at 12 million afterward (Peru's total population was 22 million).

Fujimori's longer-term economic reforms also were remarkably like those Vargas Llosa had proposed: he liberalized the exchange rate, reduced and simplified tariffs on imports, eliminated tariffs on exports, and liberalized capital markets. The government later reformed the tax system, reduced employment in government ministries and state-owned enterprises, privatized state-owned enterprises and financial institutions, eliminated job security laws, eliminated wage indexation, liberalized labor relations, and privatized social security.

Venezuela

To secure the AD candidacy for president of Venezuela in 1988, Carlos Andrés Pérez had to defeat a rival, Octavio Lepage, who had the support of President Lusinchi. Pérez relied on support from AD labor leaders in his struggle against Lepage. Once Pérez became the AD candidate, his campaign went through two distinct phases. In the first phase, from December 1987 to June 1988, Pérez pronounced himself in favor of policies that reflected his debt to labor and recalled his presidency in the mid-1970s, at the height of Venezuela's oil boom. He promised a substantial across-the-board wage increase and a major "war" against poverty.

Midway through the campaign, with a strong lead in the polls, Pérez appeared to ease toward the center on economic policy, without completely reversing any previous positions and without moving to the right of his opponent (see Martz, 1995). He began to advocate trade liberalization with some continued protection for local industry, as well as "moderate" and "selective" privatization of state activities. At the same time, he called for a multitiered exchange rate within a system of continued exchange controls and joint action by Latin American debtors. These positions suggested continuity with the economic nationalism and protections of the prevailing economic model.

Pérez's opponent, COPEI's Eduardo Fernández, advocated a floating exchange rate, reducing the role of the state in the economy, privatizing heavy industry, ports, and services, and stabilizing prices.

On December 4, Pérez became the first Venezuelan to win the presidency twice, defeating Fernández 53–40%.

As president-elect, Pérez quickly reassured the business community that he would not impose a substantial across-the-board wage increase (LAWR, September 3, 1989) and gathered around him the cabinet that would carry out *"el Gran Virage"* or the Great Turnaround: the liberalization of the Venezuelan economy. The government entered into loan agreements with the IMF and the World Bank that entailed reducing the public-sector deficit; the deficit came down from 9.9% of GDP in 1988 to 4% in 1989. Pérez raised the prices of goods and services that Lusinchi had frozen, and he eliminated price controls on all but 18 goods. The increases were steep: 100% for gasoline, 133% for natural gas, 30% for public transportation. The government adopted a single floating exchange rate, liberalized interest rates, and reduced import tariffs to below 40% on average (for descriptions, see Hausmann, 1995; Naím, 1993). It attempted tax reform but encountered resistance in the legislature, including from Pérez's own party.

Price increases set off an explosion. People in Caracas rioted on February 27 after the government announced that it would raise bus fares. After two days the Metropolitan Police had not been able to control the rioting and looting; Pérez suspended constitutional guarantees and ordered the military onto the streets. By most accounts 300 people died (see, e.g., Naim, 1993), but people directly involved claim that the number

54

was much higher.[16] Price liberalization, riots, and repression were corroding Venezuelan democracy.

The Great Turnaround backfired politically as well as economically; it was far from successful. The first in a series of "big bang" efforts to correct past policy deficiencies all at once (see Hausmann, 1995; Martinelli and Tomassi, 1994), the program unintentionally overshot its targets, causing considerably more hardship than necessary. The technical designers of the program aimed at a fiscal deficit equivalent to 4% of GDP in 1989; the actual deficit fell to 1.4%. Government economists predicted that GDP growth would merely slow to 2.0% in 1989 from 5.6% in 1988; actual growth in the non-oil economy in 1989 was *negative* 9.8%. The *técnicos* also missed their target on inflation: it was supposed to increase only 2% in 1989 over 1988 and rise to 37.5%; in fact, inflation soared to 82%.[17] In its first year, the Great Turnaround produced falling output, declining real wages, and persistent inflation. This debacle colored the public's views of the government and the program, even after growth resumed.

Summary and Conclusions

These sketches show that we should not equate the recent neoliberal era in Latin America with a groundswell of mass support for rapid market reforms. A minority of governments could claim a mandate for neoliberalism. Of the 44 governments elected between 1982 and 1995, 17 (39%) had sent clear campaign signals of an intention to liberalize; these 17 represented only slightly more than half of the 33 governments that chose neoliberalism once in office.[18]

At the outset I raised a set of questions. Why do some politicians campaign promising efficiency-oriented reforms, others security policies?

---

[16] Interviews with military personnel in Caracas, November 1998; see also Andean Commission of Jurists (1989) and Burggraaff and Millett (1995).

[17] Ricardo Haussman, an economist who took part in the Venezuelan reforms both as a cabinet member and as an official at the Interamerican Development Bank, gives details of these missed targets (Haussman, 1995).

[18] Some neoliberal candidates, it should be said, simply lost elections, and their losses were interpreted by others as object lessons. The most strident neoliberal candidate who lost was Mario Vargas Llosa of Peru. Costa Rica's Rafael Calderón of the United Social Christian Party ran on an efficiency-oriented platform in 1986 and was defeated by the more moderate Oscar Arias of the National Liberation Party. In the next campaign, in 1990, Calderón did not repeat the mistake: he ran promising welfare policies and hid his efficiency-oriented program until he was securely in office.

What determines who wins? And under what conditions will politicians reveal their real policy intentions in campaigns, intentions that then guide their early policies? The information presented in this chapter begins to suggest answers, and the next chapter will delve more deeply into the question of the conditions for violations of mandates. Here I review some suggestive points:

1. *Economic conditions influence the preferences of voters and hence the viability of efficiency- versus security-oriented candidates.* In the majority of the elections I have considered, the economy dominated other issues. When inflation was high, voters favored efficiency-oriented candidates; when growth slowed, they favored security-oriented candidates. Of course, economic policy proposals were not the whole story behind voters' choices. The economic legacy of the incumbent government, the way that legacy was framed in the campaign, and the economic proposals of the opposition all appear to have shaped voters' choices. Undoubtedly in Latin American nations as in other democracies, socialization, party, ethnic, and class identity also shaped voters' choices. Yet political parties experienced great surges in support followed by enormous drops; this level of electoral volatility argues against any simple social cleavage explanation of electoral outcomes in post-debt-crisis Latin America (see Roberts and Wibbels, 1999). Economic policy proposals and economic performance critically shaped voters' chocies.

2. *Politicians' choice of economic policy positions was shaped by ideology and technical beliefs, as well as by the desire to win votes.* A wide variety of objectives and motives animated politicians' choices of what message to send in campaigns and what policies to pursue in office. Some politicians were ideologues with strong policy convictions. Sometimes these convictions were so powerful that candidates had difficulty masking them, even when not masking them got the candidates into trouble with voters. The most startling example is Mario Vargas Llosa, who in the campaign lectured Peru's labor leadership on the nefarious effects of unions and job security laws. (Indeed, in postmortems analysts wondered whether Vargas Llosa cared more about winning or about expounding his neoliberal philosophy.) Other politicians were less ideological, but they were concerned with their place in history and thought that only "tough medicine" would save an economy in trouble and earn them retrospective accolades. The following description of Víctor Paz Estenssoro fits others, such as Carlos Andrés

Pérez, who had championed statist models in earlier eras and now switched wholeheartedly to the market model:

Along with his interest in market economics, Paz had a personal agenda that fit tightly into the neoliberal project. As one of Bolivia's major political figures in the twentieth century, Paz harbored concerns about his place in history and how the legacy of the MNR [his political party]-led revolution of 1952 would be regarded in the long run. . . . Rather than seeing the NPE [the pro-market reforms] as an indictment of the economic model he had helped set in place in 1952, Paz saw it as the only medicine that could save the modern state he had fathered. (Conaghan and Malloy, 1994:188)[19]

At the other extreme from ideologues in the mold of Vargas Llosa and actors on the stage of history in the mold of Paz Estenssoro were political chameleons who would alter their message in pursuit of votes, constrained only by the credulity of voters. The Peruvian election of 1990 pitted against each other two politicians who represented extremes of each type: Fujimori, the tactician who was ready to espouse any program to win votes, versus Vargas Llosa, who "was more interested in implementing neoliberal policies than in winning the election" (Cameron 1994:123).

In addition to having different motives, politicians also catered to different constituencies of class, region, and sometimes ethnicity. Yet these differences played a smaller part that one might guess in determining campaign messages. Latin American class structures are such that electoral rewards are concentrated in the lower classes, including both urban and rural workers and (in some countries) the peasantry. Hence bourgeois or oligarchic parties still have to make mass appeals if they are to win elections. And close elections are decided by relatively small segments of the electorate that constitute swing voters, again limiting the range of party appeals.

Apart from differences in ideology and class or sectoral orientation, politicians held varying beliefs about how policy would map onto outcomes. This variety helps explain the diversity of policy positions that we have encountered.

3. *The modification of campaign messages in pursuit of votes carried both advantages and risks.* The main advantage was increasing one's vote share

---

[19] Conaghan and Malloy are reporting the admiring interpretation of Paz's motives offered by Gonzálo Sánchez de Lozada, his co-party leader and successor in the presidency.

and hence the probability of winning. One risk was that voters would not view the shift as credible and hence that the effect would be to tarnish one's reputation for honesty and reliability. Indeed, credibility problems limit politicians' ability to refashion their identities and reposition themselves in policy terms during campaigns. The Chilean right was not believed when it advocated security-oriented reforms, and Daniel Ortega declined to change his position on the draft because he believed voters wouldn't believe him and might actually turn against him for attempting a "campaign trick."

Other risks that politicians perceived should they switch to popular positions were the alienation of party activists and the possibility of having to renege on a popular promise, a move that might bring with it longer-term electoral costs.

4. *Competitive races favored the shifts toward voters' preferred policies.* Big leads encouraged candidates to reveal their own beliefs about what sorts of economic policies were appropriate; tight races encouraged dissimulation of these beliefs, especially when politicians saw their own beliefs as contrary to those of a majority of voters. We saw instances where politicians assured of victory were willing to reveal unpopular policy intentions in the campaign (e.g., Aylwin in Chile) and where politicians shifted during the campaign to a more revealing stance as they moved ahead of their opponent (e.g., Pérez in Venezuela). I speculated that, counterfactually, Daniel Ortega in Nicaragua might have shifted in a direction closer to that of the median voters, and risked having to renege on his promise later, had he known that the race was tighter than polls were reporting. We should expect policy switches after close races – or, more accurately, in races that candidates perceive to be close.

5. *Politicians face uncertainty about the impact of policies and about the preferences of voters.* Campaign strategizing took place in a world of considerable uncertainty. Politicians were uncertain about the mapping of policies onto outcomes and about the distribution of voter preferences. Politicians and technocrats, both efficiency- and security-oriented, made big mistakes in predicting policy outcomes. Both Carlos Andrés Pérez and Alan García miscalculated the economic effects of their respectively orthodox and heterodox packages, and both paid a heavy political price for their errors. Mario Vargas Llosa was just one of several candidates who overestimated his capacity to win voters over to his economic philosophy. Daniel Ortega, reading misleading polling data that overestimated his strength, refused to

match his opponents' popular promise to end the draft – a promise that Ortega probably would have had to break – and lost.[20]

6. *A recent experience of military rule favors politicians touting efficiency-oriented programs, old democracies security-oriented ones.* Both politicians and voters may have reasoned that the new political system was fragile and would be imperiled by a sharp reorientation toward welfare and distributive goals. Hence we saw that in Chile's first election campaign in 17 years a center-left coalition was careful to send messages reassuring to the private sector.

The point is significant for the following reason. Prominent theorists of the transition to democracy advocated fashioning electoral rules so that the right would gain representation in the legislature out of proportion to its electoral strength. Their notion was that if the right fared badly in early elections, an authoritarian backlash would threaten the young democracies. O'Donnell and Schmitter write: "[P]arties of the Right-Center and Right must be 'helped' to do well, and parties of the Left-Center and Left should not win by an overwhelming majority. This often happens 'artificially', by rigging the rules . . . or 'naturally,' by fragmenting the partisan choices of the Left" (1986:62). But in Latin America, nonrightist political parties sought to reassure business and the military, and voters worked into their calculus of support the need not to provoke authoritarians. Institutional engineering in favor of the right therefore was unnecessary.

The next chapter delves more deeply into the strategic logic of policy switches, allowing a fuller assessment of the incentives that induce them and the kinds of politicians likely to make them.

---

[20] Uncertainty about voters' intentions was exacerbated by skepticism about public opinion polls, a skepticism not uncommon among the political class in much of Latin America. For example, at an informal gathering in Caracas of journalists, politicians, and academics in November 1998, a few weeks before a presidential election, the conversation focused on the question "What candidate might defeat former Colonel Hugo Chávez Frías?" Chávez was an authoritarian retired officer who had led a coup attempt and whose party had done surprisingly well in recent legislative elections. In the run-up to the presidential election, the press assiduously covered the stalled negotiations between the candidates of AD and COPEI, the presumed outcome of which would be the withdrawal of one candidate and his or her throwing support behind the other to defeat Chávez. I wondered aloud why so much attention was focused on two candidates whose pooled vote share, according to the most recent poll, would not amount even to 10%. The answer was that the poll was flawed, dreamed up by a partisan newspaper editor.

3

Explaining Policy Switches

When politicians run on one platform and implement another, people often instinctively infer that they have self-interested motives and are turning their backs on their constituents. Yet as I show in this chapter, under some conditions politicians who wish to represent their constituents will change policies, even abruptly, upon taking office. I explore the strategic settings in which politicians who are trying to represent constituents well may immediately renege on campaign pronouncements, as well as settings in which politicians switch in self-interest and at the expense of constituents. I then turn to the Latin American experiences and argue that policy switches were often carried out by politicians who were attempting to represent constituents.

Representatives and Rent-Seekers

The first model I turn to draws on the fact that voters are not always certain about the impact of policies on their welfare.[1] Although they have beliefs about how policies will affect them, these beliefs can change in response to the outcomes they observe after policies are carried out. Perceiving this uncertainty, governments may switch to policies that are initially unpopular in order to advance their constituents' interests and win reelection.

Consider a two-period world in which politicians run for office and then for reelection at the end of the term. They have beliefs about which policy is best for voters. Candidates' beliefs are not known to voters, and the can-

---

[1] The discussion in this section draws heavily on the work of Joseph E. Harrington, Jr. (1993a, 1993b).

didates must decide whether to reveal or conceal these beliefs in the campaign before the first election. The candidate who wins must then decide which policy to implement. Politicians care about maximizing voters' utility income and about holding office.[2]

Voters also have beliefs about which policy is best. Voters' beliefs are not fixed but may change once policies are implemented and their results observed. We can conceive of voters' initial beliefs about how alternative policies will affect their utility income as a Bayesian prior; once they observe the outcomes of policies implemented in the first term, they revise their beliefs to take account of both their initial beliefs and the outcomes. Voters don't know politicians' beliefs before the first election, whether a given politician is of the type who believes that policy *a* is more effective than *b* or the reverse. But they know that if the incumbent enacted policy *a* in his first term, *a* is more likely to continue if the incumbent is reelected than if he is defeated by a challenger. Voters must make two choices: whom to vote for in the first election and then whether to support the incumbent or the challenger in the second election.

To get a sense of how voters' beliefs may change, consider the voter who initially believes that her utility income will grow more under security than under efficiency policies. In the first election she votes for the politician who promises security policies. If a majority of voters (or the median voter) share her belief, the politician sending the security message in the campaign wins. Suppose that the politician then switches to efficiency policies. If by the end of the term the income of voters, who initially preferred security policies, grew more than expected but not much more, they may still believe that security policies are more effective and support the challenger. If their income grew by much more than expected, they may infer that the prior beliefs on which their prosecurity preferences rested were incorrect and that efficiency policies were in fact better. In this case, they will support the incumbent for reelection.

Voters may be fairly sure of their prior beliefs or they may be very uncertain about the effects of policies and may not trust their initial instincts much. Furthermore, voters know that policy is only one factor influencing changes in their welfare. The determinants of their income can be expressed as

---

[2] Formally, the utility politicians derive from a term in office can be expressed as $u(k,y) = k + \theta(y)$, where k is the value of holding office and y is per capita income.

$$y(x) = w_x + e$$

where y is realized income, w_x is income induced by policy x, and e is a random and unobserved disturbance. Because voters don't observe this random component (e), even though they observe income (y) they don't know how much of it is due to policy (w_x). Voters can be thought of as holding the belief that w_x is associated with a probability distribution of future income, with a mean of μ and a variance σ^2. The more uncertain they are about the effect of policy on income, the larger the variance. And the more uncertain they are, the more the outcomes they observe, rather than their initial belief, will shape their ultimate belief about the appropriateness of a policy (Harrington 1993a).

Consider a voter who is fairly certain about the effect of efficiency-versus security-oriented economic policies on her future income. She expects her income under security policies to fall within a certain range, and the mean, which we can call μ, is higher than the expected mean under efficiency policies, which we can call μ'. Because she is fairly certain, the variance of this probability distribution is small. Perhaps ideological convictions drive her certainty. If she then observes her income grow more than expected under efficiency policies, she might attribute this to a large random disturbance (e) and continue to favor security-oriented policies. Her voting behavior in the second election would be sensitive to the policy pursued by the incumbent, not to performance on his watch. In contrast, the voter with very uncertain beliefs, perhaps one who is not very ideological, would tend to weigh observed changes in income more heavily than policy when she formulates a judgment at the end of the term.

Voters' uncertainty and the consequent plasticity of their policy preferences in light of outcomes, in turn, influence the electoral strategies of politicians. Consider a candidate who believes that voters greatly underestimate the relative effectiveness of efficiency over security policies. If voters' beliefs were certain and fixed, the candidate would face three choices. Either he could campaign on an efficiency program and lose. Or he could campaign on a security program, implement efficiency policies (which, he believes, will maximize income), and fail to be reelected. Or he could campaign in favor of security policies, implement them, and improve his chances of winning reelection, but at the cost of pursuing what he believes to be inferior policies. But if voters' beliefs can change in light of the outcomes they observe, then the politician has another, more appealing choice. He may campaign in favor of security, switch to efficiency, and – if incomes rise enough – still be reelected at the end of his term.[3]

Note that because voters consider both their prior beliefs and the results they observe in formulating their preferences after the first term, all things equal the standard that they will hold a politician to if he switches policies will be higher than the one they would hold him to if he enacted the policies that he campaigned on. At a given level of realized income, the popularity of a policy switcher, relative to a consistent politician, will be dragged down by voters' prior beliefs. Politicians, who anticipate this higher standard, will therefore switch only if they believe their preferred policies are far superior to those initially favored by voters.

This model is of interest because it offers a reasonable account of politicians' strategy in switching policies and – like our Latin American examples – of switching right away, not only after conditions have changed. It is also of interest for normative reasons. According to the model, politicians who switch are attempting to represent constituents: within the bounds of what they know and believe, they are trying to promote the welfare of citizens as best they can. They are representative even though they are, in the terms introduced in Chapter 1, unresponsive: their actions are at odds with the current preferences of their constituents. Because they view voters' beliefs as inaccurate, and hence anticipate that voters' preferences about policies will change, politicians are unresponsive and violate mandates *in order to act* as good representatives.

Note, furthermore, that (given the model's assumptions) not all politicians whose policies match their campaign messages are representative, whereas *all* who switch are. Politicians fall into three groups: (1) Those whose beliefs match those of the median voter. They run revealing their true intentions and then act consistently once elected. (2) Those whose beliefs are at odds with the beliefs of the median voter but who think their preferred policy will not outperform the one preferred by voters enough to induce a change in voters' preferences. If they care enough about holding office, these politicians also implement policies consistent with their campaign messages, but ones that they think are worse for voters; they are *not* representing. (3) Those who conceal their intentions and then

---

[3] Harrington shows that the propensity to switch policies in office is also a function of the relative value to the politician of income versus holding office.

switch. They are implementing policies that they think are best for voters. Hence if we observe only politicians' messages and policies, we will not be able to distinguish representative from nonrepresentative politicians among those who act consistently, whereas switching is a sure marker of representative politicians.[4]

But now imagine a grimmer world, one inhabited not by good, representative politicians alone – ones whose utility in office is increasing in per capita income – but also by bad politicians, who want to win office in order to get something that is costly to voters. They may steal from the treasury or take kickbacks or make policy concessions in return for campaign contributions. In the Latin American context, perhaps politicians' opportunities for rents are enhanced under neoliberal reforms. Neoliberalism is preferred by market actors, and these actors can reward reformers with bribes or kickbacks or by generally making life easier for the reformers. Whereas it will be in voters' interest to implement efficiency policies only when conditions warrant them, say when the deficit is high and inflation threatens, bad, rent-seeking politicians prefer efficiency policies regardless of conditions. Voters do not observe conditions directly, nor do they observe whether a particular candidate is a representative or a rent-seeker. Voters listen to campaign pronouncements by politicians in favor of security or efficiency, which is equivalent to announcing that conditions are, respectively, good or bad.

Consider the situation in which a representative politician anticipates good conditions and hence pronounces himself in favor of security policies in the campaign. The rent-seeker type mimics this campaign, fearing that she will lose the election if she does not. Voters hear two pro-economic-security messages and choose by tossing a coin or by some other criterion. Now consider that the rent-seeker wins. She announces that she was wrong about conditions and switches to efficiency. For example, she may claim that the treasury is almost empty but that this fact was hidden by the previous government. In contrast, the representative politician will switch only when he anticipates that efficiency policies will produce a much larger improvement in income than voters expected. Representative politicians switch from security campaign messages to efficiency policies only when they anticipate considerable improvement in economic out-

---

[4] Their actions may fall short of deeper senses of representation, however, which I take up in Chapter 6.

comes; rent-seekers switch whatever the anticipated economic consequences of doing so.

Another condition will induce representative politicians to switch: when
they find themselves sharing power with other parties in postelection coalitions or facing an opposition majority in the legislature. Either coalition
partners or opposition parties may insist on deviations from the governing party's campaign platform. Given that our cases of policy switches are
all in one direction, from security campaigns to efficiency policies, minority or coalition status would be an inducement to switch only for representative politicians. The reason is as follows. If a rent-seeker runs on a
security message, he will always switch once in office, whether he forms a
majority, coalition, or minority government.[5] But a representative who
runs on a security campaign but finds himself leading a government
that is not in the majority may switch merely as a concession to coalition
partners.

The foregoing discussion suggests five test implications of the hypothesis that policy switchers were trying to act as representatives.

> *Test implication 1: Politicians' beliefs.* Politicians who switch believe that
> voters greatly underestimate the relative effectiveness of efficiency
> over security policies, that they must hide this belief to win office, but
> that switching to efficiency policies once in office is good for voters
> and improves their or their party's prospects at the next election.
>
> *Test implication 2: Voter uncertainty.* All else equal, the less certain voters
> are about the appropriateness of policies, the more likely policy
> reversals are.
>
> *Test implication 3: Economic outcomes.* All else equal, the economy
> improves more under switches than under consistent policies.
>
> *Test implication 4: Term limits.* Politicians facing term limits are no more
> likely to ignore mandates and switch than those who may run for
> reelection. If term limits were a cause of switches, this would suggest
> that politicians who switched did so in pursuit of rents.
>
> *Test implication 5: Majority status.* Policy switches are associated with
> shared rule: minority and postelection coalition governments.

---

[5] Because the bad type (like the good type) wants to maximize utility over two terms and
hence has an interest in reelection at the end of the first term, he may not switch in the
first term but wait until the second term to do so.

In the remainder of this chapter, I test the hypothesis that Latin American policy switches were carried out by politicians who were attempting to represent. I do so by exploring whether these test implications describe the reality of elections and economic policy making in post-debt-crisis Latin America.

As we move from abstract models to reality, we expect greater complexity and ambiguity. The evidence to be presented decisively argues against considering most policy switchers as ignoring their mandates in pursuit of rents in any crude sense. Yet neither do their actions conform neatly, in all ways, to those predicted by the model of representation outlined previously. It will be useful to signal from the outset some of the slippage between this model and the particular governments to be discussed in this chapter. First, the idea that government leaders are from the very outset of their term focused on the next election should not be taken literally. Some faced term limits, which meant that they would never be able to run again, or could run again only after sitting out one or two terms; much could transpire in the interim, including, not implausibly, military interventions that could draw the curtain on this democratic episode. Furthermore, economic crisis, and in some cases civil war, tended to shorten the time horizon of politicians, who might be more focused on getting through the week than on an election that might take place 4, 6, or 12 years hence. Because the institutional and political settings were so different, Latin American presidents were a far cry from, say, U.S. members of Congress, who virtually begin their reelection campaigns the day after they are elected.

These considerations should not be taken as invalidating the claim that politicians cared, and cared perhaps above all else, about their standing in public opinion, even if their concern was not tied from the outset to a new election. Why else might they care? Aldrich (1995) makes the sensible suggestion that politicians strive to have long and successful careers, a component of which is winning election and governing successfully. Success might be measured by the victory of one's own political party at the next election when a particular officeholder is kept by term limits from running again. Even term limits – the effect of which on politicians' propensity to violate mandates I will consider later – have been remarkably malleable in Latin America. In the last decade of the twentieth century, three presidents modified term limits, thus enabling themselves to run again; two of the three attempted to interpret the modified rules to enable themselves to run yet a third time (one successfully), and others instigated public discussions of modifications at times when they were popular and thought they could win.[6]

No doubt politicians desire public support for its own sake, for the same sorts of reasons that people like to be popular with their acquaintances, teachers with their students, and parents with their children – even though students don't fire teachers and children don't fire parents. Toward the ends of their careers, politicians may also begin to worry about their standing in history and to engage in what Albert Hirschman has called *obituary improvement* (cited in Domínguez, 1997). These objectives may come into conflict with one another, and when they do, it is of no small theoretical or normative import which one prevails. If I toil long hours over lectures to please my students, I am likely to annoy friends and family; and political leaders may find themselves facing a trade-off between current popularity and actions that they expect to earn them accolades in the history books. Yet when they consider these sorts of trade-offs, they worry about how to serve and what version of representation will gain them most honor and prestige; none of these considerations warrants a simple notion of rent-seeking.

If the theoretical assumption of politicians as constant vote maximizers can be modified without much damage, another set of assumptions is more problematic. These are assumptions about politicians' beliefs, in particular (1) that the beliefs are rational, that is, shaped by all information that is available at costs that the decision maker will rationally bear, and therefore (2) that their beliefs are reliable guides to action. Politicians who plausibly violated mandates in order to act as good representatives sometimes presided over policies that just didn't work or didn't work as they had predicted. Rather than enjoying the spontaneous adulation of citizens dazzled by the results, these leaders found themselves out of office or scrambling to mobilize support with end-of-term modifications in their efficiency-oriented policies. More profoundly, the belief evinced by politicians that voters would change their minds in light of good results

---

[6] Fernando Henrique Cardoso of Brazil, Alberto Fujimori of Peru, and Carlos Menem of Argentina modified term limits and, as sitting presidents, ran successfully for reelection. Fujimori and Menem, both in their second terms, claimed that they were serving their first term under the new rules and therefore should be allowed to run yet again. Menem ultimately desisted, but Fujimori ran for a third consecutive term and won in a controversial election. Popular presidents, like Alan García of Peru in the first years of his term, proposed modifying term limits, but later gave up on the proposal when it became clear that they were unlikely to win.

sometimes seems to be a product of wishful thinking – shaped by preferences – rather than rational information-gathering (Elster, 1989:37–38). Politicians whose beliefs reflect the ends they wish to achieve rather than the information they have, and who therefore make mistakes, are not rent-seekers in any simple sense, but they may also not be representatives in a broad sense of the term.

Politicians' Beliefs

What we can know about politicians' beliefs is inherently limited. We don't have access to their inner thoughts, and they have strategic reasons for hiding these thoughts. Yet we can learn a great deal about the beliefs they probably hold by examining their words, actions, the likely strategies these reveal, and the interpretation of actors who may have known and influenced these beliefs and for whom less is at stake. With these methodological caveats in mind, I will argue that some politicians who switched from security-oriented campaigns to efficiency policies believed that if they pursued security policies they risked creating economic havoc. They believed that a majority of voters nonetheless preferred security policies, and hence that to advocate efficiency policies in campaigns would be tantamount to accepting defeat. Yet they anticipated that if they sent security-oriented messages in campaigns, won, and switched to efficiency, voters would come to support them and their parties in subsequent elections.

Some politicians who pronounced themselves in campaigns to be in favor of expansionist policies but who in office reversed themselves believed that if they fulfilled the policy expectations created in their campaigns, they risked precipitating an economic collapse. These were the fears of Carlos Andrés Pérez in Venezuela. His predecessor, Jaime Lusinchi (1983–1988), presided over an expanding economy, with GDP growth averaging over 5% in the last two years of Lusinchi's term. Yet in the context of declining oil prices the expansion was unsustainable. The Lusinchi government was able to hide some signs of economic distress from Pérez, Pérez's advisors, and the broader public. For example, not until the new government came to office did it know the degree of depletion of foreign reserves, a fact that the then dependent central bank colluded in hiding (see Martz, 1995; interview with Carlos Blanco, November 1988). Even so, the overvaluation of the bolívar was readily apparent to Pérez and his advisors before the election, as was inflation. During the campaign, Pérez gathered around him economists who foretold a dark future should his government not adopt a course of austerity and liberalization. Moisés Naim, a young economist who would serve as Pérez's first minister of development, was cautious when the president-elect first approached him, expressing unwillingness to serve unless the new government adopted radical reforms. "I told him, 'Venezuela is about to experience the worst inflation in its history'" (interview, January 1993). In another interview, a former cabinet member told me that Pérez initially turned macroeconomic policy over to the liberal economists in his cabinet, led by the minister of planning, Miguel Rodríguez, and interfered little. Pérez was hesitant about the political viability of some structural reforms, such as privatization of the telephone company, but eventually was won over to these reforms as well (interview with Fernando Martínez Móntola, November 1998).

Pérez was also influenced in a negative way by observations of the presidential term of Alan García in Peru (1985–1990; Naim, 1993; interview with Martínez Móntola, 1998). García, a friend and colleague in the Second Socialist International, implemented a heterodox stabilization program; his term ended in recession and hyperinflation. The Peruvian debacle was one that the Venezuelan leader hoped not to repeat.

Alberto Fujimori was also counseled by powerful actors that his term would end in economic chaos were he to implement the policies he had outlined during his presidential campaign. After the run-off election in June 1990, several politicians with connections to conservative parties and international finance approached Fujimori. The most important, for a brief time, was Hernando de Soto, author of *The Other Path* (1989), a book that blamed Peru's economic woes on excessive state regulation. De Soto encouraged Fujimori to travel abroad to meet with government and financial leaders and offered to arrange some contacts. Adolfo Figueroa and Santiago Roca, now in charge of Fujimori's transition team, and Oscar Ugarteche, the team's expert on foreign debt, advocated delaying meetings with international financial leaders until after the gradualist stabilization program was underway. De Soto prevailed, and Ugarteche resigned. Figueroa agreed to accompany Fujimori and De Soto on the condition that the trip would be one of protocol, not substantive discussions.

The three arrived in New York on June 22 (ironically, while the furor still raged over George Bush's then-recent reneging on his "no new taxes" campaign pledge.) In an interview with me, Figueroa recalled realizing quickly that he had underestimated De Soto's business and political contacts. De Soto's brother, Alvaro de Soto, was a special assistant to United Nations Secretary General Javier Pérez de Cuellar, a Peruvian. Through Pérez de Cuellar, De Soto arranged a meeting on June 28 at the UN between Fujimori and Michel Camdessus, the managing director of the IMF; Barber Conable, the president of the World Bank; and Enrique Iglesias, the president of the Interamerican Development Bank (IDB). At the meeting, as reported to me by Figueroa (who also attended), the leaders of the international financial institutions communicated the following alternatives to Fujimori. If the new president did not carry out an immediate and sharp financial adjustment, his administration would run the course of Alan García's. If he did not adjust, he ought not to turn to the international financial institutions for help. If he did adjust and complemented "realistic" short-term stabilization measures with structural reforms, he could count on the financial institutions for full support.

The Japan leg of the trip was equally disastrous from the perspective of Fujimori's neo-Keynesian advisors. When the president-elect met the Japanese prime minister, the latter said that he planned to help Peru but admonished Fujimori first to reach an agreement with the IMF. In an interview, Santiago Roca joked that when Fujimori met the emperor of Japan, the latter's first words were "Nice to meet you, Mr. Fujimori. Reach an agreement with the IMF." It was on the plane trip back to Lima that Figueroa realized that Fujimori would no longer require his advice. Within weeks Figueroa and Roca had resigned.

When Fujimori returned to Peru at the end of his international tour, domestic forces redoubled the pressure to abandon the policies he had campaigned on. A former advisor reported to me the following illustrative anecdote. One evening shortly after Fujimori's return from abroad, he found Fujimori watching two television political talk shows simultaneously. On both, conservative economists were offering their views on how the incoming government should handle macroeconomic policy and advocated a large fiscal adjustment. Fujimori turned to the advisor and said, "You see, *everyone* wants a shock." The view of Fujimori's early advisors was that this pressure, combined with pressure from international financial institutions and governments on his international tour, persuaded him to change course. Whatever the theoretical merit of his campaign economic promises such as *el anti-shock*, and whatever their mass appeal, no good could come of a policy course that had so many powerful opponents.

The timing of Fujimori's conversion to neoliberalism is suggestive of a kind of "new information" scenario of the sort outlined in Chapter 1, whereby the politician reveals his policy intentions in the campaign but learns information once in office (or during the transition period) that persuades him that his intended policies will not have the intended effect. Pérez also was responding, in part at least, to pressures brought to bear on him as president-elect, not as a candidate. Yet, as we shall see, evidence suggests that both men, still as candidates, sensed that their campaign pronouncements might be at odds with their actual policies and suppressed these intuitions for electoral reasons.

If candidates like Pérez and Fujimori sensed that the security-oriented policies they pronounced might not be the ones they would actually pursue, why did they not simply campaign in favor of efficiency-oriented reforms? The answer is simple: they feared they would lose. Hence some policy switchers displayed a belief structure like the one that the representation model predicts will induce a policy switch. They believed that the policies preferred by a majority of voters would in fact induce bad results, in large part because of the opposition of markets to these measures, but thought they couldn't win if they revealed these intuitions.

This thought structure is well illustrated by Carlos Menem and his campaign strategists in Argentina. Various actors involved in Menem's 1989 campaign, including eventually Menem himself, suggest that the shift from a traditional Peronist position to austerity and structural reforms occurred before the election, in fact before the national campaign was in full swing.[7] In an interview I conducted in April 1993, Julio Bárbaro, Menem's campaign aide in charge of corporate contributions, reported that Menem decided to recruit his finance minister from the firm Bunge y Born immediately after his victory in the Peronist primary elections, which took place in July 1988, a full year before he became president. Other Menem insiders, such as Alberto Kohan, Julio Corzo, and Rubén Cardozo, met with representatives of Bunge y Born and other members of the business establishment, such as Carlos Bulgheroni of the Bridas conglomerate and Julio

---

[7] Palermo and Novaro (1996:128) claim that the eventual shape of reforms was not known before the election, and adduce as evidence Menem's spontaneous and volatile temperament, which would have made it impossible for him to keep the plans secret. Yet the decision to turn the finance ministry over to Bunge y Born managers carried the implication of austerity and pro-market reforms. It is plausible that the speed and depth of the reforms were not known and that the postelection hyperinflation and riots induced the government to act more quickly.

Ramos, owner of the conservative financial newspaper *Ambito Financiero* (Palermo and Novaro, 1996:214).

The belief that the candidate who revealed intentions to pursue market liberalization would lose was displayed by Roberto Dromi, a Menem insider and early cabinet member, whom I interviewed in 1994. What follows is a part of that interview:

Stokes: If Menem knew in the campaign that he would pursue austerity and liberal reforms once in power, why did he not say so in the 1989 campaign?
Dromi: In this country, 10% of the labor force were government employees. We knew that if we talked of privatizing Aerolíneas Argentinas [the national airline], we would have the airline workers on our backs, if we talked of privatization, we would have those workers on our backs. We thought we might lose the support of Left Peronists, the unions, protected industries, and public employees. And we were not confident of winning. At first we thought Cafiero would win the primary, then we thought Angeloz would win the election.

The best explanation for why Menem's campaign was misleading comes from Menem himself. In a 1993 interview with an Argentine journalist he described his strategy during the 1989 campaign:

The three golden rules of leadership are, one, to be perfectly informed, two, to keep that information secret, and three, to act by surprise. I did this all my life. If during the electoral campaign I had said to the people "we are going to renew relations with England," I would have lost 20% of the voters. If I had said, "I will privatize the telephones, the railways, and Aerolíneas Argentinas," the whole labor movement would have been against me. *There was not yet a clear consciousness of what was required.* (Cited in Nun, 1994:22; my emphasis)

Consistent with the representation model, the candidate believes that he will lose the election if he reveals his policy intentions, because voters do not understand the true costs of their own preferred policies or the true benefits of policies they fear. But, Menem suggests, they will with time come to understand that these policies were best: "There was not *yet* a clear consciousness of what was required."

Alberto Fujimori too thought that in order to win he had to persist in campaign messages emphasizing economic security, despite an intuition that these messages might not predict the eventual course of his policies. An anecdote, reported to me by Fernando Villarán, a campaign advisor, reveals Fujimori's thinking at the time. Villarán was suspicious of candidate Fujimori's dogged insistence on *el anti-shock*. Some adjustment is coming, Villarán told Fujimori, so you shouldn't place so much weight on the anti-shock. He admonished Fujimori, "Try to think more like a states-man, not like a politician." Fujimori replied, "If I don't think like a politi-cian now I'll never get to be a statesman." The difference between Menem and Fujimori was between some relatively well-formulated policy inten-tions that remained hidden and a vague intuition that campaign pro-nouncements might not be carried out. Yet both candidates believed that voters would reject them if they announced liberalization measures, and therefore both hid their intentions or intuitions.

In contrast, when candidates favoring pro-market policies believed they could advocate these policies openly without risk of losing, they did so. They may not have feared losing because an overheated economy led voters to fear efficiency policies or because no credible opponent could pronounce security beliefs. This was the case, as we saw in Chapter 2, of the Chilean *Concertación* in 1989. Patricio Aylwin's campaign strategists thought there was little to fear in electoral terms from advocating a continuation of the Pinochet regime's neoliberal model in slightly modified form because their opponents on the right could not credibly shift to a security position. (They also believed that a restrained economic message reduced the likelihood of meddling by the military.) Despite downplaying the social problems that polls showed that most voters wanted the next government to ameliorate, Aylwin defeated the right by a 29% margin.

Candidates with a neoliberal campaign stance sometimes modified their stance when races tightened. In Peru in 1990, Mario Vargas Llosa had been a distant front-runner for a full year, during which he expounded a radical version of neoliberalism. During the campaign leading up to the general election in April, Vargas Llosa's television ads, which ended with the message "It will cost us, but together we will make the Great Change," signaled his willingness to impose liberal reforms with all their costs. Despite conflicts within the campaign over this strategy, and despite polling and focus group data showing soft support among low-income people (who constituted a majority of the electorate), the campaign per-sisted with an efficiency-oriented message until after the general election (see Daeschner, 1993; Salmon, 1993; Vargas Llosa, 1993). Fighting for survival against Fujimori in the run-off, Vargas Llosa turned control of his campaign over to a faction that had pushed all along for a less strident message. Yet Vargas Llosa is an ideologue, and he had difficulty project-ing a softer image. Postelection polls cited in Chapter 2 indicate that people were not persuaded by his partial shift away from neoliberalism.

In Venezuela in 1988, Pérez pulled ahead of his opponent in public opinion polls in October for reasons that seemed to have to do more with the COPEI candidate's personality than with policy. Pérez then began to hint at exchange rate liberalization, one element of what eventually would be the *Gran Virage*.

Statistical analysis confirms that in close races, winners stuck to security-oriented messages. Using the LACAP database, I estimated a probit model of the probability that a security-oriented candidate would win. The smaller the margin of victory, the more likely that the victor was someone who made security-oriented promises in the campaign; bigger margins were associated with a greater probability that the winner had taken a chance on a neoliberal orientation in the campaign (see the appendix to this chapter).

If candidates thought voters overestimated the benefits of security-oriented policies and underestimated the benefits of neoliberalism, the question remains, why could they not simply hope to educate or persuade voters in campaigns? The question is the more compelling because, as we shall see, all things equal, politicians paid a price for switching policies. The answer is that voters seemed to perceive that the pool of politicians included some who would like to impose harsh measures for bad reasons, such as to benefit the economic elite or international financial interests at the expense of common citizens. Their lingering sense that Peru's Vargas Llosa "represented the interests of the rich" (Apoyo, 1990) is evidence of this suspicion. Candidates who believed that efficiency policies were best for their constituents would have difficulty sending campaign messages distinguishing themselves from those whose real concern was for some elite special interest. Words would not persuade skeptical voters, but good performance under efficiency policies might.

In sum, both qualitative evidence from campaigns and statistical analysis of cross-national data offer evidence that fear of losing elections induced politicians to hide their policy intentions.

Yet evidence of this belief structure does not adjudicate between the representative and the rent-seeking models of policy switches. Both kinds of politicians are expected to hide their true intentions to win office. The critical question is, Did they dissimulate and switch because they thought efficiency policies were in the best interest of voters or because they found efficiency policies advantageous for themselves, whether or not they would be good for voters?

Argentina in 1989 offers strong evidence that policy switchers were sometimes motivated by the belief that the economy would perform much better under efficiency-oriented than under security-oriented policies, and that voters would eventually see the shift to liberalization as beneficial. This view, repeated to me by several Menem strategists, was most fully elaborated by Roberto Dromi. The interview partially quoted earlier continued as follows:

Dromi: In this country, 10% of the labor force were government employees. We knew that if we talked of privatizing Aerolíneas Argentinas, we would have the airline workers on our backs, if we talked of privatization, we would have those workers on our backs. . . .

Stokes: But you believed these measures [privatization, fiscal adjustment] were needed to lower inflation. If you stated your intentions, you might have won the support of the 90% of Argentine workers who didn't work for the government and who suffered from inflation. (At this point in the interview, which took place in Dromi's law office, he pulled from the shelf *Nuevo Estado, Nuevo Derecho* [Dromi, 1994], a book he had authored, and opened to the epigraph, a quote from Machiavelli's *The Prince*, which he then read aloud):

[T]here is nothing more difficult to try, nor more doubtful of success, nor more dangerous to deal with, than to take it upon oneself to introduce new institutions, because the introducer makes enemies out of all those who benefit from the old institutions and is feebly defended by all those who might benefit from the new ones. This feebleness arises, in part from the fear of the opposition, who have the laws on their side, in part from the skepticism of men, who do not truly believe in novelties until they see them arising out of firm experience.[8]

Dromi continued: We knew that Argentines would disapprove of the reforms we planned, but would come to see that they were good. And we also wanted to send a message.

Stokes: A message to whom?

Dromi: To God and the devil, to Morgan Guaranty, the U.S. government, the World Bank.

Dromi aptly captured three pieces of our story. First, whatever the economic policy preferences of these Peronists, they saw themselves as constrained by markets. The optimal policy, given market constraints, was efficiency-oriented reforms. Hence the need to send a message "to Morgan Guaranty, the U.S. government, the World Bank." Second, Dromi anticipated a shift in the beliefs of voters regarding policy. Ex ante, before the "firm experience" of pro-market reforms, their posture was one of skepticism. Yet ex post, when they have been instructed by firm experience, Menem and some of his strategists believed voters would come to support

---

[8] The translation of Machiavelli is Paul Sonnino's (1996). The excerpt is from Chapter VI. Dromi's Spanish version differs in some details from Sonnino's English rendering.

efficiency-oriented reforms and the government that had put them in place. Third, policy makers perceived efficiency policies as best *given* constraints by powerful market actors. But it was hard to convey this strategic situation to voters, who would be likely to believe that market elites, not they, would benefit from efficiency policies. The perspective of Peronists was that, in an unfavorable world economic context, *not* to send the right signals to markets was to risk another economic breakdown. And they believed, or persuaded themselves to believe, that voters also would acknowledge the neoliberal road as having been the right one toward stability and growth. We shall see in Chapter 5 that Argentine voters did seem to be won over to the view that Menem was justified in having switched, whereas voters in other countries who lived through switches were unpersuaded.

Not all actors involved in the 1989 Menem campaign accept this interpretation of the evolution of his campaign messages and policy. An alternative explanation is that Menem's campaign messages expressed accurately his policy intentions at the time. But hyperinflation and social unrest broke out in the months following the election, and these new conditions precipitated the change of course. This was the interpretation, for example, of Rodolfo Díaz, who served as coordinator of the PJ's Platform Commission. In a written interview with the author (July 2000), Díaz wrote:

The elections were in May and Menem won. From that moment on, the edifice of institutions fell apart and hyperinflation exploded. In public opinion, the demand for stability overcame demands for redistribution. Among economic agents, uncertainty raised transaction costs to unsustainable levels. Menem had to assume power six months early. This triple circumstance (paralysis of institutions, hyperinflation, and early transition) is what motivated the new government – and legitimized in society – the option for harsh measures. (Author's translation)

Note that Díaz's account of an abrupt change from campaign message to early government policy emphasizes changed conditions postelection; these changes made the prior campaign proposals of the winning candidate inappropriate, a fact recognized by politician and public alike. Though different from the representation model, this scenario is also one in which the politician changes course in an effort to serve the interests of voters rather than in pursuit of rents.

Yet the changed-conditions account of Menem's change of course is not entirely persuasive. There is little doubt that the economic chaos and social unrest of the final months of the Alfonsín government made it easier for Argentines to accept harsh fiscal adjustment (see Echegaray and Elordi, 2001). But sharp economic decay, which came to a head after the election, was in progress well before the election. The average monthly inflation rate in 1988 was over 14%, and prices jumped sharply in February 1989 (see Smith, Acuña, and Gamarra, 1993). Still Menem persisted with a "redistributive" message: *The Productive Revolution* (*La Revolucion Productiva*, 1989), the campaign book of Menem and his running mate, appeared in early 1989 and devoted a chapter to the *salariazo* ("*El salariazo: para una economía popular*"). And right through the campaign, in the midst of a volatile economy, the Peronist proposals on inflation stabilization, exchange rate policy, and the foreign debt remained consistently statist and interventionist, in contrast to the calls for market liberalization of the other major contending parties (see Clarín, April 28, 1989).

In office, the Menem government did not limit itself, furthermore, to fiscal adjustment, but instead pursued, through successive economic ministers, a far-reaching program of economic liberalization (see Canitrot, 1993; Smith, 1991). But most at odds with the new-conditions explanation of Menem's change of course are the words of Menem himself, cited earlier. By his own account, the candidate foresaw during the campaign that in office he would undertake liberalization policies. But he suppressed these intentions because he sensed that Argentines did not yet have "a clear consciousness of what was required," and because he feared that to announce them openly would be to risk losing the election. In sum, although the searing effect of events in Argentina in the 60 days following the 1989 election cannot be understated, it seems that the representation model, rather than changed conditions, better explains Menem's policy switch.

In Peru, Fujimori's strategic choices appear to have been conditioned by extremely short-term considerations. With no real party and a highly tactical orientation, Fujimori's guiding principle was to win the election and worry later about how to govern. This was the sense of his comment to Villarán, quoted earlier, that he had to win the election before he could concern himself with statesmanship. Fujimori is a pragmatist by temperament, and the combination of economic crisis and a serious security threat from Shining Path guerrillas further discouraged him from taking the long view. It is unlikely that Fujimori in mid-1990 was looking forward as far as 1995, when a successor could run for reelection, much less to 2000, when he would first be eligible to run for reelection under the term limits then in force. In switching to efficiency reforms, Fujimori seems to have been trying not to maximize his own future electoral prospects but to avoid the risks he began to see as associated with policies unpopular with markets, and thus to put himself in the best possible political position vis-à-vis both the markets and the public.

If Fujimori's time horizon was shorter than a presidential term, Carlos Andrés Pérez's was longer. Pérez was 67 years old in 1988; he had already served one term as a popular president and was anxious to assure his place in history. This anxiety tended to shift his attention from the Venezuelan to the international stage. Nevertheless, to be remembered by history as a success, Pérez had to rule over a healthy and expanding economy and to create the conditions for reelection of his party's candidate in 1994. According to people close to him, Pérez believed that his domestic prestige would carry the government through a tough but brief adjustment, and growth would follow. What he certainly did not anticipate was what in fact happened: riots in response to price adjustments, challenges from the military, and impeachment that kept him from even serving out his full term.

Venezuelan campaign strategists and architects of the *Gran Virage* thought that the success of reforms over a relatively short period would be self-evident and hence that people would agree that this had been the right path. According to Carlos Blanco, a minister under both the Lusinchi and Pérez governments, Pérez's economists believed that the transition would be painful for a year or two, during which the government would survive "on the prestige of Carlos Andrés Pérez" (interview, November 1998). As we saw, the government's initial adjustment measures produced much worse results than had been expected; former government members blame the government's failure on these bad economic results, as well as the failure of the political leadership to sell the policy more actively.

To summarize, we have seen that in some settings politicians dissimulated neoliberal intentions in order to win elections, switched policies under pressure from markets, and were persuaded, or persuaded themselves, that voters, in light of the eventual results of these policies, would change their views and see these policies as having been the right ones.

But can we be certain that these politicians, or others who switched, did not act under the enticement of personal benefits or rents? If, as we have seen, policy switchers acted under pressure from markets, might they not have been anticipating some personal or partisan benefit, one costly to voters?

To answer this question it is useful to consider the form that rents can take:

Private financial gain, such as in exchange for bribes or in anticipation of kick-backs.

Quid pro quos for past campaign contributions or enticements for contributions in the future.

Economizing on effort or to save the psychic discomfort of sticking to a line of action that powerful actors oppose.

Pursuing ideological commitments or personal policy preferences.

In what follows, I consider the plausibility of each sort of rent as a cause of policy switches.

Private Financial Gain

Did the prospect of personal financial gain motivate politicians to change course? Certainly Latin America was rife with corrupt politicians in the neoliberal era, as evidenced by financial scandals leading to the impeachment of Fernando Collor in Brazil, as well as numerous ministers, bureaucrats, and legislators. Yet to make a plausible case, we need to show that corruption was linked to *neoliberal* programs and that the anticipation of opportunities for venality induced governments to switch at the outset of their terms.

Out-and-out bribery of officials by actors with an interest in reforms was unlikely. International financial institutions are not in the business of offering bribes, as far as we know. Even if, say, domestic exporters wanted to bribe politicians into liberalizing international trade, note that this sort of reform has qualities of a public good. It is nonrival in consumption: a general lowering of trade barriers would benefit many industries (and would hurt many others), and among those benefitting, both those who had bribed and those who had not would benefit indiscriminately. Therefore, those who stood to benefit faced substantial collective action disincentives from acting alone and legal risks if they attempted to coordinate their efforts. The only case of officials receiving bribes in return for support of liberalizing reforms that I know of is in Ecuador. But this was the case of Alberto Dahik, the zealous vice president under Sixto

Durán Ballén, who tried in 1994 to bribe legislators to support the government's liberalization program. When the press reported the bribes Dahik fled the country. This is the case of the government offering, not receiving, bribes!

A further difficulty with the proposition that politicians switched to neoliberalism in anticipation of illegal self-enrichment is that opportunities for corruption occur in many settings. It is hard to make the case that venal politicians would favor efficiency policies over other sorts. Indeed, neoliberal budget cutters eliminate many public works projects, a prime opportunity for kickbacks and bribes. When governments liberalize trade, they lose discretion over which industries to protect, and industries lose an incentive to bribe politicians. When governments eliminate multiple exchange rates, they lose discretion over whom to channel cheap hard currency to and hence opportunities to extract bribes.[9] Even Carlos Andrés Pérez, who was impeached in 1993 on accusations of the misuse of public funds, is not a good example of a policy switcher in pursuit of self-enrichment. His opponents accused Pérez not of appropriating public funds for private use but rather of illegally using funds from a discretionary account to support candidates in elections in Central America. Fernando Collor in Brazil (who announced efficiency policies, such as privatization, in his campaign) simply stole from the treasury, a form of corruption open to security- and efficiency-oriented governments alike.

One dimension of neoliberal reforms that creates opportunities for venality is privatization. Government officials have some discretion about which state-owned enterprises to sell, what sorts of investments to make before offering them for sale, on what terms to sell them and to whom, and how to write the enabling legislation. These decisions entail potential windfalls for investors, who therefore have an incentive to influence politicians with bribes. Furthermore, for the most part, few of the details of these transactions are known to common citizens.

Argentina under Menem was rife with corruption scandals, some of which ended in courts finding officials guilty. Corruption occurred in the privatization of national airlines and the telephone company (see Verbitsky, 1991). Several Menem insiders were implicated, including Roberto Dromi – ironically, the source who most eloquently laid out the

---

[9] Ricardo Hausmann, an economist and minister under Pérez, argues that the government introduced a floating exchange rate in part to fight corruption (see Hausmann, 1995).

case that the Argentine switch was in the interest of voters. Dromi, minister of public works at the beginning of the first Menem government, was forced out of office under accusations of venality in connection with privatizations.

Yet the fact that some officials extracted private financial benefit from policies is not proof that the anticipation of such benefits motivated the adoption of these policies. Is it plausible that these venal officials would not have found ways to enrich themselves had economic liberalization not occurred? But, most basically, it was the president himself in this and all other countries under consideration who initially decided on the neoliberal policy course, presidents who were embarrassed by the corruption of some of their associates but who seemed to be no more corrupt than their security-oriented counterparts elsewhere.

Campaign Contributions

Candidates and parties need financial support to compete in elections. If special interests contribute to campaigns and in return demand policy concessions, the result is a deadweight loss to consumers (see Becker, 1958; Stigler, 1975). Industry, international political parties, and foreign governments contribute to political campaigns in Latin America (see Ferreira Rubio, 1997a). The level of funding of campaigns varies widely, from multi-million-dollar efforts to shoestring operations. The most celebrated mismatch in recent memory was the 1990 Peruvian election, in which the $13 million candidate (Vargas Llosa) lost to the $700,000 candidate (Fujimori; see Barreto, 1990). The Vargas Llosa campaign relied on contributions from industry and wealthy individuals, the Fujimori campaign on self-financing and small contributions. Hence in this case, no big contributors existed who might demand policy reversal as a quid pro quo for past campaign support. Fujimori and his strategists might have anticipated future contributions; yet he knew he could win elections without them, and the inducements to change course, reviewed earlier, did not seem to include concerns about building a political party that would need major contributors.

Argentine industry contributed substantially to the Peronist campaign in 1988–1989 (Ferreira Rubio, 1997b). Among the contributors was Bunge y Born, the conglomerate that in Peronist folklore epitomized nefarious internationalized capital and that supplied Menem with his first two finance ministers.[10] Yet Menem insiders report a shift toward plans for austerity measures and market reforms early in the general election campaign, before they solicited funds from this conglomerate. In general, I find little evidence of politicians switching policies as a quid pro quo for campaign contributions or in anticipation of such contributions in the future.

Shirking

Some principal-agent models of democracy posit that officeholders will attempt to economize on effort, choosing a level of activity that is suboptimal from the perspective of their constituents (see Banks and Sundaram, 1993; Ferejohn, 1986). Consider the president of a developing country who wants not to work hard. He does what the IMF wants because he knows that otherwise it will take a lot of negotiating to secure loans. He could get a better deal for his country by expending more effort, but he doesn't. He is shirking, and hence failing to represent. With more effort, he could produce more income for voters; the utility he derives from the effort saved is therefore a rent.

It may be appealing to think of Alberto Fujimori's switch in these terms. Recall that he decided to fire his neo-Keynesian advisors under pressure from some powerful people: leaders of international financial institutions and foreign governments, as well as domestic opinion makers. By opting for domestic economic policies the IMF favored, Fujimori was saving his government work in its efforts to shed its ineligible-borrower status. Carlos Andrés Pérez saved much effort by adopting the *Gran Virage*; his team of economists could turn to the IMF for a ready-made adjustment program.

Yet there are many examples of these leaders and other policy switchers standing up to powerful actors, expending much effort, and enduring much psychic discomfort. A typical conflict, in which politicians demonstrated considerable willingness to stand up under pressure, was between governments and international financial institutions over what to do with revenues from the privatization of state-owned enterprises. The financial institutions usually pressed governments to apply these revenues to the cancellation of their foreign debt, whereas governments preferred to spend

---

[10] For an excellent discussion of this point, see Hausmann (1995).

them on public works or social programs or to cancel internal debts. In Ecuador this conflict produced many hours of tense debate in 1993 between an IMF mission and the Durán Ballén administration, which had switched policies after winning office a year earlier (interview with Pablo Lucio Paredes, 1993). Alberto Fujimori fought hard against the U.S. government over drug policy in the early 1990s, and Carlos Andrés Pérez tried to mobilize a regionwide debtors' cartel in 1989 – hardly a move likely to shield him from pressure from the international financial world. Of course, these same governments were willing to conform to the preferences of international financial and market actors; they were even willing to go overboard in order to "send a signal," in Roberto Dromi's words. But they showed this willingness only when doing so advanced an objective, generally a domestic political objective.

Ideological Commitments

Political ideologies are powerful in Latin America, and ideological predispositions undoubtedly informed the causal beliefs of voters and politicians alike. And from a certain vantage point, ideology can motivate a sort of rent-seeking. Consider the situation in which the policy ideal point of the median voter is x_v, the policy ideal point of the officeholder is x_p, and $x_v \neq x_p$. As Alesina and Spear (1988) show, even if all candidates converge on the position x_v in their effort to win election, if they care about policy and if their careers are finite, this commitment will not be credible and they will switch once in office to their ideological ideal point (see also Alesina, 1988). After some iterations, voters won't believe candidates unless they enunciate their true intentions. The "rent" the officeholder extracts is then the gap between the policy implemented and the ideal point of voters, which can be modeled as $(x_v - x_p)^2$. The gap is a rent because it reduces the median voter's utility in the governmental term, which can be represented thus: $u_t(x_t) = -(x_v - x_p)^2$.

Yet how plausible is it that ideological commitment motivated policy switchers? Some policy switchers were ideological conservatives. Sixto Durán Ballén of Ecuador was vice-president under a previous conservative administration, ran in 1992 on a moderate security-oriented platform, and then pursued austerity and pro-market reforms known as the *Nuevo Rumbo* or New Route. Rafael Calderón (1990–1994) in Costa Rica also ran promising housing for the poor and other social programs and hinted at trade protection for agricultural goods, but once in office he imposed austerity measures more in line with his and his Social Christian Party's ideology.

Yet what made many switches to neoliberalism so startling is that they were carried out by politicians whose ideological inclinations were toward the left. This was true of Menem, the Peronist, and of Pérez, the historic figure in AD; it was also true of Jaime Paz Zamora in Bolivia (1989–1993), a founder of the Movement of the Revolutionary Left; of José María Figueres in Costa Rica (1994–1998), of the social democratic National Liberation Party; of Salvador Jorge Blanco in the Dominican Republic (1982–1986), of the Dominican Revolutionary Party; and of Rodrigo Borja in Ecuador (1988–1992), of the Democratic Left. In none of these cases were ideological rents a likely explanation for policy switches.

Cukierman and Tomassi (1998) present a model in which politicians reverse long-standing economic policies and ideological commitments play a central role. They describe conditions under which parties of the left (right) will be more likely to implement policies that one would expect under a right (left) government. They want to explain *policy reversals*, which they define as policies that are surprising given the ruling party's ideological orientation. (Hence their explanandum is different from mine, which is policies that are surprising given campaign messages.) Their intuition is that governments can more credibly attribute policy reversals to extreme conditions (conditions unobserved by voters) than to party ideology (also unobserved) when reversals are carried out by the party least likely to favor them ideologically. Their motivating example is Richard Nixon's trip to China. U.S. voters would not infer that Nixon had hidden partisan-ideological motives for a trip to China, whereas they might if Hubert Humphrey made the trip; unlikely protagonists of extreme policies enjoy a credibility advantage. In Latin America both right-wing politicians (Durán Ballén, Calderón, Chamorro, Febres of Ecuador, and others) and left-wing politicians imposed neoliberal reorientations of policy. Hence Cukierman and Tomassi's model does not fully explain the Latin American turn toward economic liberalization.

There is another way of thinking about a rent that I have not considered thus far and that may help to clarify the behavior of one important actor in Latin America's unmandated neoliberalism. This is the rent as pure ego satisfaction. Perhaps some politicians were simply too self-regarding to care about designing policies that would help constituents.

Ego satisfaction, or a kind of *amour propre*, doesn't explain Carlos Andrés Pérez's switch to neoliberalism, but it does help explain the unraveling of his government under unpopular reforms. Many of Pérez's cabinet members came to believe that the president did too little to persuade the Venezuelan congress and leaders of the governing party to support the Great Turnaround, and that the declining popularity of the government, coup attempts, and impeachment of Pérez might all have been avoided had the president invested effort in the public presentation of reforms and thought harder about how to compensate those who were hurt by them. Yet obsessed as he was with his performance on the world stage – an obsession, some former cabinet members believe, fanned by his vanity – Pérez traveled frequently, appearing to be bored by Venezuelan politics and particularly dismissive of legislators from his own political party. His foreign travels became a matter of open conflict with the legislature, which tried, in late 1992, to keep him from traveling to Switzerland in the midst of rumors of a coup. Pérez's misallocation of public funds to support his Central American allies was a reason for his impeachment. Here then is an example of a politician's personal interests being perceived as a rent by domestic actors, although in this case the ego-rent is associated not with the change of course but with the failure to sell the neoliberal turn subsequently to the domestic public.

On close analysis, then, rents in their various guises seem not to have motivated policy switches. Some politicians were venal, but corruption was not policy-dependent and greed did not, on the whole, shape policy. Campaign contributions were not decisive in shaping policy switches to efficiency-oriented policies. Politicians were capable of hard work and withstanding substantial pressure when it was in their interest – above all their domestic political interest – to do so. And although these actors were intensely political, their chief motivation was not ideology but winning the domestic political game and hence enjoying a long and successful career in politics. The rent-seeking model fails because it begins with unrealistic assumptions about basic motives, motives that appear, under scrutiny, at odds with those of the politicians who changed course.

Voter Uncertainty

The second test implication of the representation model is that voter uncertainty about the mapping of policies onto outcomes increases the likelihood that politicians will change course.

There are good reasons why people everywhere would view the link between economic policy and economic outcomes as uncertain, and why this uncertainty would, in the setting of post-debt-crisis Latin America, run especially high. Why should voters be more unsure about the effects of economic policies versus other policies? It may be useful in this connection to draw a distinction between the primary and secondary effects of a policy. Primary effects are the changes it causes that are most immediate and intended. Secondary effects are ones caused by the primary effects; they may entail a longer time lag and are harder to predict than the primary effects. Now consider the contrast between one economic policy, say exchange rate liberalization, and another, such as the criminalization of abortion. Exchange rate liberalization will have a wide range of secondary effects, many of which potentially interfere with the objectives of the liberalization measure itself and which are hard to predict. For example, in addition to bringing nominal rates in line with real ones and hence inducing an efficient allocation of resources between domestic and external sectors, exchange rate liberalization may also cause inflation, a decline in economic activity, and increased unemployment. These secondary effects are shrouded in uncertainty, and yet they may undermine the initial objectives of the policy. In contrast, the criminalization of abortion will have the primary effect of reducing drastically the number of abortions performed by doctors in hospitals; it may have the secondary effect of increasing the number of illegal and unhygienic abortions and perhaps of stimulating greater investment in contraceptive technologies. But the secondary effects are likely to be fewer and to interfere less with the objectives of the initial policy: to reduce the number of abortions.

Political debate surrounding any policy is likely to center on both primary and secondary effects. Yet because economies are complexly interconnected systems, "delicate watches" (Hirschman, 1977), economic policy changes are likely to be especially shrouded in uncertainty. Greater uncertainty than usual attached to Latin American economic policy at the historical juncture of the post-debt-crisis years. Huge external shocks rocked the economies, beginning after August 1982, when international lenders withheld new loans. At the same time, experts, economists, and policy makers debated whether the country should undertake a drastic shift in the economic model. Little wonder that common citizens might have trouble distinguishing the effects of external conditions from those of domestic policy or sorting through the experts' claims and counterclaims about the benefits of alternative policy approaches. If voter uncertainty makes policy switches more likely, then the greater uncertainty attached to economic policy alternatives in Latin America in the postdebt crisis era than in the advanced industrial countries in normal times helps explain the rash of policy switches in the region.

Lacking direct measures of voter uncertainty, how can we test this hypothesis? Recall that in the representation model, when voters are uncertain, their view of whether an incumbent government is worthy of reelection will rely more on performance than on policy. Consider two voters. One is sure that economic security-oriented policies are in her interest; the other also favors security policies but is less sure. The government comes to power and switches to efficiency, and the results are good. The voter who was sure of her preferences is less likely to change her mind and decide that efficiency policies were best; she may believe that unusually good international conditions or other unobserved factors caused the good performance. The less certain voter is more willing to change her mind and decide that, against her expectations, efficiency policies caused the surprisingly good outcomes. When deciding whom to vote for the next time around, the voter who is certain will weigh economic outcomes little; the uncertain voter will weigh them a lot.

Extending this logic, if voter uncertainty causes policy switches, and if voters who are uncertain weigh performance more heavily than do voters who are certain, then the vote share of incumbents who switched at the beginning of their term should be more sensitive to performance than that of consistent incumbents. Using the LACAP database, I studied the impact of economic outcomes on the incumbent party's share of the vote, comparing this effect in settings where the term began with a policy switch and ones where it began with policies consistent with campaign messages. The analysis is indeed suggestive of an association between policy switches and uncertain voters (see the appendix). When politicians began their term by switching policies, their party's electoral performance at the end of the term was somewhat more sensitive to economic performance in the years leading up to the next election; when they began their term by pursuing policies consistent with their campaign messages, their end-of-term share of the vote was somewhat less sensitive to economic performance. This finding tends to support the interpretation that politicians who perceived voters as uncertain were prone to engage in bait-and-switch tactics.

It is also possible that policy switches *created* uncertainty. Consider the voter who places her faith in a politician who in the campaign opposes a fiscal shock on the grounds that it will exacerbate inflation. Imagine her confusion when that same politician, within weeks of taking office, announces a fiscal shock – claiming that the shock will end inflation! If politicians who changed course anticipated this confusion, they would also anticipate that their prospects at the end of the term would be all the more sharply determined by performance. It follows that they would invite such judgments only if they felt reasonably sure that their performance would be good and voters would come around. In contrast, if policy switchers were rent-seekers in any of the senses outlined earlier, we would expect varying levels of voter uncertainty not to affect the probability of their changing course.

If the representation model is a good way to think about the strategic dynamic leading to policy switches, all things equal, politicians who switch should be held to a higher standard than nonswitchers. Statistical analysis indeed suggests that, given two incumbents on whose watch economic performance has been the same, at the end of the term the consistent politician will receive more votes than the policy switcher (see the appendix). Perhaps norms of consistency and honesty lie behind this difference; perhaps, as Downs (1957) argued, voters wish to invest in the reliability of future campaign appeals. But the finding is also consistent with the representation model's assumption that voters as Bayesian updaters, whose ex-ante belief that a policy is not welfare-enhancing will depress their ex-post support for the government that imposes it, even if later the policy seems to work well.

Economic Outcomes

If the representation model of policy switches is correct, some politicians carrying out security policies believe efficiency policies would be more effective, but not effective enough to overcome voters' prior skepticism. In contrast, politicians who switch anticipate much better performance under efficiency than under security policies. Assuming that politicians' beliefs have any bearing on reality, good – representative – switches should be associated with better economic performance than consistent security policies.

The statistical analysis reported in the appendix shows that, controlling for differences in initial conditions, the economy grew 4% more under policy switchers than under governments that did not switch. The effect is startling, given what we have already learned about the impact of economic outcomes on the electoral fortunes of incumbents. For policy switchers, a 1% increase in GDP at the end of the term produced a 3% increase in the share of the vote. On average, then, the 4% increase in GDP for policy-switching incumbents was worth a full 12% of the vote that policy switchers would not have attracted had they not switched, enough to make the difference in many elections between winning and losing. And enough to overcome the electoral punishment of switching per se, the fact that on average, given identical economic outcomes, voters would tend to punish parties that, earlier, violated their mandate.

The lesson is not that all Latin American presidents should bait-and-switch if they want to improve voters' economic welfare and their own reelection prospects. Rather, our model describes politicians who switch only under certain conditions: when growth is sluggish, leading voters to favor security candidates; when voters are nevertheless uncertain that security-oriented policies are best; and when politicians believe that voters underestimate the benefits of efficiency-oriented policies. Politicians who reneged on their mandates under these conditions did so because they believed they would help voters, and hence their political careers; and on average they were right.

The cases we have followed closely in this study provide examples of the advantages that sometimes follow from changing course. When Menem first became president of Argentina, the economy had contracted on average 0.6% in the preceding two years. The average growth rate in the two years leading up to his reelection in 1995 was 5.5%. Given the model in Table 3.4 of the appendix, a leader facing similar conditions who did not switch to efficiency policies would have produced an end-of-term growth rate 4.2% lower: 1.3%. Such a sluggish economy would have added basically nothing to the share of the vote of our hypothetical nonswitching Menem when he ran for reelection. In contrast, the 5.5% growth rate for a switching Menem was worth almost a quarter of the national vote. A nonswitching Menem, then, might have received a mere 25% of the vote in 1995, rather than the 49% that the real Menem did receive, and almost certainly would have lost.

I repeat the phrase "on average" purposely. Some policy switchers saw the economy go sour, along with their or their parties' prospects of holding on to office. Others achieved some good economic results but not good enough to persuade skeptical voters that efficiency policies had been the best, and had to find other ways to mobilize support (see Chapter 5). What's important is that the expected improvement in economic conditions at the end of a policy switcher's term is hard to reconcile with a rent-seeking model of the violation of mandates. It is easier to reconcile with a model of policy switchers as interested in improving their constituents' welfare as a way to win their votes in later elections.

Term Limits

If term limits induced policy switches, we might infer that politicians had bad reasons for switching. Barred from reelection, they might be relatively indifferent to their popularity at the end of their term. They would not switch to unmandated policies believing that these were best for voters and that voters would later agree, but because they wanted to extract rents during the current term.

Consistent with the representation model – and against the rent-seeking model – statistical analyses show no effect of term limits on the probability that new presidents would change course (see the appendix). In the only estimation that achieved even close-to-significant results, term limits made policy switches less, not more, likely.

Majority Status

When politicians adjust policies because they have failed to constitute a majority government, they are not switching in pursuit of rents in any of the senses offered here. We expect deviations from the mandate in systems where institutional rules encourage coalition government. The Comparative Manifestos Project, a cross-national study of the fit between party manifestos and government programs, found that government actions deviated from party manifestos most frequently in Belgium and the Netherlands, two countries with frequent coalition governments (see Klingemann et al., 1994, chapters 12 and 13). Huber and Powell (1994) contend that proportionality systems, with their higher incidence of shared executive power, do not vitiate representation but rather implement a distinctive conception of it, the *Proportionate Influence vision*. Proportionate Influence maximizes the representation in government of the full range of constituencies, whereas *Majority Control* systems maximize the representation of the majority. Following Huber and Powell, we should interpret the violation of mandates by parties that find themselves sharing power not as a failure of representation but as an institutionally forced variation of the form of representation.

Coalition and minority governments caused policy switches in Latin America. The smaller the proportion of seats in the lower house of legislatures that the president's party occupied, the more likely the president was to change policies. Similarly, coalition and minority governments were more likely to change policies than governments controlled by a single party (see the appendix). Again, these findings favor an interpretation whereby electoral pressures and institutional features induce politicians to run campaigns that predict their policies poorly, not one whereby politicians bait and switch to indulge their ideology or line their pockets.

But we should be careful not to overstate the minority status effect on policy switchers. Latin American legislatures tend to be constitutionally weak and de facto even weaker. Presidents in many Latin American countries have wide-ranging executive decree powers and use these powers even more extensively than constitutions allow. Lack of party discipline further weakens legislatures (but see Shugart and Carey, 1992). Furthermore, in some instances, the anticipation of positive results from efficiency policies mattered more to politicians who changed course than concerns about dealing with the opposition or coalition partners. The Menem government is a case in point. When Menem faced congressional opposition, rather than make policy concessions to opponents he made ample use of the executive decree (*"decreto de necesidad y urgencia"*; see Ferreira Rubio and Goretti, 1998). Menem issued 336 decrees between July 1989 and August 1994; in the 136 years between 1853 and 1989, presidents had issued a mere 25 decrees. My interviews and secondary accounts (e.g., Palermo and Novaro, 1996) suggest that not the partisan opposition but pressure from markets, as well as future electoral strategies, shaped Menem's policy choices.

Similarly, one should not exaggerate the importance of Alberto Fujimori's minority status in determining the change of course. Fujimori faced an opposition majority, led by right-wing members of Congress who came to office on Vargas Llosa's coattails. The rightist opposition in Congress was unlikely, however, to mobilize opposition to Fujimori's neoliberal revolution, given that these were very close to the policies that their candidate had proposed. Fujimori's first cabinet was composed of representatives from a number of parties. Yet the cabinet, which included political figures from both left and right, played a small role in economic policy, and several members resigned early in response to Fujimori's economic program. By all accounts, pressures from markets played a larger role than pressure from the opposition majority in Congress, or contrary views in the cabinet, in causing Fujimori's change of course.

Minority status played a larger role in the policy reversal of Jaime Paz Zamora of Bolivia (1989–1993). Paz Zamora was a leader of the Movement of the Revolutionary Left (MIR), a Marxist party, who came in third in the popular vote for president. Constitutional rules at the time turned the selection of the president over to Congress if no candidate won an absolute majority of the vote. National Democratic Action (ADN) Congressmen joined the MIR to elect Paz Zamora president. We have little reason to believe that Paz Zamora was a convert to neoliberalism or that he believed that a continuation of his predecessor's "New Economic Program" of market liberalization was best for his constituents. But as a minority president, Paz Zamora would have had great difficulty enacting a program that diverged much from the one supported by the right. The continuation of neoliberalism in Bolivia was carried out by a cabinet full of members of Banzer's ADN, who occupied 10 of 18 positions, including the posts of finance and planning. Bolivia thus illustrates a policy reversal carried out by a postelection coalition government, one in which policy bore the imprint of a range of parties, not just the one of the president.

Summary and Conclusion

The drive to represent, not to extract rents, motivated most violations of mandate in Latin America. This is not to say that these countries were governed by angels or that democracy worked well. It is simply to say that politicians made decisions about how to campaign and then how to rule more with an eye to winning the domestic political game than to lining their pockets or caving in to raw pressure. And winning the domestic political game meant – among other things – mobilizing the support of constituents over the length of the term.

Here is a summary of some of the evidence we have seen in favor of the representation model as an explanation of mandate violations:

- Politicians who switched believed that security-oriented policies would lead to bad economic outcomes, because their countries' economies would be punished by markets; but they believed that voters would reject them if they ran on an efficiency-oriented program.

- Economic performance was better under policy switches than under consistent governments. Because incumbent parties' electoral performance was sensitive to economic outcomes at the end of their terms, superior economic performance meant that incumbents who switched also improved their electoral prospects. This happened despite the fact that, all things equal, voters showed a slight tendency to punish policy switchers in subsequent elections.
- Presidents who were under term limits were no more likely to violate their mandates and impose unpopular policies than were presidents who could run again.

It is worth emphasizing the historical context of Latin American democracies in the post-debt-crisis era that shaped these "representative" switches. Politicians were caught in a crosscurrent between voters and markets. On one side, they faced voters who feared liberalization and austerity. On the other side, politicians were buffeted even more than usual by markets, which demanded liberalization and austerity.

Caught in these crosscurrents, some politicians took a gamble, used electoral campaigns as an opportunity to pursue votes, and then appeased markets once in power. Yet they sought to appease markets, as I have been at length to show, not because doing so would benefit them personally. If they appeased markets they would shield their constituents from bad economic outcomes, and – politicians hoped – constituents would then reward them with electoral support.

The story told so far necessarily simplifies a complex reality and only begins to suggest differences from one national setting to another and across time. Yet two features of this complex reality cannot continue to be glossed over. First, we know that politics is played not by candidates or politicians alone but also by political parties. Second, we know that voters are not homogeneous; they have different identities, incomes, party affiliations, and ways of approaching politics. In the next chapter, I explore the role of parties in representation and policy switches; in Chapter 5, I turn to the strategies and reactions of voters.

Appendix: Close Races and Victory of Security-Oriented Candidates

In the probit model in Table 3.1, the dependent variable is a dummy scored as 1 when the winner of a presidential election had advocated security

Table 3.1. *Probit Model, Dependent Variable Election of Security-Oriented Candidate, 38 Observations*

Variable	Coefficient	Std. Error	z-Stat.	Prob$\lvert z \rvert \geq x$
Constant	0.43	0.53	0.81	0.47
GDP[a]	−0.21	0.09	−2.23	0.03
Inflation[b]	−0.4E−4	0.2E−4	−2.00	0.05
Transition[c]	0.08	0.03	2.58	0.01
Margin[d]	−0.07	0.04	−2.00	0.05

Maximum likelihood estimates
  Log-likelihood −15.11
  Restricted (slopes = 0) log-l. −25.86
  Chi-squared (4) 21.50
  Significance level 0.0003
  Pseudo-R^2 = 0.42

Frequencies of actual and predicted outcomes

Predicted outcome has maximum probability.

Actual	Predicted 0	1	TOTAL
0	12	4	16
1	3	19	22
TOTAL	15	23	38

[a] Average annual percentage change in GDP in the two years before the year of the election. Source: *International Financial Statistics*, IMF.
[b] Average inflation rate in the two quarters leading up to the election. Source: *International Financial Statistics*, IMF.
[c] Number of years since the return to democracy.
[d] Difference in vote share going to the winner and the second-place candidate.
Note: The same model appears in Table 2.2.

policies in his campaign and 0 when the winner had advocated efficiency-oriented policies. The model includes the independent variable MARGIN, which is the difference in the share of the vote between the first- and second-place candidates, which I use as a proxy for the perceived closeness of the race throughout. The coefficient relating MARGIN to the victory of a security-oriented candidate is negative and significant at the $p < .04$ level. The model as a whole predicts 31 of 38 of the outcomes correctly (82%). The chi-square of the log-likelihood ratio is 21.5; we would expect a chi-square of this magnitude when the null hypothesis of nonassociation is in fact true in 3 samples out of 10,000.

All four independent variables are significant predictors of the victory of a security-oriented candidate. The lower the rate of GDP growth and the lower the rate of inflation, the greater the probability that voters would elect a security-oriented candidate. The greater the number of years that had elapsed since the transition to democracy and the tighter the race, the more likely voters were to elect a security-oriented candidate.

Voter Uncertainty and Policy Switches

To test the hypothesis that policy switches reflected uncertainty among voters about the effect of economic policies on outcomes, I estimated models of the incumbent party's share of the vote in elections. If voters were more uncertain of the impact of policies on their welfare when politicians switched course, this should show up in a greater sensitivity of electoral outcomes to economic outcomes at the end of the term of a government that switched than after a government that didn't.

Because – as we saw in Chapter 2 – only politicians espousing a security-oriented program in the campaign ever switched, and because the same economic factors influencing the election of security-oriented politicians were also related to electoral outcomes at the end of the term, I estimated a Heckman selection model (see Table 3.2). The selection equation models the impact of economic and other conditions on the probability of the election of a security-oriented candidate; the outcome equation models the effect of economic outcomes and a prior policy switch on the incumbent party's share of the vote. Diagnostic statistics reported in the table support the hypothesis of nonindependence of the two equations.

We are interested here in the effect of GDP growth rates on the incumbent's share of the vote, and in comparing this effect among switchers and nonswitchers. The theoretical model of representative politicians predicts policy switches when politicians believe voters are uncertain; hence we expect policy-switching incumbents' share of the vote to be more sensitive to GDP change at the end of the term than that of non-policy-switching incumbents.

Statistically, this comparison requires that we examine the coefficient on GDP among these two subsamples – switchers and non-switchers. Following Gujarati (1995:512ff), the effect of GDP change in the base category, nonswitchers, is given by the coefficient on change in GDP. In the upper panel of Table 3.2, the coefficient on GDP is 1.3. The effect of GDP

Table 3.2. *Heckman Selection Model of Incumbent Party Share of Vote,[a] 23 Observations*

	Outcome Equation			
Variable	Coefficient	Std. Error	z-Stat.	Prob$|z| \geq x$
Constant	38.71	3.36	11.51	0.00
SWITCH	−7.29	7.28	−1.00	0.32
GDP[b]	1.30	0.84	1.22	0.12
GDP*Switch	1.70	1.38	1.22	0.22
	Selection Equation			
Variable	Coefficient	Std. Error	z-Stat.	Prob$|z| \geq x$
Constant	−1.87	0.57	−3.26	0.00
GDP[c]	−0.59	0.19	−3.12	0.00
INFL[d]	−0.07E−3	0.04E−3	−2.15	0.03
TRANS[e]	0.36	0.12	3.01	0.00
MARGIN[f]	−0.04	0.04	−1.01	0.32

LR test of independent equations ($\rho = 0$) chi-square = 7.25, Pr = 0.0071
$\lambda = -8.59$ (s.e. 1.48)

[a] Proportion of popular vote going to the winning presidential candidate. Source: LACAP.
[b] GDP growth rate in the two years leading up to the year of the election. Source: *International Financial Statistics*, IMF.
[c] GDP growth rate in the two years leading up to the year of the prior presidential election. Source: *International Financial Statistics*, IMF.
[d] Inflation in two quarters leading up to the previous presidential election. Source: *International Financial Statistics*, IMF.
[e] Number of years since the transition to democracy at the prior presidential election. Source: LACAP.
[f] Margin of victory in the prior presidential election. Source: LACAP.

change among switchers is given by the sum of the coefficient on GDP and the interaction term: 1.3 + 1.7 = 3.0. The z-score associated with the interaction term indicates that the difference between the two coefficients is not statistically significant. Still, given the small sample (23 observations), it is of considerable interest that the share of the vote going to the incumbent candidate after a switch is more than twice as sensitive to GDP change at the end of the term as it is among nonswitchers. A larger sample might well support the finding that policy switches are associated with greater voter uncertainty, and hence with greater sensitivity of voters to economic outcomes than to policies.

The constant terms in these models also support the representation model, for they tell us what effect switching had on later political outcomes when GDP growth was constant at zero. By a procedure similar to the one used earlier, I in effect split the sample into switchers and non-switchers by examining the constant of the full equation and of the sum of this constant plus the coefficient on the switch dummy. The y-intercept of the outcome equation is 38.7; this is the end-of-term share of the vote for consistent politicians when change in GDP is zero. The coefficient for switchers is 38.7 + −7.3 = 31.4. Although still statistically insignificant, the result suggests that, economic outcomes equal, policy switchers are punished for changing to unpopular policies.

Economic Outcomes

What is the effect of policy switches on economic outcomes? To answer this question, I compare GDP growth rates at the end of the term of politicians who earlier switched policies and those who did not. Yet we have reasons to believe that our sample of politicians who might switch is subject to selection effects. We saw in Chapter 2 that security-oriented candidates – the only sort that ever switched policies – tended to win when GDP growth rates were low. Thus selection filters out cases of security-oriented politicians who came to power under initial conditions of relatively high growth. And, as the probit model in Table 3.3 shows, among security-oriented candidates who won office, the probability of a switch was higher when growth was higher.[11] GDP growth is weakly associated with a heightened probability of a switch (significant at the $p = .09$ level); higher inflation shows some signs of predicting a switch, although the significance of the coefficient is reduced ($p = .15$).[12]

---

[11] GDP was robustly associated with the probability of a switch, as is clear in the model in Table 3.3, as well as in Table 3.5 and in the models reported in Chapter 4. I report here a specification that includes a variable for the majority status of government as well because it improves the overall predictiveness of the model.

[12] This finding also supports the representation model. When growth and inflation are low, voters prefer governments that emphasize growth; when they are high, voters prefer governments that control inflation. But security-oriented politicians who are elected under conditions of *relatively* high growth and inflation are more likely to switch to efficiency policies once in office. It appears that politicians were somewhat attentive to voters' preferences even when they defied their mandates, an attentiveness that we would not expect in rent-seeking politicians.

Table 3.3. *Probit Model, Dependent Variable SWITCH, 22 Observations*

Variable	Coefficient	Std. Error	z-Stat.	Prob$\lvert z \rvert \geq x$
Constant	2.44	2.05	1.20	0.23
GDP[a]	0.33	0.20	1.68	0.09
Inflation[b]	0.07	0.05	1.44	0.15
Status[c]	−0.08	0.04	−1.9	0.06

Maximum likelihood estimates
  Log-likelihood −8.70
  Restricted (slopes = 0) log-l. −15.16
  Chi-squared (3) 12.92
  Significance level 0.005

Frequencies of actual and predicted outcomes

Predicted outcome has maximum probability

Actual	Predicted 0	1	TOTAL
0	6	4	10
1	1	11	12
TOTAL	7	15	22

[a] Average change in GDP during the two years leading up to the election. Source: *International Financial Statistics*, IMF.

[b] Average inflation rate in the two quarters before the quarter of the election. Source: *International Financial Statistics*, IMF.

[c] Proportion of parliamentary seats controlled by the president's party.

Given differences in initial conditions and hence the selection problem, I estimated a Heckman selection model of economic outcomes. The model reported in Table 3.4 shows that, controlling for the economic growth rate at the outset of the term, consistent governments were associated with a GDP growth rate not significantly different from zero (constant = 1.59, standard error = 1.27). Policy-switching governments were associated with an end-of-term growth rate of 4.17% (again, holding prior growth rates constant). The difference between the two y-intercepts is significant at $p = .02$. Note the negative association between GDP growth rate at the beginning of the term and change in the growth rate at the end: a 1% lower initial growth rate is associated with a 1.1% higher rate of growth at the end of the term. The lower the initial GDP, the more room exists for improvement. Yet this improvement is improved on, as it were, by the switch to efficiency policies.

Table 3.4. *Heckman Selection Model, Dependent Variable CHANGE IN GDP GROWTH RATE at End of Presidential Term versus Beginning of Term, Selection Variable ELECTION OF SECURITY-ORIENTED CANDIDATE in Prior Election, 23 Observations (16 Uncensored)*

	Outcome Equation			
Variable	Coefficient	Std. Error	z-Stat.	Prob$|z| \geq x$
Constant	1.59	1.27	1.25	0.21
SWITCH	4.17	1.72	2.42	0.02
GDP	−1.12	0.21	−5.35	0.00
	Selection Equation			
Variable	Coefficient	Std. Error	z-Stat.	Prob$|z| \geq x$
Constant	−1.11	0.62	−1.80	0.07
GDP	−0.51	0.27	−1.87	0.06
INFL	−0.00006	0.00004	−1.32	0.19
TRANS	0.25	0.17	1.45	0.15
MARGIN	−0.002	0.03	−0.08	0.94

Log-likelihood ratio = −43.64 (null = −46.16)

Wald chi-square = 28.61 (df = 2), Pr = 0.0000

$\rho = -1$ (s.e. = 4.95×10^{-11})

LR test of independent equations ($\rho = 0$) chi-square = 5.04, Pr = 0.0247

$\lambda = -3.15$

Term Limits

I estimated models with a variety of specifications to test the hypothesis that term limits increased the probability of mandate violation, a hypothesis that would be consistent with the rent-seeking model. Table 3.5 reports one such estimation, one of the very few in which term limit variables produced close to significant results. The model includes two dummies: NO LIMITS, where the president was free to run for immediate reelection, and NOT RUN, where he could never run again. The base category, therefore, is presidents who could run again but were under some term limits – for example, they could run again once but not immediately after a second term. The negative sign on the NO LIMITS variable suggests that presidents who faced mild limits were slightly more likely to

Table 3.5.   *Probit Model, Dependent Variable SWITCH, 22 Observations*

Variable	Coefficient	Std. Error	z-Stat.	Prob|z| ≥ x
Constant	1.29	1.01	1.20	0.20
GDP[a]	0.26	0.11	2.35	0.02
Inflation[b]	0.02E-2	0.09E-2	0.25	0.80
Status1[c]	−1.55	1.07	−1.44	0.15
Status2[d]	−1.64	1.32	−1.25	0.21
No limits[e]	−0.51	1.14	−0.44	0.65
Not run[f]	−0.98	1.01	−0.96	0.33

Maximum lkelihood estimates
  Log-likelihood −8.10
  Restricted (slopes = 0) log-l. −15.16
  Chi-square (6) 14.12
  Significance level 0.03

Frequencies of actual and predicted outcomes
Predicted outcome has maximum probability.

	Predicted		
Actual	0	1	TOTAL
0	10	0	10
1	2	10	12
TOTAL	12	10	22

[a] Average change in GDP during the two years leading up to the election. Source: *International Financial Statistics*, IMF.
[b] Average inflation rate in the two quarters before the quarter of the election. Source: *International Financial Statistics*, IMF.
[c] Status 1 is a dummy for a single-party majority of the president's party or a majority of the pre-election coalition.
[d] Status 2 is a dummy for a postelection coalition government.
[e] No limits means that the incumbent faces no term limits.
[f] Not run means that the incumbent is prohibited from ever running again.

switch than those who faced no limits at all. The sign on NO LIMITS is the reverse of that predicted by the rent-seeking model of policy switches; the sign on NOT RUN is also wrong and far from significant. The results lead us to reject the rent-seeking hypothesis: that politicians switched course when they did not have to worry about the judgment of voters at the end of their term.

Majority Status

The independent variable STATUS measures the proportion of parliamentary seats controlled by the president's party. STATUS was negatively associated with the probability of a policy switch: the larger the proportion of seats held by the president's party, the less likely the president was to change course (although the effect was not strong). For example, in the model reported in Table 3.3, the coefficient relating STATUS to the probability of a switch is negative and weakly significant. In the model in Table 3.5, single-party majority governments and coalition governments are less likely to change course than minority governments, although neither effect is statistically significant. (The effect of STATUS remains in specifications that include MARGIN, the margin of victory in the election).[13]

---

[13] I follow Powell (1990), in merging preelection coalitions with majority governments and in treating postelection coalitions as intermediate between majority and minority governments. His concern is discernability: will voters be able to distinguish which party is responsible for policy and hold it accountable at the end of the term? My concern is with the ability of nonwinning parties to force programmatic changes either on minority governments or on coalition partners. I reason that leading parties are relatively more beholden to coalition partners than to opposition majorities.

4

Are Parties What's Wrong with Democracy in Latin America?

Political parties express and channel citizens' interests, provide predict-able choices to voters, link government to civil society, impose order on legislative processes, and discipline politicians: this is the conventional wisdom. To work well, democracy requires that these things happen. But observers contend that political parties in many of Latin America's democ-racies are weak or uninstitutionalized, and party systems volatile and frag-mented. They also contend that these democracies suffer from citizens with ill-defined and fluctuating preferences, campaigns that fail to predict policy, tenuous links between civil society and the state, chaotic legislative processes, and incompetent and undisciplined officeholders. It is tempting to blame weak parties for the deficiencies of Latin America's democracies.

In this chapter I evaluate these claims, in particular that weak political parties and uninstitutionalized party systems obstruct the fulfillment of mandates by elected governments. Before turning to this analysis, I will attempt a certain theoretical ground-clearing. Whether parties should be expected to induce officeholders to act consistently with mandates and to represent constituents' interests depends on one's view of what parties are: how they are structured and what their objectives are. Because the effect of parties is controversial – because in some theoretical traditions parties make governments more representative and in others less – it is not obvious a priori what the normative significance of strong parties will be.

Parties and Democracy

Parties Are Good for Democracy

The purported advantages of parties are two. First, they serve *electoral* purposes, increasing participation, elaborating programs, and symbolizing

ideology or policy orientation, all of which make governments more responsive to citizens. Governments are responsive to the subset of citizens who vote; increased participation will broaden the segment of the citizenry to whom governments must listen. Programs and manifestos state the policy intentions of parties; their dissemination in campaigns allows citizens to make meaningful choices in elections. Without strong parties, voters' choices are guided by the personal characteristics of candidates, leaving winners unconstrained by policy mandates. In light of the Latin American experience Mainwaring and Scully write, "Unfettered by party platforms, [political leaders] make policy choices that tend to be short-term and erratic. They are more prone to demagoguery and populism, both of which have deleterious effects on democracy" (1995:25).

Party labels convey to citizens the past and likely future policy orientations of alternative governments, allowing voters to choose without having to know in detail what incumbents have done or what challengers promise to do. Legitimacy of the democratic system is a side benefit of predictability and responsiveness: "The people themselves do not rule, but they make choices about who does, thereby expressing their consent to the government," and parties make these electoral choices predictable and meaningful (Mainwaring and Scully, 1995:24).

The second set of advantages offered by parties is in the realm of *governing*. They bring order to the legislative process by disciplining members and reducing the number of proposals, hence mitigating the problems of cycling majorities and agenda manipulation (Aldrich, 1995; Schattschneider, 1942). Parties may have longer time horizons than individual politicians, and use their disciplinary powers (e.g., promotions and candidacies) to force individual officeholders to follow through on programmatic commitments, and to keep them from rent-seeking, from shirking, or even from being disloyal to democratic institutions. And governments can govern better when parties are strong. When parties are uninstitutionalized and party discipline is weak, governments may have trouble dealing with legislatures, and may become immobile and unstable.

That strong parties are a cornerstone of democracy is a familiar theme in studies of advanced industrial countries. Students of U.S. politics have long bemoaned the weakness of American parties and imagined a revitalized political system under strong parties (see APSA, 1950; Fiorina, 1980; Jacobson, 1992; Ranney, 1975; Schattschneider, 1942). They credit strong parties with promoting representation and fulfilling mandates. Party government, Schattschneider contends, is effective government; and effective

government is good for the people who are not interested in "alibis for non-action" but who "want results" (1942:53). The *responsible party* thesis claims that strong parties are able to commit themselves to policies in their manifestos and carry them out once in office (Ranney, 1975). The Comparative Manifestos Project (see especially Klingeman et al., 1994) offers systematic evidence in favor of this claim, demonstrating that party manifestos have predicted policy in the OECD countries in the post–World War II period. Governments fulfill mandates, the project contends, because parties spell out their preferences in manifestos and then staff governments.

Parties Are Bad for Democracy

In the history of political theory, a more skeptical view of parties domi-nated well into the nineteenth century. Sartori (1976) notes that the term *party* derived from the Latin *partire*, to divide; *party* was used inter-changeably with *faction* until the time of Burke (see also Hofstadter, 1969). The architects of representative government in the United States were opposed to parties. In the view of James Madison, parties, like religious sects or interest groups, display

a zeal for different opinions . . . an attachment to different leaders ambitiously con-tending for pre-eminence and power. . . . [Factions] have, in turn, divided mankind into parties, inflamed them with mutual animosity, and rendered them much more disposed to vex and oppress each other than to co-operate for their common good. (Madison, 1982 [1787]:55–56).

Given the distaste for parties displayed by the architects of American democracy, it is ironic, as Hofstadter (1969) noted, that they soon collab-orated in creating the first U.S. party system.

Early-twentieth-century theorists shared in this skepticism about parties. As Offe (1984) notes, Max Weber, Rosa Luxembourg, and Robert Michels wrote in the first decades of the twentieth century from radically different political vantage points; yet all discovered mass political parties to be organizations that tamed, rather than represented, their constituents. Offe concurs in their diagnosis: "As soon as mass political participation is organized through large-scale bureaucratic organization – as presupposed and required by the model of electoral party competition . . . the very dynamic of this organizational form contains, perverts, and obstructs class interest" (184). Parties modify their programs to make themselves more

attractive as coalition partners; elevate leaders through their bureaucratic structures and hence make them less and less like their putative constituents; and reduce class consciousness and class appeals in order to reach a broader electorate (see Przeworski and Sprague, 1986). Whether cheered or chagrined by these developments, the common opinion of early-twentieth-century political sociologists was that parties subverted representation.

Among analysts of Latin American politics, the pro-party chorus has grown loud. Still, some writers, past and present, are in the tradition of democratic theorizing in which parties are at best a necessary evil and at worst a threat to democracy. Parties may become all-pervasive, structuring conflict throughout civil society, making conflicts unmanageably sharp. There is a distinctly Madisonian flavor to Valenzuela's influential analysis of the breakdown of democracy in Chile under Allende, in which he underscores the polarizing effect of parties. "The multiparty system, with its profound ideological differences, created political pressures that made it difficult to structure national policies capable of addressing the daunting problems of underdevelopment" and eventually helped bring democracy down (1994:167; see also Valenzuela, 1978). Coppedge (1994) diagnoses the same syndrome in his analysis of the afflictions of Venezuelan democracy. Parties "penetrate politically relevant organizations to a degree that violates the spirit of democracy. The sad consequence is that many of the informal channels of representation that are taken for granted in other democracies, such as interest groups, the media, the courts, and independent opinion leaders, are blocked by extreme party domination" (1994:2).

Another complaint against strong and pervasive parties in the developing world is that they function as patronage machines, consuming surplus and channeling it toward party members and voters in exchange for political support (N. Alvarez, 1999; Eisenstadt and Roniger, 1984; Gay, 1998; Kitschelt, Mansfeldova, Markowski, and Tóka, 1999; Landé, 1977; Levitsky, 1999; Mainwaring, 1999; Scott, 1969; Wilson and Banfield, 1963). The danger of strong parties lies not in their potential for polarizing the population along ideological lines or creating social conflict. Rather, it is that they may turn citizens into clients. They induce the electorate to give up programmatic choice in favor of material sidepayments from political bosses and patrons.

In sum, theorists and political analysts give us reason to wonder whether parties are good for democracy or merely a necessary evil.

Parties, Mandates, and Representation

If strong parties do make governments more responsive and predictable, why might this be so? In this section, I examine some answers to this question. I show that the predictability effect of parties and their representation effect must be considered separately. Recent theories converge on the prediction that political parties promote mandate consistency. But they disagree about whether parties promote representative (or responsive) governments or governments that cater to the views of extremists. Hence, although most theorists agree that voters benefit from parties in that parties cause campaigns to be more predictive of government policy, they disagree about whether the benefit of mandate consistency is in addition to the benefit of representation or whether parties force a trade-off between mandate consistency and representative government.

Parties as Overlapping Generations

Consider the following situation, due to Alesina and Speer (1988). A political party is composed of individual members; for simplicity, we will assume three of them. Party members care about holding office and about policy (see also Calvert, 1985; Wittman, 1977). The policy ideal point of the party is different from that of the median voter; but parties don't know the distribution of voters' preferences, so there is uncertainty about the outcome of elections. Members have a finite number of years remaining in their careers, and when they retire, young new recruits will take their place. Imagine that Member 1 has one political term left in her career, Member 2 has two terms left, and Member 3, the youngest, has three terms left. Member 1, the most senior, will hold office if her party wins. If, counterfactually, she were not a member of a party and found herself in office, Member 1 would impose her ideal policy, x_p, which (by assumption) is different from the ideal point of the median voter. Alesina and Speer show that the more the candidate values policy over office, the more policy will diverge from the preferences of the median voter.

Yet the behavior of the unconstrained incumbent is bad for the party. It is particularly bad for Member 2, who will be the candidate in the next election and whose prospects for winning are reduced when the incumbent (Member 1) has indulged her ideological preferences and pursued unpopular policies. Hence the party has an incentive to impose discipline on the incumbent and force her to pursue policies that the median voter favors. According to Alesina and Speer, parties can compensate incumbents by offering them services in exchange for policy moderation, such as help in getting the leader's agenda through the legislature or defending her before the press and public. Zielinsky (1997) shows that internal party democracy has the same effect of imposing voter responsiveness on incumbents. If the party chooses government policy by majority rule, Member 1, the officeholder, whose instinct is to indulge her ideological predisposition, is outvoted by party Members 2 and 3, who want to hold office in the future. By a two-to-one vote the party chooses a policy, x_v, the one preferred by the median voter, over x_p. Whether the mechanism of control is internal democracy or compensation, the impact of the party is to make government more responsive to voters.

At the same time that parties cause responsiveness in this model, they also force governments to fulfill their mandates. Alesina (1988) notes that a candidate with preferences at odds with constituents' and unconstrained by parties will announce herself in favor of the policy voters want (x_v) in the campaign but switch to her preferred policy (x_p) in office.[1] Anticipating this switch, voters won't find her announced intention of supporting x_v credible and will only believe her when she announces x_p. Mandates will be fulfilled, but policy will not be in line with constituents' preferences: mandate consistency will be achieved by unresponsive governments. Now bring back Alesina and Speer's political party: it wants the officeholder to announce popular measures in campaigns and fulfill them in office, and it has ways of inducing its leaders to do both. Campaign pronouncements become credible and policies responsive.

Parties as Extremist: The Law of Curvilinear Disparity

But perhaps parties are not overlapping generations of members all of whom will some day be candidates. Instead we can conceive of parties as organizations of activists, most of whom will never run for office, and leaders, who regularly do run.[2] If candidates care about holding office, and

---

[1] In contrast to Harrington's model, which motivated the discussion in Chapter 3, here (in addition to other differences) officeholders are not reelectable and hence the desire for reelection has no power to induce candidates to reveal their true intentions. Here these intentions are common knowledge, whereas in Harrington's models they were private information.

[2] The definitional question is more than that and reduces to the question "Who controls the party's platform – members who will some day be candidates or activists who care about policy and will never run?" See Stokes (1999).

if voters' preferences are single-peaked, then, as demonstrated by Downs (1957), the candidates will converge to the policy ideal point of the median voter. They converge because voters at the extremes, though discontented, have no power to induce their candidate to return to a more eccentric position. If extreme rightists abstain, they simply improve the chances of the candidate of the left; if extreme leftists withdraw from politics, the left-of-center party will merely drift closer to the center.

Albert Hirschman (1970) challenged the idea that extremists are powerless. They can exercise "voice" rather than self-defeating "exit." Voice amounts to making life miserable for party leaders until they shift away from the median voter and toward the policy position preferred by activists. Because voice is more effective when it is exercised by people inside party organizations than by outsiders, parties will be populated by activists with extreme positions in comparison with those of the general electorate. May (1973) labeled the resulting preference structure *curvilinear disparity*: the median voter is in the center of a finite Euclidean space, party militants are at one extreme, and leaders are at some point between the median voter and activists (for discussions see Iversen, 1994, and Kitschelt, 1989).

What if activists in parties care not about policy but about sharing the spoils of office? In rent-seeking models of politics, such as Ferejohn's (1986), officeholders try to appropriate the surplus, and voters' interest is in minimizing this appropriation and maximizing the benefits to themselves of government actions. In these models there are typically no political parties. But we can speculate about what would happen if parties entered the picture. If we suppose that the officeholder requires some minimum level of rents, then if he has to share rents with fellow party members who also demand the spoils of office, more rents must be extracted and less is left for citizens. Party members are also members of the citizenry, so a portion of the rents collected is channeled back to a segment of society. Parties, therefore, in addition to causing a transfer of social resources to the state for private consumption by officeholders, also cause an intrasocietal transfer, from the rest of the citizenry to the party's members and clients. Yet theorists of clientelism and machine politics generally imply that the mitigating effect is not sufficient to overwhelm the nefarious effects of rent-seeking.

Note the different structure of parties implied by curvilinear disparity and overlapping of generation models. In curvilinear disparity, parties are internally heterogeneous. They contain both activists, who care little about office for its own sake but seek it to pursue good programs, and leaders who care about office independent of the policies it will allow them to pursue. In overlapping generation models, parties are internally homogeneous. They contain only leaders, all of whom will be candidates sooner or later and all of whom care about holding office for its own sake (and also have personal policy preferences.) The critical difference between these two models is that the power parties wield over leaders in overlapping generation models makes incumbents more responsive to voters; the power parties wield in curvilinear disparity models makes incumbents less responsive.

Hirschman and those who followed him in developing the law of curvilinear disparity were not concerned with mandates. Yet the model, with its emphasis on tensions between leaders and activists, suggests a novel way to think about mandates. Consider the dilemma of party activists, whose views are at odds with those of the median voter. Once they have helped leaders win office, how can they be assured that the incumbent will enact their preferred policies? And who is to say after the fact what sort of implicit agreement was worked out between leaders and activists at party congresses and conventions? If the law of curvilinear disparity gets at something real about the structure and dynamics of parties, perhaps it also suggests why parties produce preelectoral manifestos. Party manifestos may help resolve the activists' dilemma. They may function as a contract, or perhaps more accurately as a sort of letter of understanding, between activists and party leaders. They provide activists with a public document that they can cite when they believe the officeholder has reneged. Manifestos also serve as the outline of a script for speeches, television advertisements, and other campaign communications, providing people with a picture of where the parties that will constrain governments stand and a choice over which set of constraints they want their future leaders to observe. Because parties are able to impose mandates, voters learn something about what to expect from a future government under candidate x versus candidate y, and can choose the party closest to their own positions.

Thus we need not stretch the law of curvilinear disparity far to see that it implies that parties cause governments to act consistently with their mandates. Stated differently, all else equal, a government under a strong party is more likely to make good on campaign promises than a government under a weak party. This much curvilinear disparity shares with the model of overlapping generations. Yet whereas in overlapping generations models governments constrained by parties are *both* consistent *and* responsive, in curvilinear disparity models, governments constrained by parties are consistent but unresponsive.

Curvilinear disparity and overlapping generations models can both accommodate policy switches, but they predict switches that go in opposite directions. According to curvilinear disparity, we should expect policy switches, conditional on weak parties, to be *toward* the preferences of the median voter: parties that are weak are unable to keep incumbents from acting as vote seekers. According to overlapping generations, we should expect policy switches, conditional on weak parties, to be *away from* the preferences of the median voter: candidates run campaigns that appeal to popular positions, and once in office they indulge their ideological whims.

We are a long way from knowing what parties are. What should be clear is that the impact of strong parties on democracy is a more complex matter than recent writings on parties in new democracies recognize. In the next section, I study the impact of Latin American parties on mandate responsiveness. The hypothesis derived from the theoretical models of parties discussed earlier – the stronger the ruling party, the more prone the government is to act consistently with its campaign pronouncements – finds some mild support. Yet the reader should keep in mind that this causal effect tells us little about the impact of political parties on government responsiveness or representation.

Latin American Parties and Mandate Consistency

A review of the experience of several South American policy switchers suggests a connection between weak parties and policy switches. Alberto Fujimori, as we have seen, carried out the biggest policy reversal on record. His run for the presidency of Peru in 1990 was without the support of a political party. His campaign organization, such as it was, consisted of leaders of informal-sector organizations, Protestant churches, and politically independent, neo-Keynesian economists. Fujimori's opponent, Mario Vargas Llosa, had the support of the rightist Partido Popular Cristiano and Acción Popular parties, as well as his own Movimiento Libertad; together the three formed the FREDEMO coalition.

Fujimori won the election and swiftly shed his campaign advisors in favor of a more partisan group, one that included people associated with Vargas Llosa, FREDEMO, and its constituent rightist parties (Fujimori

110

also picked up some cabinet members from APRA and the United Left, but most deserted soon after the neoliberal change of course began.) One notable figure recruited from the camp of Fujimori's erstwhile right-wing opponent was Juan Carlos Hurtado Miller, an Acción Popular member who had been minister of agriculture under the Belaúnde government (1980–1985); Acción Popular was one of the parties that backed Vargas Llosa's candidacy. Hurtado Miller became Fujimori's first finance minister. Another notable recruit from the other side was Hernando de Soto, author of *The Other Path*. De Soto was a pronounced neoliberal who was associated with Vargas Llosa in the early days of Movimiento Libertad; De Soto's views on economic policy could not have been more at odds with the gradualism and neo-Keynesianism proposed by Fujimori in the campaign. As we have seen, he played a significant role in Fujimori's change of course. Through his brother, an aide to UN Secretary General Pérez de Cuellar, De Soto arranged the meeting, described in Chapter 3, in July 1990 between President-Elect Fujimori and the heads of international financial institutions.

One can imagine a counterfactual scenario in which Fujimori, the candidate of a long-standing social democratic party, is subjected after the election to pressures from domestic policy elites, the IMF, and the Peruvian bourgeoisie to abandon positions announced in the campaign. But Fujimori is kept from drifting too far by members of the party's leadership who will become cabinet members and who control valuable political resources, such as access to party committees around the country.

Ecuador provides another example of policy switches in the context of uninstitutionalized parties. In Ecuador, presidents seem always to do just what they promise in campaigns not to. León Febres Cordero was the presidential candidate of the Social Christian Party in 1984, a party affiliation that would have suggested to attentive voters a right-of-center orientation. Still his campaign slogan was "Bread, roofs, and jobs," and, as Conaghan and Malloy (1994) note, he emphasized a social agenda. (Other campaign positions meant that Febres did not merit being coded as a switcher in the LACAP database. In particular, he advocated a freeze on public spending.) Febres won the election in May and aggressively pursued trade liberalization and the elimination of domestic price controls, with little attention to his social agenda. Four years later, the two leading candidates were Rodrigo Borja of the Democratic Left and Abdalá Bucaram, a populist eccentric. As we saw in Chapter 2, Borja ran promising no fiscal shock, won in May, and in August imposed a 125% increase in fuel prices and other price increases.

In 1992 the two leading candidates, Sixto Durán Ballén and Jaime Nebot, were conservatives who went to great lengths to emphasize a progressive social agenda. Durán Ballén promised massive new housing campaigns and a reduction of the prices of basic foods and medicines (Cornejo Menacho, 1992). The two barely edged out Abdalá Bucaram in the general election. Durán Ballén won the run-off in July 1992 and on September 3 switched to the New Route (*Nuevo Rumbo*): austerity and economic liberalization. In turn in 1996, Bucaram won the Ecuadoran presidency promising to protect real incomes and create jobs, and railed against the country's upper class. In office his government quickly increased the prices of energy, public transportation, and telephones rates and began to privatize state-owned enterprises. Six months later, in the midst of daily street demonstrations against austerity measures, Congress impeached Bucaram, declaring him mentally unfit. Graffiti on the streets of Quito read: "Ablablabla" (Schemo, 1997.)

There is a priori appeal to the idea that the Ecuadorean experience shows that weak parties cause policy switches. By some counts, Ecuador has the most volatile party system in South America. Coppedge (1995) measured party system volatility in Latin American legislative elections during the twentieth century. Ecuador's average volatility index between 1954 and 1992 was 54, which means, as Coppedge explains, that parties that won 54% of the vote in one election disappeared in each subsequent one.

In Ecuador as in Peru, strong, well-institutionalized parties were not available to produce manifestos, staff cabinets, and anchor officeholders to preferred positions. For example, recall that in 1992 Sixto Durán Ballén ran as the candidate of the newly created Partido Unidad Republicana (PUR). His opponent, Jaime Nebot, was of the Social Christian Party (PSC). Durán Ballén had himself been a member of the PSC until 1988 and had served as vice-president of Ecuador in the Social Christian administration of Febres Cordero. He left the party after performing dismally as PSC presidential candidate in the 1988 election and later created the PUR. Key cabinet members who tried to implement the *Nuevo Rumbo* had held positions in the prior PSC government of Febres (recall that the PSC's Nebot was Durán Ballén's opponent in the recent elections). Pablo Lucio Paredes, Durán's planning minister, had been an advisor to the Junta Monetaria under Febres Cordero; Mario Ribadeneira, Durán Ballén's minister of finance, was Febres's ambassador to Washington; and Ana Lucía Armijos, Durán's Central Bank chief, had been the head of monetary policy at the bank under Febres.

If Ecuadorean parties had been stronger, would presidents have acted consistently with their campaign positions? In a less volatile party system the incumbent party's share in the 1988 elections might not have fallen as sharply (by definition: this abrupt change of electoral fortunes, along with short-lived parties, is what produces high volatility indexes). And Durán Ballén would have been less likely to create a new party after losing the presidential race. He might well have foreseen a future in his own party, including another run for the presidency. It is common in the better-institutionalized party systems for parties to run candidates repeatedly even when they have lost before. Had Durán Ballén not jumped the PSC ship after 1988, he would not have been in the odd position of opposing his former co-partisans and feigning ideological discrepancies with them in the campaign of 1992, only to incorporate these people into his government once the niceties of the election were behind him.

We could find many examples of policy-switching governments that drew ministers and technical advice from the parties they had just defeated. In Bolivia in 1985 the main contenders for the presidency were Víctor Paz Estenssoro of the National Revolutionary Movements (MNR) and General Hugo Bánzer of National Democratic Action (ADN). Bánzer's main economic advisor was Juan Carriaga, a businessman who, together with Jeffrey Sachs, the Harvard economist, drafted a blueprint for pro-market reforms. Bánzer defeated Paz Estenssoro in the popular vote, but the Bolivian Congress elected Paz Estenssoro president. But Bánzer's defeat did not kill Carriaga's and Sachs's program of pro-market reforms. Instead Paz Estenssoro recruited Carriaga into his transition team, and the key features of the Carriaga–Sachs program found their way into the New Economic Program (*Nuevo Programa Económico*, or NPE), Paz Estenssoro's economic liberalization package. The NPE ran counter to Paz's past record and he did not anticipate it in his campaign.[3] In contrast to Peru and Ecuador, Paz's party (MNR) did dominate the cabinet that would

[3] The political dynamics of Bolivian economic policy making bore a strong resemblance to those in other countries where politicians changed course. However, because Paz Estenssoro provided some hints in the campaign that he would pursue austerity policies and liberal reforms, I did not code this case as one of a policy switch in the LACAP database.

implement the NPE. Yet the MNR cabinet members were figureheads. Real policy was being decided by Carriaga's team. (The only member of the more important behind-the-scene policy team from the MNR was Gonzálo Sánchez de Lozada, a businessman who would later succeed Paz as president.)

In sum, policy switches did happen in countries with uninstitutionalized parties where "governing" parties were either absent (Peru) or marginalized (Ecuador) or where the parties' presence in government was symbolic (Bolivia). Therefore it is tempting to conclude that uninstitutionalized parties caused mandate unresponsiveness.

Yet policy switches also occurred in countries with relatively well-institutionalized parties, such as Venezuela, Argentina, and Costa Rica. In these countries too, activists from "ruling" parties found themselves marginalized or had to accommodate themselves to the government's about-face.

Consider Argentina. Some Menem insiders in 1989 were aware that the campaign they were witnessing was misleading. But many Peronists were surprised and unhappy after the election, when Menem announced austerity measures and surprising cabinet appointments (see Levitsky, 1999). Surprised and unhappy Peronists had no choice but to acquiesce or leave. And some did leave: Menem's policy switch provoked a split in the Peronist labor confederation, the Confederación General de Trabajadores (CGT), with followers of Saúl Ubaldini abandoning the CGT and the government in the wake of its neoliberal turn (see McGuire, 1997). In sum, Argentine political parties, especially the Peronists, appeared relatively institutionalized *until* Menem's radical policy switch, at which point the party cracked.

Venezuela is another country in which the government under an apparently well-institutionalized ruling party ignored its electoral mandate. Venezuelan parties, as we saw earlier, were if anything too institutionalized and pervasive, none more so than AD (Coppedge, 1994). The cabinet that Carlos Andrés Pérez appointed to carry out the Great Turnaround tilted toward non-AD economists and businessmen, including "IESA (Institute for Advanced Study of Administration) boys," named for the think tank with which they were associated, such as Miguel Rodríguez (minister of planning) and Moisés Naím (industrial development). Pedro Tinoco, a powerful businessman and banker, became president of the Central Bank. When Pérez attempted to deepen the reforms in mid-1990, he added three more IESA boys: Roberto Smith (transport), Jonathan Cole (agriculture), and Herbert Torres (investment fund). Pérez's neoliberal turn and the prominence of nonpartisans in the cabinet were all the more surprising given his debt to labor unions in winning a contentious inner struggle for the AD presidential candidacy in 1988. As in Argentina, a strong, enduring, highly structured party was no guarantee of party government or of mandate responsiveness.

In Venezuela as in Argentina, the weakness of the governing party was more the consequence than the cause of mandate unresponsiveness. Pérez's relations with AD deteriorated under the Great Turnaround; party members who held cabinet positions were eclipsed by their technocrat colleagues. The impression even among these same technocrats was that Pérez went too far in turning his back on AD's congressional delegation (interviews with former cabinet members, November 1998). The party in Congress retaliated by refusing to pass a tax reform package that was a critical piece of the Great Turnaround and that would have eased Venezuela's fiscal dependence on oil.

Time, Volatility, and Mandates

To further test the hypothesis that weak parties and unstable party systems explain policy switches in Latin America, I turn to the LACAP database. It includes three measures relevant to party strength: the age of parties, the volatility of the party system, and the age of democracy.

What justifies using the age of a party as a proxy for its strength? In overlapping generation models, party strength means the ability of nonincumbent members to induce officeholders to follow the policy preferences of constituents against the idiosyncratic preferences of the officeholders. Junior members can control senior officeholders only if the officeholders expect the party to last into the future. If incumbents lack confidence in the continued existence of the party, they will not fear sanctions or pursue postretirement inducements the party may offer; and if the party is expected to be short-lived, young members will have little reason to invest in constraining the behavior of current officeholders. And it seems reasonable that members of old parties will expect the party to last, whereas members of young parties will doubt their party's durability. From the vantage point of curvilinear disparity as well, older parties may be ones in which activists have honed their influence and are better able to control party leaders than young parties in which activists are relatively disorganized.

Electoral volatility is a second measure of the strength of parties. When parties are weak and have little leverage over leaders, they are also likely to be incapable of sustaining electoral support from voters over a series of elections. It is conceivable that a political party that is good at mobilizing electoral support will be bad at controlling its own officeholders, but it seems fair to assume that the two capabilities usually go together.

A third measure of party strength is the age of the democracy, measured as the number of years since the transition. My measure of the age of *parties* simply counts the number of years between the original founding of the party and the post-1982 election bringing its candidate to the presidency. It ignores the fact that military dictatorships repressed party organizations and leaders; even when the transition resuscitated these same parties, the interruption may have lessened the expectation of ongoing careers within the party. Therefore it is useful to estimate the effect of age of *democracy* on mandate consistency as well as that of the age of parties.

If strong parties force leaders to adopt policies consistent with campaign pronouncements, we should expect a negative statistical association between the age of the governing party and the probability of a switch, a positive association between party system volatility and the probability of a switch, and a negative association between the age of the democracy and the probability of a switch.

Age of Parties

The age of the president's party, measured as the number of years elapsed between the original founding of the party and the election bringing him or her to power, varies greatly. Some Latin American political parties are venerable: the Colombian Liberal Party was 146 years old when Ernesto Samper came to office in 1994; the Uruguayan Blanco Party was 153 when Ernesto Lacalle led it to power in 1989. At the other extreme were *Cambio '90* in Peru and the PUR in Ecuador, founded less than a year before Alberto Fujimori and Sixto Durán Ballén, respectively, led them to victory. I estimated a probit model of the impact of the age of the president's party on the probability that, once in office, he would renege on his campaign pronouncements (see Model 1 in Table 4.1). The age of a president's party was significantly and negatively associated with the probability of a switch. The younger the party, the less its ability or willingness to force the president to stick to the program announced in the campaign.

Table 4.1. *Binomial Probit Models of Policy Switches (Coefficients, Standard Errors in Parentheses)*

	Model 1	Model 2	Model 3
Constant	0.45	−1.1	−0.15
	(0.72)	(0.9)	(0.66)
GDP[a]	0.31*	0.25*	0.28**
	(0.16)	(0.15)	(0.14)
Inflation[b]	0.003	0.001	0.001
	(0.006)	(0.001)	(0.002)
Age of president's party[c]	−0.03**		
	(0.01)		
Volatility[d]		0.03	
		(0.03)	
Years since transition[e]			−0.02
			(0.03)
Number of observations	21	19	22
LR chi-square[f]	15.23	5.20	8.89
Prob > chi-square	0.002	0.157	0.03

[a] Average change in GDP in the last two years before the year of the election.
[b] Average inflation rate in the last two quarters leading up to the election.
[c] Number of years between the original founding of the president's party and the election bringing him or her to power.
[d] Volatility, as defined in footnote 5, in the election bringing the president to power.
[e] Number of years elapsed since the first competitive election for presidency.
[f] Chi-square of log-ratio, 3 degrees of freedom.
* significant at $p = .10$.
** significant at $p = .05$.

Figure 4.1 simulates the effect of parties the ages of which are within the range in our sample on the probability of a switch, holding the level of GDP constant at its mean and inflation constant at its median (0.9% and 30.3%, respectively).[4] We see that the probability of a switch by a president from a party that was 146 years old (the oldest in the sample) was

[4] The simulation follows procedures recommended by King, Tomz, and Wittenberg (1998) and was produced by their software, "Clarify: Software for Interpreting and Presenting Statistical Results," available at http://gov.harvard.edu. Because of very high extreme values, the mean inflation rate was 3,695%. At this level there was little variation in the probability of a policy switch. Therefore, in the simulation, I held inflation constant at its median.

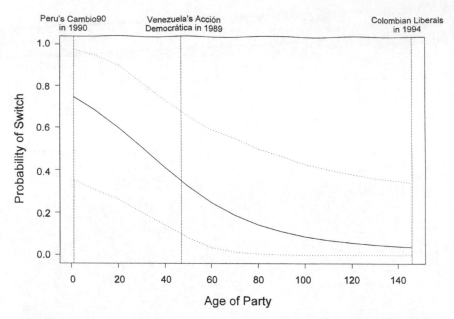

Figure 4.1 Impact of the age of party on the probability of a switch. Note: For this simulation, GDP was held at its mean (0.9) and inflation at its median (33.1); dotted lines indicate the 95% confidence interval for the estimated probability.

0.04 (standard deviation 0.10) and the probability of a switch by a president from the youngest party (1 year) was 0.75 (standard deviation 0.17). Hence the youngest parties were much more likely than the oldest ones to switch. The probability of a switch by a party at the mean age of 46.5 – roughly the age of Bolivia's MNR when Paz Estenssoro came to office in 1985, Costa Rica's PLN when Arias came to office in 1986, and Venezuela's AD when Pérez came to power in 1989 – was 0.35 (standard deviation 0.15). A shift from the age of the youngest party in our sample to the mean – 1 year to 46.5 – was associated with a reduction in the probability of a switch of 39%; moving from the mean to the maximum (146 years) was associated with a further reduction of 31%. Hence we should expect parties of median age, when they find themselves in office, to abandon their mandates about one time in three.

We saw that presidents from old parties were capable of turning their back on their announced programs, as did Belisario Betancur of

Colombia, whose Conservative Party was 133 years old when he came to office in 1982. And presidents from new parties were capable of acting consistently with their pronouncements, as did Alfredo Cristiani of El Salvador's ARENA, which was eight years old when Cristiani came to office in 1989. Still, candidates from older parties tended to be better anchored by their campaign appeals and more likely to reveal their true intentions in campaigns.

The appropriate theoretical inference may be the one suggested by overlapping generations models: when parties are expected to endure into the future, younger members induce current officeholders to stick to the popular policies, those espoused in the campaign.

Volatility

Volatility measures capture the shifts in voter preferences or electoral outcomes from one election to the next. The measure of volatility used here is based on the sum of differences in the share of votes going to each party in each election in comparison with its share of the vote in the previous election.[5] Latin American party systems are very volatile. Volatility indexes range from a low of 3.9 (Costa Rica in 1994) to a high of 66.2 (Peru in 1990). The highest average volatility index across elections in the 1980s through the mid-1990s was Guatemala's (54.1); the lowest was Honduras's (7.3). The volatility index averaged 28 across the full set of Latin American elections. (Coppedge, 1995, analyzing a slightly different set of countries over a longer time period, calculates a volatility index virtually identical to this [26.9].) To put this figure in perspective, Bartolini and Mair (1990) report the average volatility index for European party systems as 8.6. Yet volatility was not significantly associated with switches in Latin America. I tested probit models of switches with varying specifications; the sign on the coefficient relating volatility to the probability of a switch tended to be positive but far from significant (see, e.g., Model 2 in Table 4.1).

---

[5] Volatility index: $V = 1/2 \sum_{i=1}^{j} |p_{i,t} - p_{i,t-1}|$

where i is a political party, elections are held at time $t-1$, t, etc., and $p_{i,t}$ is the proportion of the vote going to party i in the election at time t.

Years Since Transition

Most Latin American democracies were still new in the 1980s and 1990s. In 1995 the region's oldest democracy, Costa Rica, was 51; its youngest, Chile and Brazil, were 6.[6] The probit model of policy switches in the third column of Table 4.1 includes, along with controls for economic conditions, a variable that measures the number of years that had elapsed since the transition to democracy at the time of the election. The sign on the coefficient is negative, as expected, but the effect is weak, significant at the 0.5 level.

Conclusions

The case studies and statistical analyses in this chapter provide evidence relevant to theories of the impact of political parties on democracy. The theories I considered predict that when parties are weak, governments will be less bound by their campaign pronouncements. We found muted evidence that this was true in Latin America. But the theories offer different reasons why parties cause mandate consistency. Curvilinear disparity implies that activists enforce mandates through the exercise of voice: because the strategy of exit is self-defeating, extremists join parties and pressure candidates and governments toward their views. Overlapping generations says that party members (future candidates) force current incumbents to implement popular policies to enhance their own electoral prospects in the future. Only the second mechanism should be sensitive to the age of the party, the explanatory variable that was significantly related to the probability of policy switches in the Latin American dataset. When parties are born and die quickly or when party life is interrupted frequently by military intervention, we expect party members' vision to be focused on the short run, reducing their incentive to control incumbents. But it is also not inconceivable that as parties evolve, the voice of activists is strengthened. Nor is it impossible that older clientelist parties are more adept at extracting resources for members. Hence, although the Latin American data provide fairly clear evidence that party age is related to

---

[6] Depending on how one interprets the events of 1992 in Peru, democracy in that country in 1995 might be only two years old. In the LACAP database, however, I code 1980 as the most recent transition to democracy in Peru and do not treat the coup in 1992 as a full breach of democracy.

the predictiveness of campaign messages, they do not adjudicate clearly between overlapping generation, curvilinear disparity, or clientelist models of parties.

The limitation is critical because, depending on which model is most appropriate, parties either enforce mandate responsiveness at the same time that they secure a greater measure of representation of voters' interests, or they secure mandate responsiveness at the price of representation. The broader point is that our theoretical understanding of the effect of parties on democracy is far from complete. Until this theoretical understanding grows, and until theory-driven research can bring us more conclusive results, we should temper our expectation that new democracies will function much better when their parties grow stronger.

5

Neoliberalism without Mandates

CITIZENS RESPOND

Introduction

How citizens react to governments that change course will deeply shape our normative judgment of these governments. If a government that abandoned campaign promises early in its term later wins the support of voters, there is a certain a priori power to the notion that the change of course was in voters' interest. If a government that switches is later reviled by voters, a priori we would tend to believe that the government had betrayed the voters' interests.

Yet scholars who have looked at public opinion in the aftermath of policy switches have derived very different impressions. One describes a dynamic whereby the president ignores his mandate and does as he deems best; as "failures accumulate . . . the country finds itself stuck with a widely reviled president whose goal is just to hang on until the end of his term" and concludes that representation is not part of this system (O'Donnell, 1994:67). Another scholar notes that "voters later had opportunities to pass judgment on the liars and the relative merits of the programs eventually adopted." They "sometimes punished the liar's party in the next presidential elections." But sometimes after switches "voters approved a change in the constitution to permit the incumbent president's immediate reelection, and then reelected him" (Domínguez 1998:78–79). He implies that at least accountability restores some citizen control. In this chapter I offer a more systematic assessment of citizens' responses to dramatic postelectoral changes of course.

Parallel to these sharply contrasting empirical impressions, positive theory offers sharply different predictions about how people will react when politicians abandon their mandates and impose unpopular policies.

122

Neoliberalism without Mandates: Citizens Respond

In the spatial model of party competition, people have policy preferences, and there is no uncertainty about how policies will map onto outcomes. Therefore politicians who change course are imposing policies that are unpopular and will produce outcomes that are unsatisfactory. Voters would withdraw support from such governments, which would then fail to be reelected. In contrast, the model of policy switches evaluated in Chapter 3 starts with the assumption that people are uncertain about the effect of alternative policies on their welfare. Therefore they might hesitate before rejecting a government that abandons its mandate and, if outcomes are eventually sufficiently good, embrace the government and favor it for reelection – a picture not unlike the one Domínguez paints. Yet people may suspect that politicians are sometimes tempted to change course for bad reasons. Then, if governments change course and outcomes are bad, people may infer not that these were well-intentioned actors who made a mistake but malign actors who abused the people's trust – a scenario in line with O'Donnell's picture of the reviled politicians barely hanging on to power.

In this chapter, I use electoral and public opinion data to explore citizens' reactions to policy switches, with an eye toward empirical and normative theory debates. I begin by reviewing what we learned in Chapter 3 about the systematic differences in the later electoral fate of politicians who switched course and those whose actions were consistent with their campaign messages. I then shift gears and look closely at three instances of governments that imposed economic liberalization by surprise. In two instances, governments that switched remained popular and were reelected – as Domínguez notes, after striking down term limits that would have barred the president from running. Do these two instances support the representation model of switches outlined in Chapter 3? The model would be supported if the outcomes of the initially unpopular policies were sufficiently good and people's policy preferences therefore shifted in favor of efficiency policies. In the Latin American context I call this the *rise of mass neoliberalism* hypothesis.

Ex post support for politicians who changed course early in the term should not, however, be taken as sufficient evidence in favor of the representation model. It is conceivable that policy switchers might retain popularity and be reelected even when efficiency policies remain unpopular. Under what conditions might this be true? Perhaps politicians who switch to unpopular policies may generate support by shifting attention to other issues and changing the electoral alliances on which they draw support.

For example, a politician might be brought to power after campaigning against pro-market reforms and then win reelection at the end of her term by engineering a greater salience of some popular policy, such as law and order. In this case, neoliberal economic policies remain unpopular but their salience declines.

The dynamic may entail a version of cycling majorities (see, e.g., Arrow, 1963; McKelvey, 1976; Riker, 1980). For example, imagine that an anti-neoliberal discourse before the first election was attractive to the informal sector (reliant on state transfers) and to urban interests (reliant on trade protection) but alienated rural sectors that would benefit from an opening of trade. The government that shifted attention to law and order might lose the support of urban informal-sector workers, who suffer repression, but pick up support among rural sectors. Shifting salience may then be associated with a shifting composition of electoral constituencies.

In neither of these hypothetical instances did voters' preferences about economic policies change, only the alliances governments forged and the issues they used to mobilize support. I call this rival hypothesis *changing calculus of support*.

I examine the dynamics of public opinion under three Latin American governments that switched to neoliberal economic policies: those of Carlos Menem in Argentina and Alberto Fujimori in Peru, each in his first term (1989–1995 and 1990–1995, respectively), and that of Carlos Andrés Pérez in Venezuela (1989–1993). One reason to focus on these cases is that they vary in terms of the success of the economic programs undertaken and in ex post support for the government. Therefore we will get a sense of the role of economic performance in the dynamics of public opinion in the course of economic liberalization. The Menem government in Argentina and the Fujimori government in Peru are generally credited with ending hyperinflation and presiding over robust growth, whereas in Venezuela under Pérez, inflation persisted and growth was uneven. Another reason to focus on these three cases is that they may provide variation on the dependent variable, policy preference change. That preferences changed in Argentina and Peru but not in Venezuela is hinted at by the reelection fates of the three governments. Despite abandoning their mandates and adopting unpopular policies, Menem and Fujimori mobilized sufficient support during their first terms to be reelected by larger majorities than had brought them to power in the first place. Pérez, in contrast, lost support after announcing unpopular policies, failed to serve out his term, and watched his party go down to defeat in the next presidential election.

Citizen Responses to Policy Switches

Were governments that switched policies less likely than consistent ones to win reelection? We saw in Chapter 3 that, all else equal, voters tended to punish policy switchers at the polls. When GDP growth was held at zero, on average the share of the vote going to the incumbent party of consistent governments was 39%. The share of the vote for parties of governments that had switched was 31%.

Yet all things were not equal; specifically, economic outcomes were on average better when politicians changed course than when they didn't. The expected growth rate at the end of the term of policy switchers was a little over 4%; for consistent governments it was 1.5% – in fact, not statistically different from zero (see Table 3.4). The difference between economic outcomes was statistically highly significant.

It must be stressed again, however, that these were the results we would expect on average, and that the small sample of cases on which the analysis in Chapter 3 drew was sensitive to outstanding results in a few cases. In fact, most governments were not reelected, whether they switched policies or remained consistent. And the proportion of those reelected was somewhat lower among the policy switchers than among consistent politicians: 3 of 12 (25%) of the switchers and 9 of 23 (39%) of the consistent governments. The examples that Domínguez cites of policy switchers who were later reelected were two of only three such instances in the full set of Latin American elections that I study. Following Wilson (1999), we might add the Costa Rican National Liberation Party as one that unexpectedly adopted neoliberal policies (under Luis Alberto Monge in 1982) and won the next election.[1] The fact remains that Latin Americans tended not to reelect incumbent ruling parties, neither those that switched nor, in large numbers, those that didn't (see also Remmer, 1990, 1991).

---

[1] I coded Monge's campaign as vague rather than as security-oriented for reasons given in Chapter 2. Therefore the adjustment and structural reform policies that his government initiated did not count as a switch in the sense of this study. Wilson is correct, however, that the PLN's historical role left voters unprepared for these policy initiatives, and Monge's campaign positions did little to prepare them.

Table 5.1. *Argentina: Problem Issues Deserving Government Attention, February 1995*

Economic Issues	Percent Responding	Noneconomic Issues	Percent Responding
Unemployment	41%	Education	7
Salaries	14	Corruption	6
Pensions/retirees	10	Health	4
Poverty/social	5	Crime	2
Recession	5	Drugs	1
Taxes	1	Justice system	1
Inflation	1	Housing	1
Tax evasion	0.4	Press/individual freedoms	0.2
		Environment	0.1
TOTAL	77%		22%

Note: N = 1,093. Totals do not add to 100% because of rounding.
Source: Romer survey, February 1995.

Changing Calculi of Support

Argentina

Did the focus of political debate shift in Argentina from 1989, when Carlos Menem was first elected promising an immediate economic expansion and wage growth, to 1995, when he was reelected after presiding over a neoliberal austerity program?

The 1989 presidential campaign was mainly about economic issues such as inflation and wages. Economic issues dominated the campaign again in 1995. A poll conducted in February 1995 asked people to mention problems to which the government should pay attention.[2] Table 5.1 lists the economic and noneconomic issues mentioned and the frequency with which they were mentioned.

Economic issues prevailed over noneconomic ones by a rate of three to one. Table 5.1 makes clear that no noneconomic (or indirectly economic) issue, such as corruption or crime, came to overshadow the economy as

---

[2] Romer and Associates conducted the survey between February 17 and 21 to a stratified random sample of 1,165 Argentines between the ages of 18 and 70. It was administered in the Federal District, Greater Buenos Aires, and the 14 next largest cities.

a source of public concern. Most Argentines were worried about unemployment and income.

That no prominent issue dimension emerged in 1995 to compete with the economy in the calculus of support of Argentine voters casts doubt on the hypothesis that voters changed their calculus of support. Voters rejected the incumbent Alfonsín government in 1989 because of the economic debacle over which the government had presided, and voters continued to use economic criteria in 1995.

A strategy for testing the hypothesis of changing calculi of support is to examine the stability of the electoral coalitions supporting Menem in 1995 versus 1989. Consider a hypothetical electorate comprised of three voters, Worker, Capitalist, and Peasant. The Populist Party offers a program of economic expansion and trade protection, which appeals to the Worker and Capitalist and wins, despite opposition from the Peasant. Because the Peasant is at the bottom of the social order, the relation between social class and support for the Populist Party is positive. The new Populist government then implements a program of austerity and trade liberalization. In the run-up to the next election, the Populist candidate says that reforms are complete, the economy is on a sound footing, and it is time to commence a program of redistribution. The Populist Party is reelected, now with the support of the Worker and the Peasant against the Capitalist. The relation between social class and Populist Party support, positive in the first election, has now turned negative.

Did the class basis of Menem's support undergo this sort of transformation in 1995 versus 1989? The May–June 1992 Romer survey asked respondents whom they had voted for in the 1989 presidential election.[3] Three years had elapsed between the election and the survey. Still, the self-reported votes were close to the 1989 election results: 41% in the poll versus 47.4% in the election for Menem, 31% in the poll versus 32.5% in the election for Angeloz of the incumbent UCR, and 5% in the poll versus 6.6% in the election for Alsogaray of the rightist UCD. We can therefore be confident that self-reported votes were reasonable proxies for actual votes.

I estimated a logit model of reported votes in 1989 as a function of education and employment. Because the two surveys did not include

---

[3] Romer and Associates administered the survey between May 25 and June 6, to a stratified random sample of 1,230 Argentines age 18 and over in the Federal Capital, Greater Buenos Aires, and the five largest remaining cities.

Table 5.2. *Argentina: Binomial Logit Estimates of Vote for Menem, 1989 and 1995*[a]

	1989	1995
Constant	1.07**	−0.60**
	(0.16)	(0.10)
Education	−0.30**	−0.01
	(0.03)	(0.01)
Self-employed	−0.10	0.27
	(0.17)	(0.18)
Part time/temp. workers	0.87**	0.24
	(0.30)	(0.28)
Employee	0.31*	0.05
	(0.16)	(0.15)
Unemployed	−0.37	−0.46
	(0.34)	(0.30)
N	1,148	1,093
Chi-squared	123.44	6.83

[a] Recalled 1989 vote in 1992 Romer survey and intended vote in 1995 Romer survey (three months before elections). In both models, the dependent variable is the dummy for a recalled or intended vote for Menem. Cell entries are coefficients; standard errors all in parentheses. Self-employed, part-time/ temporary, employee, and unemployed are dummy variables scored 1 for respondents who identified this as their work status.
* significant at $p < .05$ level.
** significant at $p < .01$ level.
Source of data: Romer and Associates/Roper Center.

comparable questions on income, I used education as a proxy for social class. Education was negatively and significantly associated with a vote for Menem: the lower the education level (social class), the greater the probability that an individual voted for Menem (see Table 5.2). Turning to employment status, part-time or temporary workers and employees were more likely to vote for Menem. Social class was a reliable predictor of the presidential vote in 1989. (I was interested in voters' choice of Menem as opposed to any other choice in both years. For this reason, I used a dichotomous dependent variable for the Menem vote.)

By 1995 the class base of Peronist support had disappeared. A model of intended vote in a February 1995 Romer survey reveals that none of our measures of social class predicts a vote for Menem.

These results cast some doubt on the rival hypothesis of cycling class coalitions. We see no evidence of an inversion of class support. Had class coalitions in favor of Menem cycled in this manner, we should have seen changing signs on coefficients for education and employment categories. In fact, we see the strong class basis of Peronist support in 1989 giving way to cross-class support for Menem's reelection in 1995. In 1995 not class but some other factors caused people to support or reject Menem; later we shall see that a sense of economic improvement and approval of the government's neoliberal program are what distinguished Menem's supporters from his opponents.

Peru

Did the salience of issues or Fujimori's bases of support shift between 1990, when he first came to power, and 1995, when he was reelected? The 1990 presidential election polarized Peruvians along class lines. As we saw in Chapter 2, Fujimori, a political unknown at the beginning of the campaign, crafted an image of himself as a non-European *chinito*, a man of the people, an image shaped as much by his pronouncements against price increases and in favor of workers and small business as by his ethnic identity. His opponent, Mario Vargas Llosa, was perceived as white, wealthy, and aloof, an image shaped as much by his pronouncements against unions and the state sector as by his physical appearance and political allies. After the run-off election in June, in which Fujimori prevailed, a survey asked those who voted for him why they had not supported Vargas Llosa. Recall from Chapter 2 that the most frequent responses were that Vargas Llosa "represents the interests of the rich" (43%), "because of his right-wing ideas" (17%), and "because I don't trust him or don't like him" (17%).

The candidates' starkly different economic policy messages – Vargas Llosa in favor of a radical liberalization of the economy, Fujimori in favor of an industrial policy, subsidies to consumers, and a gradualist approach to inflation stabilization – had deep class resonances. In a May 1990 poll, 74% of the wealthiest respondents but only 17% of the poorest favored a "shock program" to end inflation (which was 30% per month), and 74%

of the wealthy but only 21% of the poor thought that Vargas Llosa's party (FREDEMO) was more capable than Fujimori's (*Cambio '90*) of fighting poverty.[4]

The polarization persisted after Fujimori announced a painful fiscal shock. As we would expect if people's opinions of the president were shaped by his economic discourse (and not, say, by ethnic characteristics alone), Fujimori's surprise adoption of *el shock* caused an inversion of his class support – exactly the sort of inversion not in evidence over the course of Menem's first term, as we just saw. A poll taken the day after the price adjustment (August 9, 1990) showed that support among the poor dropped 40% compared to a poll taken one week earlier: from 70% approval to 30%. And support among the wealthy rose 12%, from 48% to 60%.

But once the initial panic subsided, Fujimori's supporters showed some willingness to exonerate him for his about-face. Approval of Fujimori among poor respondents rose to 57% in September. In the same September 1990 Apoyo survey, of those who said they had voted for him, 63% agreed that "he did not plan a shock but once in office found no alternative" but 27% stated that "he tricked the people when he said 'no shock'." (The corresponding figures among Vargas Llosa supporters were 29% and 69%; Apoyo, *Informe de Opinión*, September 1990.)

Note that this response by Peruvian voters to Fujimori's change of course was more in line with the representation model presented in Chapter 3 than with the spatial model. The spatial model gives us little reason to expect a government to change policies abruptly upon reaching office and even less reason to expect voters to exonerate it if it does. Politicians have just learned which policies the people preferred: those on which it conducted a successful campaign. They should conduct policy as though the term in office were simply a long campaign for reelection. And voters have two reasons to punish inconsistent governments. Their policies are reviled and they show themselves to be unreliable, depriving voters of the ability to make predictions about the future. In the representation model, in contrast, voters' uncertainty gives them good reason to hesitate before they withdraw support for a popular politician who switches to unpopular policies. They use both policy pronouncements and other information (party affiliation, ethnic identity) to draw inferences about whether this is

[4] The poll was of a stratified random sample of 600 Lima residents; see Apoyo, *Informe de Opinión*, May 1990.

Table 5.3A.   *Peru: Vote Intentions of Lima Residents, by Class, May 1990*

	Wealthy	Middle Class	Working Class	Poorest	Total
Fujimori	4%	24%	51%	56%	43%
Vargas Llosa	91	58	33	21	39
Blank vote/no vote	2	7	7	8	7
No answer	3	11	9	15	11
TOTAL	100%	100%	100%	100%	100%
N	43	136	220	201	600

Note: Significance = 0.014.
Source of data: Apoyo, S.A./Roper Center.

Table 5.3B.   *Peru: Vote Intentions of Lima Residents, by Class, March 1995*

	Wealthy	Middle Class	Working Class	Poorest	Total
Fujimori	47%	45%	50%	51%	50%
Pérez de Cuellar	40	22	19	14	17
Other	—	15	12	11	12
No answer	13	18	23	15	21
TOTAL	100%	100%	100%	100%	100%
N	15	130	554	817	1,516
Chi-square	10.6 (3 df)				

Note: Significance = 0.014.
Source of data: Apoyo, S.A./Roper Center.

a politician who wants to promote their interests or his own; even if the politician makes unexpected policy moves, they have good reason to wait and see how things turn out.

Did Fujimori retain support from his original lower-class constituents over the full presidential term? Tables 5.3A and 5.3B show the impact of social class on vote intentions in 1990 and 1995. In 1990, support for Vargas Llosa declined monotonically with class, from 91% to 21%; for Fujimori it increased monotonically, from 4% to 56%. In 1995, in contrast, Fujimori enjoyed universal support. Although he remained particularly a favorite of the lower classes, he enjoyed significant upper- and middle-class support as well. As in Argentina, in Peru changing support for the president was an additive process: he gained adherents at the top of the class structure but didn't lose them at the bottom.

In Argentina, I inferred from this additive dynamic and from the continued prominence of the economy in voters' calculus of support that Menem did not benefit from majority cycling. Did issue salience and voters' calculus of support also remain stable in Peru? Did economic policy remain a reason why poor Peruvians wanted Fujimori to be their president?

The obvious other issue that might have eclipsed the economy during the early 1990s was political violence. Terrorist attacks by Shining Path were met by counterattacks from the armed forces; over the course of a 12-year war, at least 30,000 were killed. Violence was a classic valence issue, one that "involve[s] the linking of the parties with some condition that is positively or negatively valued by the electorate" (D. Stokes, 1966). Outside of Shining Path itself there was no constituency for a continuation of violence.[5] And peace was basically achieved under Fujimori. Not unconnected with the valence issue of violence was the April 1992 coup d'etat, in which the armed forces collaborated with Fujimori in closing the courts and suspending Congress. The coup, which many Peruvians believed helped restore order, was hugely popular. Five months later, detectives captured Shining Path's leaders; Fujimori seemed to be a politician who delivered on matters that generated near-unanimity among the Peruvian public.

Table 5.4 lends support to the view that people favored Fujimori in 1995 for different reasons than in 1990. It reports answers to a national opinion poll conducted in March 1995, one month before the presidential election. People who intended to vote for Fujimori (50% of the sample) were asked why. We see that wealthy respondents answered "economic program/the economy has improved" twice as frequently as did poor respondents. In turn, poor people were more than twice as likely as the wealthy to vote for Fujimori because "he defeated terrorism."

Something important changed between 1990 and 1995. Poor people, by far a majority in the Peruvian electorate, were drawn to Fujimori in 1990 because of his pronounced security-oriented intentions on the economy. After his government switched to an economic liberalization program, his supporters seemed willing (after a brief revolt) to believe the

---

[5] Certainly there were divisions among Peruvians over how heavy a hand the armed forces should use in fighting Shining Path, and human rights abuses were occasions for periodic criticisms of this and earlier governments.

Table 5.4. *Peru: Reasons for Voting for Fujimori (March 4–11, 1995)*

	Middle Class	Working Class	Poor	All Respondents
The works he's realizing	19%	31%	36%	33%
Economic program/the economy has improved	36	22	17	21
He defeated terrorism	9	15	20	17
Other	35	30	23	26
No answer	2	2	5	3
TOTAL	100%	101%	99%	100%
N	93	395	545	1,033

Source of data: Apoyo S.A./Roper Center.

president had good reasons for changing course and to delay judgment. Yet by the end of the term, these initial working-class supporters were not on the whole happy with economic performance under the neoliberal program. Still they remained supportive of the president for reasons other than the economy. In the lead-up to Fujimori's reelection in April 1995, the poor were more likely than the wealthy to point to the defeat of terrorism as a reason to reelect the president. The wealthy, in contrast, voted against Fujimori the anti-neoliberal in 1990 and for Fujimori the neoliberal in 1995. (Note that among the full sample the most frequently mentioned reason for supporting Fujimori in 1995 was public works. I return to this fact later.)

To summarize, in Peru we see clear evidence of changing salience of issues and changing calculi of support for the president. Neither fact is consistent with the representation model, in which voters support politicians who impose unpopular policies because the policies become popular with these same voters.

Venezuela

Carlos Andrés Pérez's Great Turnaround toward market liberalization was indeed a big surprise. It was not predicted in his campaign pronouncements, and Venezuelans who remembered his first presidency in the mid-1970s, at the height of Venezuela's oil boom, were taken aback. Unlike the two other presidencies discussed here, Pérez's was a failure. Riots broke out when the government announced price increases in February 1989; social unrest flared up repeatedly; military officers attempted coups d'etat twice; and Pérez was impeached on corruption charges before the end of his term. The Pérez presidency began a period in which support for the country's two leading political parties, which had monopolized electoral politics for decades, dwindled (Alvarez, 1996; see also Crisp, 1998). They were displaced by independents and military officers, such as Hugo Chávez, a leader of a coup attempt, who won presidential elections in 1998 and 2000. It is tempting to infer that this debacle reflected the bad results of the initially unpopular policy that Pérez switched to. I test this proposition later. But do we see any evidence of shifting issue salience or electoral alliances during the Great Turnaround?

In fact, as in Peru, new valence issues came to the fore in Venezuelan politics between the beginning and the end of the policy switcher's term. In 1988 Venezuelans were worried about the economy; by 1989 they were worried about the economy and political stability; and in 1993 they were still worried about the economy and stability, but they were also deeply worried about corruption.

Economics dominated political debate in Venezuela in the late 1980s. Although during the 1988 campaign the crisis had not hit in the same way as in Argentina or Peru, Venezuelans sensed decline. A March 1989 poll asked, "Thinking about Venezuela, what are your main fears or anxieties?"[6] The most common answer (in the month following social protests that the military was brought in to quell) was a coup (21%), followed by acceleration in inflation and the cost of living (9%), civil war (9%), economic crisis (7%), and a repetition of riots like those the month before. Only 2% mentioned corruption.[7]

By the end of Pérez's term, people were still worried about the economy and stability, but they were also deeply worried about corruption. In a survey conducted in July 1993, soon after Pérez was removed from office, people were asked the open-ended question "What is the principal

---

[6] Datos, C.A.'s March 1989 survey was of a stratified random sample of 2,000 adults.

[7] Venezuelans had also been concerned about corruption under Pérez's predecessor, Jaime Lusinchi. In the October 1988 poll, more than half of respondents thought that "administrative corruption" was a bigger problem than unemployment, the cost of living, or delinquency. But this concern dropped out when Pérez was elected, even though he was from Lusinchi's same party, AD. And corruption was not widely debated or discussed in the 1988 campaign.

problem of Venezuela at this moment"?[8] The most common answer was "inflation/cost of living" (23%); the second was "corruption" (20%). And in response to the question "What problem should the new president address?," "corruption" was the third most frequent answer (16%).

Did the Venezuelan scenario then recapitulate the Peruvian one? Did a new valence issue emerge, changing the contours of political debate – with the critical difference that in Venezuela the president was on the wrong side of the issue? Certainly corruption is a classic valence issue. And certainly the linkage with the government was negative. In the 1993 survey people were asked, "Who would you say was mainly at fault or what is the main cause of Venezuela's current problems?" A full quarter of respondents answered "Carlos Andrés Pérez"; this was the modal answer.

Yet I suspect that concern about corruption was a by-product of Venezuelans' dissatisfaction with economic performance under Pérez and with the bungled political management of the Great Turnaround. Templeton (1995) presents evidence that Venezuelans see theirs as an oil-rich country in which the venality of the political class, more than inappropriate economic policies or international market conditions, depress the average person's standard of living. In fact, corruption as a moral issue has little resonance. As Templeton shows, Venezuelans are tolerant of behavior that in other countries would be defined as corrupt. Accusations of corruption are more likely to arise when economic times are bad than in response to solid evidence of misbehavior by politicians. Rather than a separate valence issue that drove Pérez's popularity down, corruption was the explanation Venezuelans offered themselves for why people in a rich country struggled economically. Given the tight linkage between corruption and economic outcomes in the minds of many Venezuelans, I conjecture that had political management and economic performance been better, accusations of corruption against Pérez would not have stuck.

Summary

The economy dominated the campaigns that brought Carlos Menem, Alberto Fujimori, and Carlos Andrés Pérez to power. In the Argentine case there is little evidence of changing calculi of voters' support in the

---

[8] Consultores 21's July 1993 survey used a stratified random sample of 1,500 adults residing in major urban areas.

president's reelection. It therefore seems plausible that improvements in economic conditions under initially unpopular policies changed voters' policy preferences, a possibility I study further in the next section. In Peru there did occur a shift in the salience of issues and in the calculi of support among social classes. Peruvians perceived Fujimori as having achieved peace and order in his first term. These achievements helped him hold on to his core constituency of lower-class voters, who in the end were un-persuaded that his economic policy switch was justified by the results. He was also aided, as we shall see, by economic outcomes, but outcomes that were only tenuously linked with his program of economic liberalization. Carlos Andrés Pérez in Venezuela suffered negative valence shocks with the corruption and stability issues, but economic outcomes also worked against him. In Venezuela, bad economic performance enhanced people's willingness to believe that corrupt leaders caused economic hardship and reinforced their belief that neoliberalism was the wrong course.

The Rise of a Mass Neoliberalism?

Argentina

In the period 1989 to 1995, the Argentine Peronists piled one electoral victory on another. Menem won the 1989 presidential election with 47.4% of the popular vote; in simultaneous elections for the lower house of Congress the Peronist party won 66 seats, for a total of 106 in a 254-seat assembly. The Peronist contingent in the assembly increased steadily in mid-term elections in late 1989, 1991, and 1993. Peronists also gained control over more and more state governments. In the presidential elections of 1995 Menem defeated his closest rival, José Bordón of the left-of-center Frepaso, 49.8% to 29.2%. Did the Peronist government's endur-ing popularity in Menem's first term and the president's reelection in 1995 reflect a mass conversion of Argentines to the neoliberal project?

Figure 5.1 traces public approval of the economic program and the president from September 1989 through March 1996. Three important facts emerge from this figure. First, for most of Menem's first term, the president's popularity appears closely keyed to the popularity of the eco-nomic reform program.[9] As we shall see, this was not the case for all of

---

[9] If presidential approval and approval of the program overlapped throughout the period, the concern might arise that survey respondents were not making a distinction between

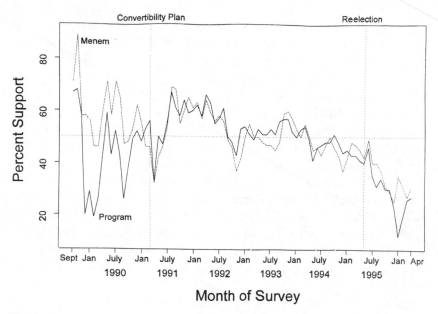

Figure 5.1 Argentina: support for Menem and the economic program.

our three presidents. Beginning in March 1991, when Finance Minister Domingo Cavallo implemented the *convertibility plan* and inflation fell, both the level of presidential popularity and its direction of change are predicted well by the popularity of the economic program.

The second fact suggested by Figure 5.1 is that the implementation of the convertibility plan boosted the approval of the president and the economic program, and sustained both at a sufficiently high level to keep Menem's approval close to 50% by May 1995, permitting him the plurality support required for reelection. Fabián Echegaray and Carlos Elordi (2001) explain that rhetorical framing and economic results drove popular support of Menem and his economic program. The Peronist government came to office in the midst of hyperinflation and social unrest, disarray that gave the new government breathing space as it embarked on its surprising neoliberal program. People's uncertainty about the wisdom of

the questions "Do you approve or disapprove of President Menem?" and "Do you approve or disapprove of the government's economic policy?" But clearly, people were making a distinction between the two questions early in the term, before the implementation of the Cavallo plan.

Menem's policies was tempered by their admiration for his boldness and perseverance in the face of resistance from within the Peronist party and the labor movement, in contrast to the timidity and vacillations of his predecessor. When hyperinflation returned 18 months into Menem's term (95% inflation in March 1990), he deployed two rhetorical stratagems. The first was to step up the *intertemporal framing* of reforms (Przeworski, 1993; Stokes, 2001a). Having admonished Argentines in July 1989 to accept "painful surgery, no anesthesia," he returned to the theme that things had to get bad first if they were ever to get better, declaring, "we are ill but improving" (*estamos mal pero vamos bien*; cited in Echegaray and Elordi, 2001). The second stratagem was to remind Argentines that the current status quo was still an improvement over the past. In April 1990 Menem declared, "I have the certainty that we are on the right path"; the only other path open to Argentina was to return to "a system that drove us to the depths of hyperinflation and worse still, to the depths of national hyper-frustration, to hyper-poverty" (cited in Echegaray and Elordi, 2001).

Inventive framing notwithstanding, real economic improvements lay behind the Menem government's continued electoral successes through the mid-1990s. The critical achievement was inflation stabilization. Inflation fell from 26% in March 1991 to 1% by the end of the year, never again to threaten. As Figure 5.1 shows, public support for the government's economic policies nearly doubled immediately after implementation of the Cavallo plan. Echegaray and Elordi show that changes in inflation affected public opinion as one would expect: the lower the inflation rate, the greater the proportion of Argentines supporting the government and its economic program, in relation both to those opposing the government and its program and to those expressing no opinion.

A third conclusion emerging from Figure 5.1 is that support of the president and the economic program, though boosted by the government's success in "pulverizing inflation," trended slowly downward over the remainder of the president's first term. Ex post support for the neoliberal policies was sufficient to sustain Menem to reelection. But in the second term, support continued to trend downward. This erosion of support, reflecting, as Echegaray and Elordi show, public unease about unemployment, lay behind the Peronists' loss of their congressional majority in 1997 and was a factor in Menem's eventual decision not to seek reelection in 1999. The president and his campaign advisors were well aware of the public's shifting concern toward unemployment in 1995. Hence the reelection campaign promise to "pulverize unemployment as we pulverized inflation" (*Southern Cone Report*, 1995:2).

Unemployment worries notwithstanding, Menem secured reelection in 1995 in large part because many voters sensed that the economy was improving. A survey conducted in February, three months before the election, probed respondents' sense of the economy, the government's economic policy, and vote intentions. People who planned to vote for the incumbent Peronists (35% of the sample) were decidedly more optimistic about the economy than those who planned to vote for someone else.

Table 5.5 presents a probit estimate of the effect of views of the economy and the government's policies on vote intentions. All coefficients are highly significant predictors of support for the Peronists. People who intended to vote for Menem tended to see the Argentine economy as growing, the government as handling the economy well, and economic policy as heading in the right direction. They were also less nervous than non-Menem supporters about a financial crisis like the one Mexico was experiencing. (Recall, in contrast, many Peruvians' noneconomic reasons for supporting Fujimori in 1995.) Hence the views of many Argentines that the government's economic policies were the right ones and that economic performance had been good drove Menem's reelection. These results support the hypothesis that Argentines were uncertain about the wisdom of neoliberalism ex ante and supported it when they witnessed economic improvements, especially price stability, ex post.

To further probe the evolution of Argentine mass neoliberalism, I took advantage of a series of questions, asked in several surveys, concerning the appropriate role of the market versus the state in the economy (see Table 5.6). In May–June 1992 and October 1995, pollsters asked questions about the role of the state and the market in setting prices, in determining social welfare, and in production. The first fact that emerges starkly from the table is the large number of people who agreed with the neoliberal statements – in all but one instance, over 40%. For example, well over half of those sampled in 1992 agreed that a country is most likely to develop "when the economy is left to free competition" and when "social services are in private hands." Over half thought the state should reduce public expenditures to control inflation "even though it might have to reduce social assistance." Without earlier benchmarks we cannot know whether these figures represent growth, stability, or decline in mass neoliberalism. But whatever the trajectory of mass opinion, a substantial segment of the Argentine population seemed prepared to embrace free markets.

Table 5.5. *Argentina: Binomial Logit Estimate of Intention to Vote for Incumbent Peronists,[a] February 1995*

Variable	Coefficient	Marginal Effects
Constant	−7.81**	−1.72**
	(0.57)	(0.17)
Future[b]	0.60**	0.13**
	(0.15)	(0.03)
Policy[c]	0.54**	0.12**
	(0.15)	(0.03)
Direction[d]	1.05**	0.23**
	(0.26)	(0.06)
Mexico[e]	0.66**	0.14**
	(0.16)	(0.04)
Growth[f]	0.56**	0.12**
	(0.19)	(0.04)
N	750	
Chi-squared	351.99	

[a] "In the presidential election of May 1995, which party do you plan to vote for?"; scored 1 if Peronist, 0 otherwise. Cell entries are coefficients, and standard errors are in parentheses; marginal effects are evaluated at the mean of the independent variables.

[b] "How do you think the economic situation of the country will be in one year: better, the same, or worse than now?" (scored in ascending order from worse to better).

[c] "What is your opinion about how the national government is managing the progress of the economy?" (scored in ascending order from very bad to very good).

[d] "Do you think the overall economic policy pursued by the current government is in the correct direction or a mistaken direction? (correct = 2, mistaken = 1).

[e] "What possibility do you think exists that Argentina would go through a financial crisis like the recent one in Mexico?" (scored as much = 1, little = 2, none = 3).

[f] "In economic terms, do you think that the country is showing signs of growth, stagnation, or decline?" (scored as decline = 1, stagnation = 2, growth = 3).

Source of data: Romer and Associates/Roper Center.

Table 5.6. *Neoliberalism in Argentine Public Opinion, 1992 and 1995*

1992		1995	
		Which aspects of the economic	
A country is most likely to		*model do you agree with, and*	
develop when:	Agree	*which do you disagree with?*	Agree
The economy is left to free competition	**59%**	A free market without state intervention	**49%**
		Disagree	33%
or		Don't know	19%
The state intervenes or plans economic life	35%		
A country is most likely to			
develop when:			Agree
The state privileges order and reduces public expenditures to control inflation, even though it might have to reduce social assistance	**51%**	Control of the public deficit even if it means reducing personnel and social expenditures	**43%**
		Disagree	41%
		Don't know	16%
or			
The state invests in social assistance even though increased expenditures might risk inflation	38%		
A country is most likely			
to develop when:		Privatizing public enterprises	
		Agree	**47%**
Social services are in private hands	**65%**	Disagree	45%
		Don't know	8%
		Privatizing public works	
		Agree	**36%**
or		Disagree	45%
Social services are in the hands of the state	24%	Don't know	19%

Source of data: Romer and Associates/Roper Center.

On the other hand, mass neoliberalism declined slightly between 1992 and 1995; the number of respondents who opposed a preponderant role for markets versus the state or who expressed no opinion rose somewhat. This hint of a dropping off of mass neoliberalism is consistent with the

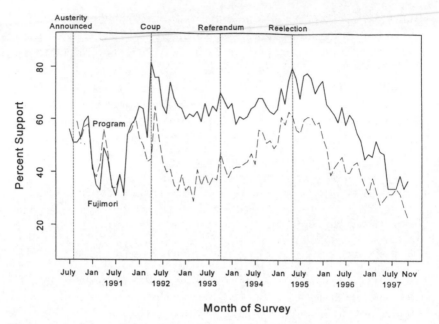

Figure 5.2   Peru: support for Fujimori and the economic program.

slow downward trend in support for the government's economic program between 1991 and 1996, which we observed in Figure 5.1.

Peru

Earlier we saw evidence that Peruvians who had been skeptical of economic liberalization remained unpersuaded, and hence that factors other than the economy explained the Fujimori government's enduring popularity. Figure 5.2 offers additional evidence. It traces approval of President Fujimori and of his government's economic program from September 1990 through September 1997. Opinions of the economic program and of the president are almost indistinguishable for the first 18 months. Then a gap first opens between them, and support for the economic program remains well below that of the president for the remainder of his first term.

Tepid support for the Fujimori government's economic program appears paradoxical, especially in view of the parallels between the Peruvian and Argentine experiences. As in Argentina, in Peru the new gov-

142

ernment came to power in the midst of extraordinarily high inflation, and, as in Argentina, it achieved price stability. Inflation fell from 63% in July 1990, when Fujimori took office, to 3% in May 1993, never again to rise above this level. And Peruvians supported the economic program and the government when inflation fell. Elsewhere (Stokes 2001b) I show that a 5% decrease in the inflation rate, from 8% to 3% (the mean monthly rate in the period 1990–1997), was associated with a 4.5% increase in support for the government's economic program. Given Peruvians' responsiveness to success on inflation, why did the Fujimori government not reap greater rewards for economic performance?

One explanation is that, as in Argentina, in Peru the economic program also increased unemployment. Job loss was particularly acute in well-paying industrial sectors. An index of employment in firms in Lima with 100 or more workers (1979 = 100) fell nearly monotonically, from 97 in July 1990 to below 75 in March 1995, the month before Fujimori's reelection. Job loss made Peruvians pessimistic about future economic performance and turned them against the government. When the employment index fell from 95 (its maximum) to 62 (its minimum), support for the economic program fell from 51% to 40% (Stokes 2001b).

The puzzle remains: in both Peru and Argentina, the surprising neoliberal adjustment lowered inflation and raised unemployment, yet Argentines seemed more favorable toward the economic program than Peruvians. Greater income disparities in Peru may explain the difference. Poor Peruvians responded to GDP growth during Fujimori's first term as though they were stuck in Hirschman's (1973) tunnel, watching the lane of traffic next to them move ahead. Rather than inferring that they also would soon advance, they inferred that they were being left behind. Under conditions of economic growth, poor Peruvians became optimistic about the future overall performance of the economy, believing that growth would be followed by more growth (Stokes 2001b). But they believed that others, not they, would benefit from future growth.

The challenge facing Fujimori was to retain the allegiance of poorer voters – a large segment of the electorate – despite their lack of enthusiasm for his neoliberal economic program. Figures 5.3 and 5.4 testify to his accomplishment. Figure 5.3 tracks support for the president and the program among the poorest stratum that the Lima Apoyo polls interviewed (generally about one-third of the sample.) Beginning in mid-1991, a gap appeared in lower-class popular opinion between support of the president and support of his economic program. During the first term, on

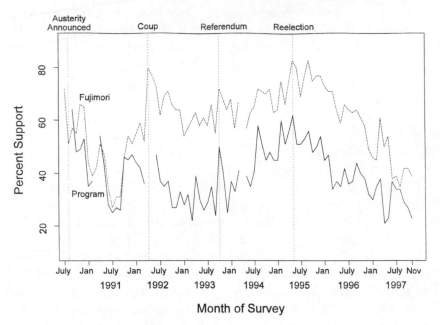

Figure 5.3 Peru: support for Fujimori and the economic program among the poor.

average 59% supported the president; only 39% supported his economic program. The story was very different among the wealthiest stratum of respondents (see Figure 5.4). Here support for the economic program was high, averaging 60%, and very close to support for the president, which averaged 61%.

Why did Peruvians support Fujimori even when they opposed his economic program? The policy switch itself is one piece of the puzzle: in a stroke, he won the allegiance of wealthier voters by adopting the economic program their candidate had advocated. He then retained support of poorer voters by appearing to solve the problem of political violence and, with the coup, by imposing order in the midst of chaos.

Yet it would be a mistake to conclude that Peru's poor were indifferent to economic performance and would vote to reelect Fujimori regardless of the economy. Certainly the government made no such assumption. On the contrary, although poor Peruvians showed little evidence of being won over to the government's economic program, they did come to see themselves as benefiting economically under the Fujimori government; indeed,

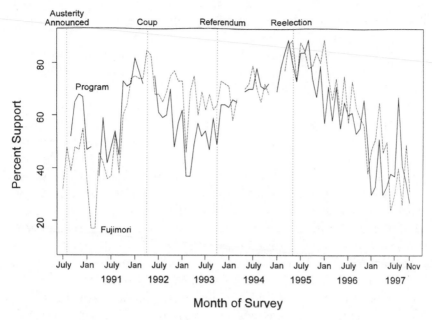

Figure 5.4   Peru: support for Fujimori and the economic program among the wealthy.

the government worked hard to cultivate this belief on the eve of elections.

Consider again Figure 5.2, and note the sharp rise in support of the government's economic program in the six months before the national elections in May 1995. The cause of this spike in support was a concerted spending spree by the government.

Sensing that voters might not think of job loss as a fair trade-off for price stability, to help the president's chances of reelection the government embarked in late 1994 on a major program of social spending (Kay, 1996; Roberts and Arce, 1998), devoting the equivalent of 0.5% of GDP to an antipoverty program (Schady, 2000). Electoral considerations weighed heavily in decisions on where to spend the money. Schady shows that the government directed spending through the Peruvian Social Fund (FON-CODES) antipoverty program to communities that supported Fujimori in 1990 and to communities where the president's support in 1990 hovered around 50%. These last districts were ones where the political productiv-ity of expenditures was greatest; FONCODES programs could tip the

145

balance in favor of the government, whereas funds would be wasted, from an electoral vantage point, on individuals who would never be persuaded to support Fujimori.[10]

Targeted social spending in the run-up to elections, rather than pro-market reforms in general, mobilized support for Fujimori among the poor. Hence the most frequently cited reason poor respondents offered for their intention to vote for Fujimori in 1995: "he is accomplishing many works" ("*Está realizando muchas obras*"; see Table 5.4). The term *obras* connotes public works, such as the creation of infrastructure or community development projects, mostly of a physical sort. Alternatively, the poll offered them the response "economic policy/the economy" as a reason to vote for the president, but fewer poor respondents chose this answer. Monthly Apoyo surveys made no such distinction: they simply asked people whether they approved or disapproved of the government's economic program. The apparently growing support for the government's economic policy in the period leading up to Fujimori's 1995 reelection, visible in Figure 5.2, probably confounds people's opinions of neoliberal policies (privatization, reduced spending in traditional social programs) with their opinions of targeted antipoverty programs. This targeted spending, along with the president's accomplishments in the areas of order and peace, drove poor Peruvians to support Fujimori in 1995, not a spontaneous conversion of Peru's poor to the neoliberal economic model.

Over-time data offer additional evidence that the preelection spending spree helped compensate for mixed economic results of the government's liberalization program. Holding all economic variables at their means, in a month during the spending spree the expected proportion of respondents supporting the economic program was 57%. In a month falling outside of the spending spree, again with economic variables at their means, support falls to 43% (Stokes 2001b).

People's views of the ideological underpinnings of neoliberalism are another window on changing mass beliefs in this period. Table 5.7 reports responses of Lima residents to questions about the proper role of the state in the economy. The left side of the table reports responses by social class, the right side responses at various moments between 1989 and 1994.

Large numbers of people were willing to endorse pro-market views. In 1994 a large majority agreed that "private enterprise is good for the country," and a majority believed that "the state should leave productive

---

[10] Schady shows that poverty was also a criterion guiding FONCODES funding decisions.

Table 5.7. *Peru: Opinions of the Market Economy by Social Class and Over Time*

Opinion	Class (March 1994)				Date				
	Upper	Middle	Working	Poor	April 1989	July 1990	Aug 1991	April 1993	March 1994
Private enterprise is good for the country	89%	87%	71%	59%	63%	70%	80%	73%	70%
The state should leave productive activity to the private sector	75%	67%	56%	49%	51%	56%	59%	57%	56%
The state should be small	69%	51%	43%	33%	39%	52%	54%	48%	41%
Prices for most products should be determined by free competition	72%	66%	57%	45%	—	—	—	—	—
N	85	120	169	140	514	600	516	517	514

Source: Apoyo, S.A., cited in Carrión (1996).

activity in the hands of the private sector." Yet support for pro-market positions declined monotonically with social class. This class dynamic is consistent with other evidence we have seen that the lower classes, in 1990 Fujimori's chief constituents, were not won over to his market reform program.

Over-time data show growing support for neoliberal economic ideology at the outset of Fujimori's reforms but erosion after mid-1991, still at an early stage of the reform process. Unfortunately, we lack deeper longitudinal data that would allow us to place these shifts on a longer historical horizon. Still, the data do not support the hypothesis that Fujimori's reelection in 1995 grew out of a sustained rise of neoliberal mass beliefs.

Venezuela

I argued earlier that poor economic performance and negative valence shocks played a part in the political demise of Carlos Andrés Pérez and his Great Turnaround. In the 1993 presidential election, Venezuelans were in an anti-neoliberal mood. The winner, Rafael Caldera, blamed Pérez for Venezuela's economic problems and promised a reversal of some pieces of the Great Turnaround (*Andean Report*, 1993:2).

Figure 5.5 traces support for the president and the Great Turnaround over the course of Pérez's term. As in Argentina early in Menem's first term, the Venezuelans' initial reaction was to support the president despite disaffection with his government's economic program. Opinions of the program and the president become more tightly interwoven in the second year of the term (1990). Support for both declined in 1991, from the mid-40s to the mid-to-high 20s. Although we lack data on this point, the view of Venezuelan experts whom I interviewed is that this decline reflected people's disappointment that inflation remained high despite the sacrifices entailed by the reform effort. Whatever the Menem and Fujimori governments' failings, they clearly ended inflation. Not true of Pérez: inflation remained around 35% annually in 1991 and 1992 – higher annual rates than for any year between 1970 and 1988. Pérez's approval rating continued to decline after a February 1992 coup attempt in this, Latin America's second oldest democracy. The coup makers accused Pérez of indifference to the economic plight of the people (see, e.g., Naím, 1993).

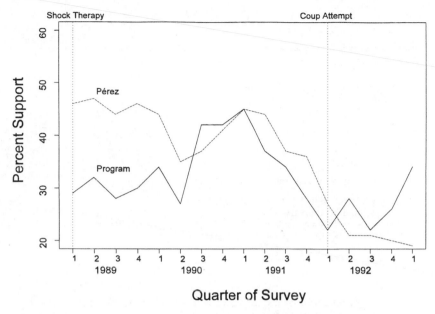

Figure 5.5   Venezuela: support for Pérez and the economic program.

These dynamics support my earlier contention that bad economic performance under the Great Turnaround lay behind Pérez's eventual fall
from grace; accusations of corruption were more a symptom than a cause
of his tarnished presidency. As Figure 5.5 makes clear, Pérez's support was
already thin by early 1993, when the Congress accused him of corruption.

It comes as little surprise, then, that Venezuelans showed less support
for neoliberal ideology than was evinced by Argentines or Peruvians. Table
5.8 reports responses to questions on economic ideology in the June 1993
survey, cited earlier, conducted after Pérez's impeachment.[11] Majorities
disagreed with pro-market statements in four of the five questions. Overwhelming majorities favored statist intervention in setting prices and
subsidizing goods, and substantial majorities opposed privatization of
state-owned enterprises and price liberalization. A slender plurality
favored foreign investment in oil.

---

[11] The July 1993 survey was conducted by Consultores 21.

Table 5.8.   *Venezuela: Responses to Questions of Economic Ideology, 1993, 1,500 Respondents*

	Yes	No	No Response
Should the government maintain social programs such as food grants?	76%	20%	4%
Should food prices be subsidized?	70%	22%	7%
Should the government sell state-owned enterprises to private capital?	39%	53%	9%
Should prices be freed to stimulate production?	41%	52%	7%
Should the government permit foreign investment in the national oil industry?	47%	43%	10%

Source: Consultores 21/Roper Center.

Summary

Voters' later judgment of incumbents who switch policies at the beginning of their term could focus on these same policies or their attention could be diverted to other matters. When voters remain focused on the issue area where the government imposed unmandated policies, voters could still support the government despite the change of course, as long as outcomes are sufficiently good – for example, prices stabilize and growth resumes. This is the Argentine story. When voters' attention doesn't change and outcomes are bad under unmandated policies, support for the government erodes. This is the Venezuelan story. When outcomes of unmandated policies are not very good, the government need not simply face defeat but still has some stratagems at its disposal. One is to divert attention to other, more popular policy dimensions, such as from the economy to peace and order. Another is to modify the unpopular policy – for example, to replace cost-cutting with spending. The Peruvian government deployed both of these stratagems.

Discussion

This analysis of the dynamics of public opinion in the wake of policy switches invites a reassessment of the representation model. The model assumes that voters' policy preferences are determined by causal beliefs about the impact of policies on their welfare. These beliefs take a probabilistic form and hence are subject to some uncertainty. Because of this uncertainty, beliefs can change when outcomes are sufficiently at odds with prior expectations. The malleability of voters' causal beliefs, that is, voters' tendency to update beliefs in light of outcomes, in turn has implications for the electoral strategies of politicians. Because voters may come to support policies ex post which they opposed ex ante, politicians may send misleading campaign signals and switch. The bait-and-switch strategy, in short, can be a good one for winning election to a first term and reelection to a second.

The analysis in this chapter offers some support of the representation model. At a simple level, people's policy preferences were not fixed but could change considerably. Support for Menem's economic policy varied in his first term between 30% and 95%; support for Fujimori's economic policy varied between 25% and 65%; support for Pérez's Great Turn-around varied between 25% and 45%. The data do not allow me to analyze uncertainty directly (as do, for example, M. Alvarez, 1997; Bartels, 1991; and Buendía Laredo, 2000), and some of this variability may reflect public perceptions that economic policies themselves changed. Yet it is fair to infer that changing economic outcomes drove much of this variability, and hence people updated their beliefs.[12]

Yet we have also learned that our model is too simple to account for the dynamics of public opinion when governments change course, nor does it fully specify the possible fates of policy-switching governments. The model leaves little room for politicians' beliefs to be wrong, and thus for the kinds of overly optimistic predictions the Venezuelans fell prey to. Governments may be representative but incompetent. They may change course, believing it to be in the best interest of voters, only to turn out to be wrong. I return to a discussion of beliefs, competence, and representation in the final chapter.

To the extent that politicians' beliefs are wrong and outcomes turn out to be as bad as voters initially feared, the representation model predicts

---

[12] We might think of purely retrospective voting, as conceptualized by Key (1966) or Fiorina (1981), as an extreme form of uncertainty about the effects of policy on outcomes, where the voter is entirely agnostic, employs no prior probabilities at all, and bases judgment entirely on outcomes. Yet we have seen evidence that voters did seem to have prior preferences concerning policy: they paid attention to what campaigners said and reacted to policy changes, if only briefly, before the outcomes had materialized. My data do not allow me to weigh the relative importance of people's prior beliefs versus the outcomes they observe on their posterior beliefs or on their willingness to support an incumbent.

that voters will reject policy switchers for reelection. Yet in making this prediction the model simplifies away the multidimensionality of politics. The Peruvian experience reminds us that many matters can come into play over the course of a four- or five-year presidential term; terms of debate may shift; and the president can win (or lose) support from actions that were not central to people's considerations when they brought him to power in the first place.

If politicians are wrong and unmandated policies turn out not to produce sufficiently good effects to win people over, the government can also modify unpopular policies. This is a second implication of the Peruvian story. Unexpected positive valence shocks were, after all, just half of the story of Fujimori's success. The other half was the government's targeting of expenditures at electorally critical communities to compensate for the failings of the surprise policies. Pro-market reforms did not perform sufficiently well to persuade the skeptical. But the government, rather than risk going down to defeat (defeat that the model would predict), had an additional tool available: modifying the policy or compensating for its ill effects, at least until it was safely returned to power. The model's (useful) reduction of politicians' choices to, first, which campaign promises to make and, second, which policy to implement at the beginning of the term leads us to ignore this alternative available to incumbents.

Still, such an 11th-hour reconversion to state intervention might run into credibility problems. If voters believe that the pool of politicians includes people who may renege on their mandates for good and bad reasons, might they not expect incumbents who switch back to popular policies when they try to get reelected to switch back yet again to unpopular policies after reelection has been secured? Our abstract model tells us little about credibility.[13] But Peruvians who believed that Fujimori's government would continue to spend lavishly on antipoverty programs were disappointed in his second term, and declining public approval ratings probably reflect this disappointment. Similarly disappointed were Argentines who believed Menem's promise to "pulverize unemployment as we pulverized inflation."

---

[13] What it does tell us is that (by assumption) an incumbent is more likely to implement the same policy if reelected than to change; but if we depart from the model and allow politicians to change again at the end of the term, which policy is she then more likely to implement?

Neoliberalism without Mandates: Citizens Respond

This chapter calls for a deeper consideration of theoretical and normative issues, a task I take on in the next two chapters. The facts of two of our cases are simply not consistent with the picture painted by Guillermo O'Donnell of "failures accumulating" under politicians who ignore their mandates, and countries finding themselves "stuck with a widely reviled president." Yet Domínguez's more sanguine appraisal of democracy as "self-correcting," in turn, fails to capture the hard realities of electoral politics. Accountability, the contingent renewal of incumbents, allows voters to make general ex post judgments about how incumbents have performed over a range of actions and policies. Voters may not be able to hold governments to account for particular actions they have taken or policies they have mounted. Most Peruvians were skeptical of neoliberalism when in 1990 they elected Alberto Fujimori, the anti-neoliberal candidate, president; they remained skeptical as of mid-1994, nine months before the election that returned him to power. Intensive and politically targeted expenditures brought them around in time for the election, but by early in the year following the election their skepticism had returned. Hence it is clear that a politician may mislead voters to win office, abandon his mandate, and be reelected even without persuading people in any lasting way that the unmandated course was the right one.

The conclusions, then, are mixed. Politicians who switch to unpopular policies may be reelected; they may even be acting as good representatives in the sense of pursuing the policies that they believe are most beneficial for their constituents. Accountability, however, is not sufficient to ensure that politicians will be reelected only if they violate campaign promises in the people's interest. Politicians may be lucky and people may forget as new issues arise, issues that cut in the government's favor; or they may be able to target compensation strategically and take advantage of divisions among voters. And to the extent that politicians anticipate these loopholes in accountability, they may be tempted to switch to unpopular policies even in the absence of good, constituent-oriented reasons to do so.

6

Mandates and Democratic Theory

The House of Commons has no more right to initiate legislation, especially imme-
diately upon its first meeting, of which the constituencies were not informed, and of
which the constituencies might have been informed, and as to which, if they had
been so informed, there is . . . the very greatest doubt as to what their decision might
be.

  Marquess of Hartington, addressing the British Parliament (1886)

Power was delegated to the president, and he did what he deemed best.

  Guillermo O'Donnell (1994)

Guillermo O'Donnell believed he had discovered in *delegative democracies*
a new "species" of the genus democracy. But a long tradition of theorists
of representative government would find much that is familiar in the Latin
American scenarios he observed. The scenario – voters seem to elect a
government to carry out some policies, governments don't seem to follow
voters' wishes, and voters turn against them – is not at all foreign to
representative governments that O'Donnell would be unlikely to call
delegative democracies. In the first preceding epigraph, a British Member
of Parliament railed against William Gladstone, a fellow Liberal, because
of his government's immediate postelection change of course (on the
question of Irish home rule.) The Marquess of Hartington's criticisms
would be repeated, a century later, by critics of Latin American policy
switchers.

Just how important mandates are to democracy has been a topic of
perpetual disagreement. The abandonment of campaign promises, many
claim, is not a perversion of representative democracy but part of its
normal functioning. Many theorists believe that campaign messages are
hollow, or unenforceable, or keep governments from pursuing the best

154

policies. In this chapter, I make the case that campaign pronouncements are meaningful and should constrain the actions of government; when there are good reasons for governments to change policies, they should take actions that restore the sense that the people's views count.

The controversy over legislator judgment versus the will of constituents is germane to *any* representative democracy. Its relevance is heightened in contemporary Latin America not because these democracies are of a fundamentally different sort ("species") from representative ones, but because the tension between the judgment of representatives and the will of citizens has been especially acute in this region at this historical juncture. To sort out these issues, we need not an adjective to specify a new species of democracy, but a deeper consideration of the relation of government to citizenry in all representative systems.

In this chapter, I explore the proposition, prominent in many theories of representative government, that representation requires that officeholders make policy without regard for the opinions of constituents, and the opposite proposition, put forth by other theorists, that representation means (at least in part) responsiveness to constituent opinion. The debate is closely related to the central one of this book: whether prior campaign messages do, and should, constrain the policies of politicians once in office. If officeholders ought to act independently of constituent opinion, it might still be desirable that they state their intentions in campaigns, but these intentions should hardly be binding. If, in contrast, officeholders ought to be responsive to constituent opinion, then candidates must signal policy intentions in campaigns. The winning candidate's message will then reflect voters' preferences, and this message should (under normal circumstances) shape the winner's actions.

In support of the view that representatives' actions should be in line with constituents' opinions and campaign messages, I will present two propositions. First, against the common view that constraints arising from constituent opinion and campaign messages are detrimental to politicians, it is important to see that such constraints can also be enabling of governments and of good public policy. Second, if (as we have been assuming) political representation means action in the interest of constituents, a strong case can be made that constituents have an interest in becoming good decision makers in matters of public concern and that only informative campaigns make them good decision makers. Looked at this way, politicians who emit misleading campaign messages and then switch policies for good reasons are not fully representing their constituents, as I have been claiming in previous chapters that they are. I develop both points later in the chapter.

The Case Against Mandates

In representative democracy, representatives are people who are more capable of governing: this is the position that many champions of representative government defend. Representatives have more *information* than constituents, information that they gain by specializing in government and by exposing themselves to the deliberative arguments of other representatives. Yet, if the only difference between representatives and constituents were that representatives have more information, then representative government might appear at best a practical solution to governing large polities: if popular democracy were feasible in large nation-states, normal people would gain knowledge through deliberation and skill through the practice of governance. The argument in favor of representative institutions goes further. Representative government is superior to popular democracy because representatives have *qualities* that constituents lack and that make them inherently better legislators. Representatives are wiser, more impartial, and more patriotic than those they represent. Therefore an attempt to reproduce popular democracy in representative systems by inducing the representatives to follow the will of the people would drain these systems of exactly that which makes them better than popular democracies. In this section, I critically evaluate the work of several historical and contemporary theorists of representative government who favor the independence of representatives from the preferences of constituents.

When the opinions of constituents and of their legislators conflict, who should prevail? In answering this question, Edmund Burke outlined a theory of representation that minimized the role of citizen opinion in policy making.

When Burke was elected Member of Parliament from Bristol in 1774, it was not uncommon for constituents to write instructions for their MPs, directing them in matters of policy. The practice, promoted by English radical democrats, was opposed by Burke. In his "Letter to the Electors of Bristol" he explained why. A representative's

unbiased opinion, his mature judgment, his enlightened conscience, he ought not to sacrifice to you, to any man, or to any set of men living. These he does not derive from your pleasure – no, nor from the law and the constitution. They are a trust from Providence, for the abuse of which he is deeply answerable. Your representative owes you, not his industry only, but his judgment; and he betrays, instead of serving you, if he sacrifices it to your opinion. (1949 [1774]:115)

The critical distinction is between the "judgment" of the legislator and the "opinion," "will," or "inclination" of constituents. A legislator's judgment is a special gift of divine origin ("from Providence") that the representative has in greater measure than his constituents. The implication, not developed by Burke, is that elections function to select those of particularly wise judgment for governmental service. Moreover the representative participates in a deliberative body, and deliberation enhances the rationality of decisions. Burke wrote:

My worthy colleague says his will ought to be subservient to yours. . . . But government and legislation are matters of reason and judgment, and not of inclination; and what sort of reason is that in which the determination precedes the discussion, in which one set of men deliberate and another decide, and where those who form the conclusion are perhaps three hundred miles distant from those who hear the arguments? (115)

Unlike the judgment of the representative, constituent opinion may be tainted by prejudice and by interests that are narrow and parochial. A representative should not promote the narrow interests of his constituents, but collaborate with other representatives in discovering the broader interests. "Parliament is a *deliberative* assembly of *one* nation, with one interest, that of the whole" (116). Hence "interests," in Burke's usage (like ours), may be local, adhering to small groups in a given place, or (as Pitkin, 1967, notes) they may adhere to occupational or economic groups such as agricultural interests; but there exists also a national interest, "a general good, resulting from the general reason of the whole" (116). The interests within a great commercial nation like Britain, Burke allows, are not uniform but "various, multiform, and intricate," yet all "must be considered – must be compared – must be reconciled, if possible" (116). It is the task of Members of Parliament to carry out this consideration, comparison, and reconciliation, a task that requires that they know their constituents' opinions but give them no disproportionate weight when making policy. Mandates as instructions impede the completion of this task.

Many contemporary theorists share Burke's view that deliberation enriches legislation (for a review see Elster, 1998). His contention that legislators are unusually well endowed with wise judgment, not just once

157

they have heard the arguments of other representatives but even before their term begins, is more controversial. But the latter view is not without contemporary advocates, as we shall see. A central difficulty with this view, which Burke never dealt with adequately, is to explain why the common people ought to be allowed to elect representatives at all. If the people lack the judgment and impartiality to govern, why should they be entrusted with the task of choosing the governors?

James Madison, a contemporary of Burke's, offered more compelling reasons why the citizenry should elect members of the legislature while maintaining Burke's sense that constituents' opinions should not constrain representatives. Madison's theory of representative government is subtler and fuller than Burke's; for example, he does not simply assert that legislators are people of superior judgment or public-spiritedness, but instead explains why elections function to select superior people for office. Hence his (largely implied) defense of the policy independence of legislators represents a more substantial challenge to those who see voters as appropriately signaling policy preferences to representatives in elections and representatives as therefore constrained by their own preelectoral policy signals to voters.

Madison and his co-authors of the *Federalist Papers* faced two rhetorical tasks. They needed to persuade their readers that the republican system they proposed would not repeat the failings, real or imagined, of popular democracy. Yet they also had to answer critics, such as the anti-Federalists, who feared that the system they proposed would amount to a usurpation of political control by the wealthy and prominent against the common people.

To achieve the first task and quell fears of the excesses of popular democracy, Madison developed a theory of representative government as quite distinct from popular democracy. In Federalist 10, Madison argues that elected representatives are better equipped than the average citizen to pursue the public good over the passions and interests of factions. The effect of representative government, Madison wrote, was to

refine and enlarge the public views, by passing them through the medium of a chosen body of citizens, whose wisdom may best discern the true interest of their country, and whose patriotism and love of justice, will be least likely to sacrifice it to temporary or partial consideration. (1982 [1787]:46–47)

Wisdom, love of justice, patriotism, the ability to discern the country's interests and place them above partial interests: these are qualities not widely distributed in any population. Madison implies that those who don't possess these qualities are nevertheless capable of recognizing them in others, so that the problem is to produce a candidate pool that will include enough superior people whom voters may choose. If the polity is sufficiently large in relation to the legislature, enough candidates will present themselves for office. In large districts, people's choices will "more likely ... centre on men who possess the most attractive merit, and the most diffusive and established characters" (47).

That common people, who may be particular and parochial, will recognize and elect candidates who are wise, impartial, and public-spirited means that elections should not be feared but instead regarded as institutions that produce a refined body of decision makers. This is one of several benefits that Madison ascribed to government by elected representatives. The election of people from diverse places with different laws and circumstances also ensures that government will act with sufficient local knowledge of the component parts of the federation. Note, however, what Madison does not mean by local knowledge. Local knowledge is not something that common people possess and must communicate to their representatives. On the contrary, in Federalist 56, Madison is at lengths to explain that the federal legislature can glean whatever local knowledge it needs from the laws of individual states. "[A]s far as this information [about commerce] relates to the laws and local situation of each individual state, a very few representatives would be very sufficient vehicle of it to the federal councils" (285; see Rehfeld, 2000).

To achieve his second task, to quell anti-Federalist fears of an elitist and detached government, Madison outlined the ways in which elections would function to select representatives worthy of the people's trust. Elections ensured a bond of sympathy between representatives and their constituents. Without this bond the danger would arise of a government above the people, its aim "an ambitious sacrifice of the many to the aggrandizement of the few" (289). In Federalist 57, Madison adduces several reasons why elections will create a virtuous "dependency" of representatives on constituents (291). Representatives will feel gratitude toward the people who elected them, and self-regarding representatives will wish to retain the good favor of their constituents. "There is in every breast a sensibility to marks of honor, of favor, of esteem, and of confidence, which, apart from all considerations of interest, is some pledge for grateful and benevolent returns" (290). Politicians whom the people elevate to office by popular election, furthermore, are unlikely to wish to modify the form of government in order to reduce the people's sovereignty.

Above these considerations, however, is the fact that the representative who wishes to continue in office depends on ongoing support from constituents. Frequent elections remind the legislator of his dependence on constituents, and this dependence, in turn, influences his behavior in office:

Before the sentiments impressed on their minds by the mode of their elevation ... can be effaced by the exercise of power, they will be compelled to anticipate the moment when their power is to cease, when their exercise of it is to be reviewed, and when they must descend to the level from which they were raised; there for ever to remain, unless a faithful discharge of their trust shall have established their title to a renewal of it. (291)

Note that Madison here implicitly attributes to voters another capability. They are capable not only of recognizing good qualities in candidates but also of knowing at the end of the term whether a given representative merits reelection. If voters lacked this capacity of ex post discernment, then representatives who abused their trust would not have to fear being turned out of office. Yet the very phrase Madison chooses, the "faithful discharge" of the people's "trust," indicates that he has in mind not that representatives will fear losing reelection if they deviate from a *policy course* preferred by constituents. Rather, the anticipation of the next election keeps the representative from self-aggrandizement or from granting legislative favors to a powerful class of friends.

To twenty-first-century readers, Madison's confidence in a clear and discoverable public good may seem strained, his concept of tyranny of the majority ill-considered, and his institutional antidotes against the mischief of faction flawed (see Dahl, 1956; Gibson, 1991; Morgan, 1974; Wills, 1981).[1] I would add that his confidence in the superior wisdom, judgment, and public-spiritedness of (most) legislators compared to their constituents seems increasingly anachronistic in later eras of universal public education, widespread literacy, skepticism about politicians, and consciousness of rights. Madison's understanding of the role of information in democratic systems also appears limited. Recall that he believed that the only local knowledge that national legislators needed they could find in state laws.

---

[1] In the early years of the Republic, Madison's worries about the tyranny of a powerful few displaced his earlier fears, expressed in the *Federalist Papers*, about the tyranny of the majority (see Hofstadter, 1969).

Yet surely the local impact of policies will vary with local conditions, and legislators can scarcely act wisely without knowledge of these conditions. Constituents' opinions of policy draw on this knowledge, and legislators' need for this information suggests a larger role for the expression of constituents' opinion than eighteenth-century theorists like Madison or Burke anticipated.

We have seen, then, that early theorists of representative government held that legislators should act independently of the opinions of constituents because, they believed, representatives are better endowed than common people with the qualities needed to govern well. Citizens would recognize these qualities at election time. Constituents' particular views about policy, should they hold any, ought not to constrain representatives, whom constituents choose, after all, for their superior judgment. Yet representatives should be elected and should face reelection fairly frequently. Reelection forces them to remain aware of their dependence on voters and expectant of voters' retrospective judgment. Burke seemed to believe that representatives should show concern for constituent opinion more as a matter of etiquette than of politics. Madison, a more egalitarian spirit, nevertheless emphasized the refinement of legislators' judgment in contrast to that of their constituents.

The belief that representatives have better judgment than the common people, central to the eighteenth-century discovery of the superiority of representative government over popular democracy, was in tension with the belief that governments should be elected by, and answerable to, the people. We saw that Madison resolved this tension in two ways: by implying that the people could *recognize* in candidates the qualities required to govern, even if they did not themselves *possess* these qualities; and by suggesting that people would be able to recognize self-aggrandizing, cronyist, and corrupt politicians at the end of their terms and vote them out of office. This second ability would help ensure that when the occasional bad legislator was elected, his tenure would be short.

Some contemporary theorists of representative government have developed more explicitly than did those of the eighteenth century the proposition that elections bring to office people of superior ability to govern rather than to translate voter preferences into policy. Bernard Manin (1997) draws out and defends the implications of this "aristocratic theory of elections": that representatives, elected for their superior abilities and judgment, should be unconstrained by constituents' opinions and that campaign messages should not be binding on representatives.

161

I turn now to a consideration of Manin's theory of representative government.

As a matter of historical fact, Manin notes, elections have tended to elevate to office people who are socially superior to the mass of their constituents. Fourth-century Athenian institutions distinguished between functions that required no specialized expertise and those that did. Athenians filled positions requiring no specialized expertise by lot, whereas they filled ones requiring such expertise by election. Most magistrates, for example, were chosen by lot among those who wished to be considered. This practice encouraged rotation in office, in accord with the democratic principle of obeying someone today in whose place one might find oneself tomorrow. Selection by lot also accorded with *isēgoria*, the belief that political virtue was universally allocated. In contrast, Athenians filled posts such as general and top military administrators, in which they believed competence was not universally allocated, by election. And the people who were elected to fill these posts tended to come from prominent families – in the fifth century from the old aristocracy and in the fourth from families whose fortunes derived from slave-manned workshops (Manin, 1997:14–15). Selection by lot remained a feasible technique with the rise of representative government in the seventeenth and eighteenth centuries. That it was and still is almost never used reflects our assumption, Manin contends, that election is a better device for choosing the especially prominent and wise.

The social prominence of those elected might make us suspect that representatives differ from their constituents not in wisdom or impartiality, as Burke and Madison believed, but merely in social and economic power, and that elections serve as public acknowledgments of this power. Perhaps in eras when most people lacked education and access to culture, power produces cultivation and cultivation is rewarded with office. Or perhaps the common citizenry favors the prominent in elections merely out of a habitual deference, whether or not the powerful are also wise and cultivated. If so, the claim that representatives are uniquely equipped – even before deliberation – with wisdom to discover the general interests becomes suspect.

Manin's "pure theory of the aristocratic character of elections" attempts to allay such suspicions (134ff). He intends to prove that election always means the selection of the best. Elections, he notes, are antithetical to some principles of democracy, such as the universal application of rules to all. Because voters must always choose a *particular* candidate (or, in some systems, a particular party or list), they are intensely personal and nonuniversalistic. Elections also fail to embody the principle of meritocracy. In elections we do not necessarily reward someone for his efforts or activities rather than because he possesses desired traits or circumstances that he has inherited or passively absorbed. We might wish that voters used criteria of hard work or organizational skill in evaluating candidates. But we cannot stop them from rewarding good looks or a prominent family name when they vote.

These points are important, but the crux of Manin's aristocratic theory is what follows. It is inherent in elections that voters choose one candidate over another. To choose between two candidates who are equal, say by flipping a coin, is not election, not decision making or choice properly understood, and it is not how voters choose. Candidates must therefore distinguish themselves from all others; they must appear unique by some important criterion. Yet mere uniqueness is insufficient. Candidates do not wish to appear merely distinct, but *better*; and voters favor the candidate whom they deem not just different, but *superior* to other candidates and to themselves. Voters therefore do not chose someone who is most like them or someone who is typical of people in their community; to use Pitkin's (1967) term, they do not pursue *descriptive representation*. They will not choose the person of average intelligence or talent, or common training or achievement, but someone who stands out for being more intelligent, talented, and accomplished – more than the average and more than any other candidate. Hence the "aristocratic" nature of elections, their inherent quality of selecting the best.

The aristocratic theory of elections is powerful but also contains some sizable flaws. Manin's empirical claim that in all social contexts people are drawn to candidates who are different and better than themselves is overstated. At the very least, a mix of descriptive and aristocratic principles animates our voting choices. I may seek the candidate who is unlike me in that he excels in organizational skill and leadership, but I may want that same candidate to be most like me in ideological orientation, social circumstances, and perhaps personal experience. How else can I expect her to make good use of her talents? John Stuart Mill, who (as we shall see) subscribed to his own version of an aristocratic theory of elections, nonetheless recognized the importance of combining the search for the best with the search for the most similar in elections. He wrote:

The ablest candidate may be a Tory, and the electors liberals; or a Liberal, and they may be Tories. . . . [H]e may be a High Churchman, or a Rationalist, while they may be Dissenters, or Evangelicals. . . . His abilities, in these cases, might only enable him to go greater lengths, and act with greater effect, in what they may conscientiously believe to be a wrong course. (1962 [1861]:236)

If Mill is right, voters pursue not one but multiple objectives. They seek to elect politicians who are competent *and* who will pursue the course that accords with their basic convictions. If they elect someone is who competent but holds discordant convictions, they merely advance aims that they oppose; if they elect someone who shares their convictions but who lacks competence, they merely fill a seat without advancing their convictions.

In response to this sort of proposition, that elections involve the selection by voters of politicians who, inter alia, share their policy preferences and convictions, Manin advances two counterclaims. First, he believes as a matter of fact that voters in general do not use elections to further their policy preferences or convictions. I will offer evidence to the contrary. Second, even if voters wish to use elections to select representatives to pursue some particular policy course, Manin believes they can't. The reason is that politicians cannot legally be held to policy claims they make in campaigns. Campaign messages therefore lack credibility, because politicians will adopt any position that is convenient in order to win votes. Manin's *distinction requirement*, that successful candidates must possess some distinctive trait attractive to voters,

sets no limits on the programs offered by candidates and their policy positions, it affects only the selection of persons. The candidates can propose the programs they wish, whereas they are constrained by their personality traits. Any policy position may be preferred by most voters and, thus, be adopted by a candidate seeking to win. But not anyone adopting that position is equally likely to be elected. Election is indeed irreducibly . . . a choice of persons. (1997:141–142)

Manin's claim that candidates cannot or do not distinguish themselves in policy terms but only in personal traits is untenable. In fact, candidates *are* constrained in the positions they adopt. They cannot fruitfully adopt positions that voters don't believe predict their actions, as we saw in Chapter 2. And they often cannot adopt positions counter to the ideological commitments of party activists, as we saw in Chapter 4. Candidates' inability to shift policy positions freely in pursuit of votes explains the well-established fact that, rather than converging on the same policy position, parties adopt distinctive positions in campaigns. Furthermore, Manin may overstate the degree to which personality traits as they appear in campaigns are anchored by the real personalities of candidates. One might just as well say that any personality trait may be preferred most by voters and thus may be feigned by a candidate.

Is it true that the policy pronouncements candidates make have no binding power on officeholders? As a matter of constitutional design it is, and for good reason. As Manin notes, no representative democracy legally sanctions *imperative mandates*. Because conditions may change in unpredictable ways, imperative mandates are impractical. With only slight exaggeration, we might say that imperative mandates would be tantamount to firing the meteorologist whenever he gets the weather prediction wrong. And there are other reasons not to legally bind representatives to campaign messages. Politicians' beliefs about the appropriate policy course may legitimately change; and as we have seen at length in the previous chapters, politicians may believe that voters' policy preferences will change.

Yet although politicians are never legally bound by campaign promises, they frequently face *political* incentives to follow through on campaign messages. Voters may punish them if they don't. There is much anecdotal evidence of such punishments. In the United States, as we have seen, President George Bush in 1990 reneged on his "no-new-taxes" pledge, thus angering many members of the Republican Party and probably contributing to his failure to be reelected two years later. In New Zealand in the 1980s, voters were so outraged by the economic policy switches of the Labor Party that they revolted, starting a movement, ultimately successful, to change from proportional representation to a mixed-member parliament and thus breaking the monopoly of the two leading parties (see Nagle, 1996; Vowles, 1995). Perhaps excellent economic performance might have persuaded New Zealand voters that their leaders had been right to switch. But the movement for constitutional change began immediately after the change of course, and by the next elections it had acquired a life of its own. More systematically, we saw that politicians who switched course in Latin America tended to lose votes in subsequent elections, all things equal, in comparison with candidates whose policies were consistent with campaign messages. Imperative mandates are nowhere law, but campaign pronouncements are almost everywhere politically constraining.

Manin's picture of voters as self-consciously electing representatives who are different from – better than – themselves draws on an interpretation of the historical trajectory of electoral politics in the advanced industrial democracies. He argues that early *parliamentary* systems were replaced by *party government*, in which people were socialized into party identities. Their votes expressed these identities rather than a sense of the superiority of nameable candidates. The aristocratic character of elections subsided, and their identity-expressing character grew; yet what remained was the irrelevance of programmatic or policy considerations in voters' decisions and the (partial) policy independence of representatives. If I vote for a candidate because he is from the party my parents supported, how could my choice be seen as sending specific policy messages? In the most recent stage, the decline of party government marks the beginning of *audience democracy*, in which candidates send messages about their character and leanings to a public that is increasingly independent of party attachments. Here again it is not precise policy intentions or even ideological stances but vague images that motivate audience-citizens. The reliance of politicians on their own judgment remains the appropriate method of governing. Manin writes:

What led to their election is a relatively vague commitment, which necessarily lends itself to several interpretations. . . . The partial independence of the representatives, which has always characterized representation, is reinforced by the fact that electoral promises take the form of relatively hazy images. (228)

Yet Manin contends that the ability of voters to cast retrospective judgments on their representatives at the end of the term appropriately limits the independence of legislators. Here Manin's theory resonates strongly with Madison's. Legislators during their term anticipate this future retrospective assessment and attempt therefore to act in a manner that will earn them future votes. Manin's "anticipation of the future retrospective judgment of voters," endogenous to systems of repeated elections, gives accountability, or what Madison called *dependency*, to the relation between representative and constituent.

Manin does not explain in detail why voters will consider the past *actions* of governments when casting a retrospective vote, but only the personality traits of candidates while making the future-oriented choice of whom to install in office. We might suppose that two different kinds of knowledge are involved in judging policy positions prospectively and policy accomplishments retrospectively. If we are to make judgments in advance about what policies are best, we will judge better if we have technical knowledge of the impact of policies across a range of areas, familiarity with past governmental actions and their effects, and information about the effects of policies in other places. Representatives may have the inclination, time, and resources to accumulate such knowledge; common citizens do not. In contrast, common citizens know whether they are better off at the end of the term than they were at the beginning; whether they are more secure or less; whether in general the impact of governmental actions and policies has been for good or ill.

Advocates of retrospective voting models rely on just such a distinction between expert knowledge needed to judge policies and common knowledge needed to judge outcomes (see especially Austen-Smith and Banks, 1989; Fiorina, 1981; Key, 1966). Whereas spatial models assumed that people would pay attention to policies enacted by incumbents and the policy proposals of challengers, retrospective models assumed no such attentiveness. Instead, voters set some standard of performance and judge the incumbent government retrospectively by this standard at the end of the term. Yet these models overstate the simplicity of retrospective judgments. If performance is correlated with the wisdom of policies, then retrospective voting will elicit the best policies that we can expect from governments that are imperfectly monitored. But the inefficiencies can be enormous, and the method falls far short of maximizing welfare in a broader sense.

To get a sense of these shortcomings, consider the example of voters who pay attention to economic outcomes, as we know they do in most democracies (see Bartels, 1992; Lewis-Beck, 1988; Paldam, 1991). All else equal, voters are more likely to reject an incumbent on whose watch real-wage growth is flat than one whose term ends with wage expansion. But perhaps a recession in a major trading partner depressed demand for exports, with the ultimate effect of driving wages down. Or perhaps demand for the country's exports surged and wages grew, but less than they might have had the government's exchange-rate and trade policies been better conceived. In the first example, citizens run the risk of setting the standard too high and voting out of office a government that performed well under bad conditions; in the second, they may set it too low and reelect a government that performed badly under good conditions.

And perhaps there are institutional features that impede ex post judgments, such as government by coalition, or the overturning of leaders by their parties, or term limits (see Cheibub and Przeworski, 1999; Powell, 1990). Manin acknowledges that the "verdict of the people" may be right or wrong (183). But if people are as likely to make mistakes ex post as ex ante, Manin's claim that voters can induce good policy making by voting retrospectively is weakened. Perhaps instead the democratic quality of elections lies in part in their function as a device for translating the people's will into policy.

Modifying the Case Against Mandates

What is a *mandate*? Its etymological origin is in the Latin verb *mandare*, to commit, enjoin, command. The popular mandate, understood as an authorization from the people to the government to pursue a given policy course, has its roots in seventeenth-century England. Emden (1956) notes that in the 1640s freeholders began to present "instructions" to their parliamentary representatives. Instructions, though frequently used, were controversial, because they were seen as debasing the representative, turning him into a mere delegate or agent of his constituents. In the evolution of British thought, Members of Parliament came to be seen not as representatives or emissaries of their local constituencies but as servants of the nation as a whole. As such, it was inappropriate for them to receive directives from their own districts. Burke famously laid out this objection, but others had voiced it as early as 1630 (Emden, 1956:23). Written instructions were superseded by petitions, which thousands of people from a single region or from the country at large might sign and then present to the Parliament (see also Pole, 1983).[2]

By the end of the nineteenth-century, petitions fell into disuse. The extension of the franchise, which meant that virtually no segment of the population lacked representation, and the rise of a national press, which quickly signaled trends in public opinion, made instructions anachronistic. Yet the notion of an electoral mandate, meaning that the people could decide matters of policy at the general election, was widespread. Mandates in this sense carried the implication that parties and candidates should not abandon the policy positions they adopted in campaigns; if they did, voters might well punish them at the next election. The Liberal Unionist Marquess of Hartington, quoted in this chapter's epigraph, expressed this view after Gladstone changed course on the Irish question. The Liberal Party split over the Irish question in 1886 and lost the subsequent election. This sense of mandate is expressed in the norm that Members of

[2] Petition movements were sometimes massive: Emden reports that an antislavery petition presented in 1833 had a million and a half signatories.

168

Parliament who changed parties during their term should step down until their authority to represent constituents could be renewed in a new election.[3]

Hence, by the late nineteenth century, the principle of independence of representatives was balanced by the view that this independence was properly limited. The utilitarian conception of people as knowledgeable of their interests and uniquely capable of defending them undercut arguments in favor of the independence of legislators. Utilitarianism influenced the democratic theory of John Stuart Mill. In the 1860s Mill was concerned, as Burke had been a century earlier, about the proper course for representatives when their opinions differed from those of the people who elected them. Mill believed that representative government ought to be government by the well educated and wise. So deep was this belief that he favored *plural voting*: giving additional votes to the highly educated. Burke thought excellence in judgment was a gift from God; Mill thought it was the result of learning; both believed that deliberation among representatives improved decisions. By slightly different routes, then, both arrived at the same conclusion. Mill sounds distinctly Burkean when he writes that constituents

who sufficiently value mental ability, and eagerly seek for it, will generally succeed in obtaining men beyond mediocrity, and often men whom they can trust to carry on public affairs according to their unfettered judgment; to whom it would be an affront to require that they should give up that judgment at the behest of their inferiors in knowledge. (1962 [1861]:241)

Mill also seems in this passage to anticipate something akin to an aristocratic theory of elections, with elections functioning to select the especially competent. But in two key respects Mill's theory of representative government departs from Burke's and from Manin's. First, Mill saw the

---

[3] The critical years in the emergence of this principle were those leading up to the great Reform Bill of 1832. In the general election of 1826, the Tories were pledged against the relief of Catholics. But in 1829 Sir Robert Peel introduced a measure in favor of such relief. To justify his change of opinion, Peel claimed that the electorate in 1826 had supported Roman Catholic relief, hence suggesting that he was merely acquiescing to public opinion. In a second episode involving Peel, in 1834 he found himself prime minister after the dismissal of his predecessor, and realized that he would not be able to form a majority without recourse to popular mandate. The "Tamworth Manifesto," Peel's legislative program, published in the press and otherwise widely diffused, was the first party manifesto. Twice then, as Emden notes, a politician whose motives were entirely opportunistic helped secure the principle of popular mandates, which Emden characterizes as a constitutional principle.

selection of the competent as an ideal that was not always achieved in his time. (And he celebrates the loss of reverence for "mere social position," as opposed to real wisdom and learning, a loss caused by democracy [239].) Second, he also held the semi-Benthamite view that individuals are the best guardians of their own interests, and that people in different social circumstances will neither know nor feel sufficient sympathy for the conditions of others (see Thompson, 1976). For both reasons, he placed limits on the independence of representatives.

Mill identified two conditions under which constituents should insist that representatives defer to constituents' opinions. The first is when no able candidate is available to represent voters in a descriptive sense. The examples he offers, mentioned earlier, is of voters who are faced with no good candidate who shares their party affiliation or religious conviction. But he devotes more consideration to the problem of class. He writes that under the existing system

in which the electors are almost always obliged by the expenses of election and the general circumstances of society, to select their representative from persons of a station in life widely different from theirs, and having a different class-interest, who will affirm that they ought to abandon themselves to his discretion? Can we blame the elector of the poorer classes, who has only the choice among two or three rich men, for requiring from the one he votes for, a pledge to those measures which he considers as a test of emancipation from the class-interests of the rich? (237)

In developing the second condition under which representatives should defer to constituent opinion, Mill draws a distinction between a person's relatively superficial preferences and "convictions on national affairs which are like his life-blood," "primary notions of right" (243). When such deep convictions separate the opinion of constituents from their representative, right or wrong the opinion of constituents should prevail. If constituents have deferred to their representatives' opinion on lesser matters but find him acting against their deep convictions, they are justified in dismissing him, in particular if his vote in Parliament against their preferred position affects the legislative outcome. Mill does not explain why constituent opinion should prevail under these circumstances, except to say that

[s]uch convictions, when they exist in a people, or in any appreciable portion of one, are entitled to influence in virtue of their mere existence, and not solely in that the probability of their being grounded in the truth. A people cannot be well governed in opposition to their primary notions of right . . . (243)

The implied reason is that a government will lose legitimacy and authority if it acts contrary to the fundamental convictions of its citizens.

Closely connected with Mill's thoughts on the role of constituent opinion are those concerning what a representative or an aspiring representative must tell constituents in campaigns. Even though a good representative should not ordinarily be constrained by constituent opinion, before he is elected he should tell constituents "what opinions, on all things which concern his public duty, he intends should guide his conduct" (243). If his opinions differ from theirs on some matters but he nevertheless seems worthy to represent them, they should ignore the differences. But if his views are at odds with theirs on matters of deep conviction, on "primary matters of right and wrong," he cannot expect them to elect him. And if his opinions change once in office, so that his actions are surprising given the intentions he expressed in the campaign, he must explain why. Especially when a representative is new to the post and is not well known to constituents, lest a change of course induce them to "withdraw his confidence," the representative should "honestly avow" his change of sentiments and leave "grounds" for the change "undisguisedly stated" (242).

Mill does not elaborate on why representatives who change course must explain the change, but given what he has said about the perils of representative government, his reasoning is apparent. If constituents were sure that their representative was wise, if they were able to choose a wise representative who shared their class interests, religious convictions, or partisan attachments, and if he was not tempted to act against their deep convictions, perhaps they would not need ex ante messages about his intentions or ex post explanations of changes of sentiment. But Mill knows that these conditions do not inhere in representative democracy.

Representative governments today have hardly outgrown the flaws that Mill in his day believed justified some limits on representatives' independence. In a skeptical discussion of mandates, Stanley Kelley (1983) agrees with Mill that legislators should defer to public opinion on many matters; to do otherwise is to undermine the authority of governments. Kelley finds little evidence in U.S. presidential politics of mandates, which he stringently defines as "messages plain to all and specific enough to be directive" and supported by "more than a bare majority" (126). His skepticism lies in the fact that few specific policy positions advocated by winning presidential candidates in the United States in the period 1964–1980 garnered majority, or even sizable plurality, support in public opinion. What's more, unlike Britain in the era of Burke or even Mill, where the number of constituents rarely rose above 1,000, today's legislative districts in most democracies contain tens or hundreds of thousands of people. Then it was easy to know what constituents wanted; now it is not. Still, Kelley holds, most people believe in mandates and hold the view that "democracy implies the normal acquiescence of government in the will of the majority"; a failure to acquiesce to its will places the government's legitimacy in question (132). He notes that between one-third and two-thirds of the American public between 1964 and 1978 agreed with the statement that government was run by "a few big interests looking out for themselves" (130). Like Mill's voters, who might have legitimate fears that their representative was influenced by "hostile particularities," today's voters are likely to infer from unpopular actions that the representative is beholden to special interests.

For two centuries, then, representative democracy has held in tension the principles of popular mandates and the independence of representatives. As Table 6.1 makes clear, arguments in favor of the independence of representatives have shifted. Burke offered no adequate explanation for why representatives should be elected, given the parochialism and deficiencies of judgment he attributed to voters. Madison agreed that only legislators would have the wisdom and impartiality to govern in republican systems. But popular election was justified for several reasons: voters would recognize virtuous candidates before they served, and they would recognize and turn out of office self-aggrandizing incumbents. Manin agrees that representatives hold a monopoly on policy competence, but hints that voters are also able ex post to discern not only corrupt representatives but also bad policy. Mill balances a belief in the superior competence of representatives with the belief that individuals are uniquely equipped to know and defend their own interests, and to hold basic convictions to which representatives should defer.

A Case for Mandates

If politicians signal policy intentions in campaigns, voters take these intentions into account when voting, and governments generally carry out their announced intentions, is the quality of democracy improved? My claim in the remainder of this chapter is that it is. Even when (as in some of our Latin American cases) governments believe they have to violate mandates to govern well, governments should take actions to reintroduce constituent

172

Table 6.1.   *Knowledge and Qualities of Constituents and Representatives*

	Constituents	Representatives
Burke	Opinions Will Local knowledge	Judgment Understanding of national interest

Madison	Interests
	Passions
	Ex post ability to discern public-
	  spirited from self-interested
	  representatives
		Wisdom
		Impartiality
		Love of justice
		Patriotism
		Local knowledge (e.g., state laws)
		  but possibly
		Self-serving, factious

Mill	Knowledge of and capacity to
	  protect own interests
	Deep convictions tied to
	  partisanship or religion
	  (for example)
		Competence
		Judgment
		  but possibly
		Inattentiveness to basic convictions
		  and interests of constituents

Manin	Ability to discern good candidates
	  ex ante
	Ability to discern good outcomes
	  ex post
	No adequate knowledge of policy
		Judgment
		Prominence
		Expertise

preferences into the policy process. Doing so both enhances social welfare and reduces political risks for governments.

If the theorists appearing in Table 6.1 (with the partial exception of Mill) are right, little would be lost if candidates for office did not send messages indicating policy intentions in their campaigns; even if they did send such messages, little would be lost if voters ignored them; and even if voters took these messages seriously, little would be lost if governments felt unconstrained by their own campaign pronouncements. Before showing what is in fact lost when any link in the chain connecting citizen preferences to policy is broken, I will first show that the chain is intact in most established democracies most of the time.

Candidates Send Signals of Their Intentions

In many democracies, candidates use campaigns to send messages about policy intentions, and these messages distinguish them from other

173

candidates. The prediction of the economic theory of democracy was that, under certain minimal conditions, candidates' (parties') positions in campaigns would converge to the same point, the preferred point of the median voter.[4] In reality, candidates' and parties' messages don't converge. Downs (1957) recognized this from casual observation, and later researchers demonstrated empirically that in the advanced industrial democracies, party manifestos are consistently far apart in policy and ideological terms (see especially Klingemann et al., 1994). Explaining this theoretical anomaly has occupied theorists ever since Downs. Some have proposed ideological parties and uncertainty about the distribution of voters' preferences to account for the theoretical anomaly (see Chapter 4). Whatever the reason, electoral campaigns in most of the world's democracies feature parties that send signals about their policy intentions, signals that distinguish them from other parties.

Voters Pay Attention to These Signals

In the United States, where the study of public opinion and voting behavior has for decades been intensive, the evidence suggests that voters take account of policy messages when deciding how to vote. Policy messages are not the only factor determining their votes, but they are an important one.

This conclusion is more surprising than one might think. The view coming out of founding studies of voting behavior was that people had little information about candidates or positions; their vote was shaped by early socialization into an affective identification with one political party or the other (Campbell, Converse, Miller, and Stokes, 1960). Another early study showed that most people did not change their minds about whom to vote for over the course of congressional campaigns (Lazersfeld, Berelson, and Gaudet, 1944). Subsequent empirical studies emphasized the retrospective considerations of voters: they might not know what candidates stood for or, in detail, what governments had done, but they could assess changes in welfare over the course of the term and vote accordingly (Fiorina, 1981; Key, 1966). The retrospective voting model suggested that elections could easily be forecast with economic and other data before

---

[4] The critical assumptions are that voters' preferences are single-peaked and unidimensional. For a recent review see Ferejohn (1995).

campaigns even began, and scholars tried to demonstrate the power of such forecasts (Abramowitz, 1988; Campbell and Wink, 1990; Hibbs, 1982; Rosenstone, 1983). Now it appeared that changes in the real wage rather than early socialization drove voters; still campaign messages played little role.

But in recent years, the image of the U.S. voter emerging from many studies is of a more rational and information-seeking sort, one potentially attentive to campaigns. Some claimed that earlier studies overstated voters' lack of information and inattentiveness (Brody and Page, 1972; Sniderman, Brody, and Tetlock, 1991). Others noted that even ill-informed voters could use cues, heuristics, and free information to make reasonable, forward-looking choices (Conover and Feldman, 1989; McKelvey and Ordeshook, 1986; Neuman, 1986; Page and Shapiro, 1992; Popkin, 1991; Rabinowitz and McDonald, 1989). Sniderman, Glaser, and Griffin (1990) show that the more highly educated voters are, the more they pay attention to what candidates say in campaigns as opposed to what incumbents have done in office.

In a recent study entitled *Do Campaigns Matter?*, Thomas Holbrook (1996) notes that electoral forecasting studies failed to account for substantial changes in public opinion during campaigns or for the fact that a sizable minority of voters – 37% on average in U.S. presidential races between 1952 and 1992 – made up their minds during the campaign, enough to change the outcomes of elections. The campaign events that tend to produce changes in public support are conventions and debates, both moments when voters can scrutinize candidates' positions, personal styles, values, and qualities (see also Brody and Page, 1972; Gelman and King, 1993). Bartels (1993) finds that exposure to campaign information has an independent effect on voters' evaluation of candidates (see also Ansolabehere, Behr, and Iyengar, 1993). Other authors as well stress the informational function of campaigns. Salmore and Salmore (1989) argue that campaigns have displaced parties in American politics as sources of information about candidates. Jamieson and Birdsell (1988) studied the effect of presidential debates on voters. They concluded that debates informed voters about the policy differences among candidates, gave them insights into candidates' characters, and produced substantive expectations about presidencies. Holbrook (1996) studied the impact of people's evaluations of how candidates had performed in debates on their voting intentions, controlling for predebate vote intentions and partisanship. He found that, independent of other factors, the better the candidate's perceived performance in the debate, the more likely people were to intend to vote for him or her.

In other democracies as well, the evidence is that voters pay attention to more than the policy intentions of candidates, and they frequently view politicians' campaign rhetoric with some skepticism. Still, voting decisions are conditioned by substantive signals candidates send about their intended policy course. And voters in European democracies have been shown to make remarkably fine-tuned judgments. For example, Anderson (1995) shows that Norwegian and Danish voters, faced with the task of judging coalition governments, meted out punishments and rewards differentially according to the popularity of policies undertaken by ministries under the control of different parties.

Governments Act Consistently with Their Campaign Pronouncements

Even if elections are rarely directive, they are predictive. In Chapter 1, I reviewed the now substantial evidence that campaign pronouncements, programs, and manifestos are predictive of government policy. Voters who care (as many do) about the future course of policy will do well to pay attention to the competitive rhetoric of campaigns. Even in Latin America, where campaign pronouncements about economic policy were hardly a sure prediction of the actual course of policy, voters who cared did better to listen to campaign messages than to ignore them.

Governments generally act consistently with the expectations their campaigns create; they are also generally responsive to shifts in public opinion between elections. Bracketing for the moment the question of whether this responsiveness is a good thing, it is worth noting that as a matter of empirical fact, officeholders in democracies seem to be much more constrained by constituent opinion than Burke, Madison, and perhaps even Mill believed they should be. In the United States, so responsive are officeholders that the complaint that politicians are unprincipled and merely blow with the winds of public opinion is as frequent as the complaint that they ignore constituent opinion. Stimson et al. (1995) show that between 1950 and 1990, a 1-point shift of public opinion to the left or right on an ideological scale was followed by a 0.74-point shift in the same direction by the president (see also Stimson, 1999). Each 1-point shift in public opinion produced a 1.01-point shift in the same direction in the policies of the House of Representatives. So powerful were shifts in public opinion that they dwarfed the effect on policy of changing partisan composition of the House: a 1% increase in Democrats (about four additional Democratic members) produced only a 0.48% increase in policy liberalism.

If in most democracies most of the time campaigns signal policy intentions of candidates and voters pay attention to these signals, is this a good thing? It is good most obviously, I believe, for voters; but it is also good for politicians. To see how voters benefit from the continuity of policy with campaign messages, let us begin with some assumptions about voters and politicians, about what they know and what their competencies are. It will be helpful to consider a continuum of knowledge along which both citizens and politicians may fall. At one end is recondite knowledge about the effects of policies, a sort of knowledge that would allow meaningful preferences over the fine details of alternative policies. Examples might include the impact of changes in the exchange rate on overall economic output or the revenue implications of fine-grained changes in the tax code. Somewhat less demanding is the sort of knowledge that would support meaningful preferences about trade protection or the use of taxes as an instrument of redistribution. Least demanding is knowledge needed to support valence preferences, such as for prosperity or good government.[5] To hold meaningful preferences in this case, we would need no knowledge beyond a basic linguistic competence: knowing the meaning of terms such as *prosperity* or *corruption*. Indeed, we would expect relatively young children to be able to enunciate meaningful preferences on valence issues. Another slightly different example is moral issues. When these come up in public life we may feel some confusion or ambivalence, but the source of these feelings is not generally a lack of knowledge but something else, such as competing moral schemes.

We can distinguish the theorists discussed earlier according to where they locate citizens on a continuum of knowledgeability. Burke, and to a lesser degree Madison, placed them toward the low end. Passions and parochial interests taint voters' perceptions; therefore their perceptions do not support wise policy preferences. The concession by Madison is that electors are able to discern public-spirited from self-interested representatives, especially after observing them in office. Manin and Mill concede

---

[5] Of course, it may take substantial sophistication to discern appropriate policy tools for arriving at universally desired ends or to recognize the underlying "positionness" of what politicians might frame as a valence issue.

somewhat more extensive knowledge and capabilities to citizens. Mill thought people were better judges of their own interests than were representatives who came from a higher social class; he believed they knew their own convictions, which they should appropriately press on those who represent them. Manin was skeptical that voters had any detailed knowledge except that which came from direct observation of the effects of a government's actions.

None of the research reviewed earlier argues for placing citizens at the opposite extreme of detailed knowledgeability. We usually do not have the information we would need to support firm preferences on, say, whether the government should vigorously support the exchange rate or allow it to slip a few percentage points, or what impact a small adjustment in monetary policy will have on inflation or unemployment. Nor would it make sense for most of us to acquire such knowledge so as to better assess the claims of political campaigns; campaigns rarely involve such details anyway.

But the research reviewed earlier does show that people are more knowledgeable and have better-informed opinions than some democratic theorists concede. We don't know, nor do we think we know, the revenue implications of small changes in the tax code; but we do know whether we want bigger or smaller governments, and these opinions are informed by our own experience and by the values we have been exposed to and may have critically assessed. We don't know or think we know whether a unified or multiple exchange rate regime is best; but we do know whether rising inflation or the loss of jobs threatens our welfare more. And most campaign messages are well matched to our opinions and concerns at this level of generality. If we concede that this is a level of debate at which citizens have opinions or preferences and these preferences are based on a reasonable base of knowledge, then under most circumstances it is in the interest of citizens that campaigns generate expectations at this level of generality and that governments fulfill these expectations.

Representative systems institutionalize a mix of legislative independence with responsiveness of officeholders to the preferences of voters. This institutional mix appears appropriate given the assumptions about voters outlined earlier. Voters know a good deal about their own situations and about which general policy direction will best serve their interests. Hence they appropriately have opinions about how future policy should evolve. Yet their grasp of technicalities, the complex causal interdependencies of policy, is limited. It is this sort of knowledge that officeholders

178

have a virtual monopoly on, particularly in bureaucratic and technocratic states. Officeholders are also more knowledgeable than voters about the conditions in which policy unfolds, conditions that can change in ways that render a policy that was appropriate today inappropriate tomorrow. For example, under unstable international economic conditions and a highly interdependent capital market, officeholders and bureaucrats can define (as citizens cannot) appropriate monetary policies. Furthermore, citizens know that officeholders possess this superior technical information and information about conditions; therefore citizens will wish to concede some independence to their representatives.

Citizens in democracies new and old also know that politicians may have reasons for ignoring their interests, helping their friends, or simply shirking. Officeholders have access to technical expertise and information about conditions that voters lack, and voters are aware of this asymmetry. There is no guarantee that those who have this knowledge will use it to further voters' welfare. Hence one function of campaign messages and manifestos is to set a common understanding of what a government ought to do if it is able and if conditions remain such that the announced policy course remains appropriate. Without such a benchmark, voters would have little ability to claim ex post that their preferred course of action was violated.

Another reason why it is in voters' interests that candidates send policy-relevant messages in campaigns is that campaigns are *educational*. We pay more attention to politics when campaigns are underway and are better informed the more attention we pay. This civic education should be celebrated even by those who think representatives should act independently of the people's will. As Mill noted, divergence between public opinion and government actions is bad: voters don't know if representatives are following their best judgments or are beholden to special interests or simply lack wisdom. Hence divergence undermines legitimacy of governments; to minimize it is to sustain legitimacy. If campaigns are short courses in civic education, if they have some of the same effects that legislative deliberation has on representatives, then they should make voters wiser and hence their opinions should diverge less from those of representatives.

Without public debates about policy, policy matters would not become salient to citizens, as numerous studies show that they do during election campaigns. Our policy opinions – general and vague as they may be – would be even more general and vague were we not subjected at repeated intervals to the competitive rhetoric of campaigns. According to a recent report on campaign reform in the United States:

Campaigns provide prospective voters with the information necessary to recognize and interpret the state of the country and the candidates' backgrounds and records – and the motivation necessary to act on that information. They also stimulate democratic deliberation and communication between citizens and their political leaders – and create a record of public commitment and popular legitimation which significantly influences the behavior of winning candidates after they take office. It seems obvious that these functions will be better served by campaigns that are substantive, truthful, and engaging than by campaigns that are vacuous, misleading, and dull. (Bartels, Task Force on Campaign Reform, 1998:12)

More strongly, political representation as a normative concept may require the education and refinement of constituent preferences, an education and refinement in which politicians play a more active part than they did in the Bayesian process of the representation model described in earlier chapters. Let us begin with a minimalist definition of political representation: to represent constituents, politicians must maximize their interests or welfare over an appropriate time horizon.

Let us assume, as I did in Chapter 3, that the pool of candidates includes those who are voter-oriented, wishing to maximize voter welfare, and those who wish to extract rents: pursue their own interests at constituents' expense. Voters cannot readily discern voter-oriented politicians from rent-seekers; the politicians' "type" is private information. Again we assume that the policy choice facing the eventual officeholder is dichotomous, let's say austerity or expansion. The appropriateness of each policy is determined by conditions, which voters do not observe.

Voters risk electing rent-seekers. They are less prone to do so if they learn to interpret conditions independent of campaign messages. A reasonable assumption is that this learning is more likely to occur when candidates do not mislead them about conditions and the appropriateness of policy, even though, as we have seen throughout this book, voter-oriented candidates may have an incentive to mislead. Voter-oriented politicians may be able to teach voters to read conditions accurately by steadfastly sending accurate messages in campaigns. If so, then even politicians who mislead and switch for good reasons would be failing to represent. The perpetuation of voters' inability to interpret conditions accurately is a cost to voters, a cost that voter-oriented politicians impose on them to win office; it is, in short, a rent.

To make the point more concrete, let's assume that unemployment is a good indicator of general economic conditions in the near future, and that the appropriate policy for a government to take depends on the current level of unemployment. At moderate levels of unemployment, the government should pursue expansion; at high levels, austerity. The voter-oriented politician observes levels of unemployment high enough to call for austerity but prefers to promise expansion and switch to austerity, anticipating that voters will later believe that austerity was the appropriate policy. If he instead explained in the campaign the reasons why experts see conditions as bad, and discussed publicly the unemployment rate and what it said about future conditions, voters might not vote for him but would begin to learn a skill that would leave them less prone to the seductive optimism of rent-seekers in the future. By baiting and switching, instead, the "voter-oriented" politician has in fact pursued a rent (office) at voters' expense. She has failed to represent.

Why, one might ask, would voters not learn this same skill of interpreting conditions and their policy implications simply through the Bayesian process whereby voters observe policies and update beliefs based on outcomes? They might, but the learning would be slower and more difficult. It is more difficult to recall the conditions (say the unemployment rate) that prevailed several years earlier than to observe current conditions, ones that are being made salient by political leaders. Furthermore, as we shall see, when politicians change course, even for good reasons, they tend to give less than straightforward explanations for the change. Their obfuscation perpetuates voter ignorance.

Note that I have not arbitrarily added "voter education" to a wish list of activities that an ideal representative should pursue. I have tried to show that, under certain assumptions, representation as the pursuit of voters' basic interests requires voter education.

I have been outlining reasons why predictive campaign messages are good for voters. Why might they be good for politicians?

The common perception of the theorists discussed in this chapter is that legislative independence is something that representatives enjoy and that voters threaten to wrest from them against their will. Yet casual observation suggests that politicians care about mandates as much as, or perhaps more than, do voters. Candidates spend much time and money getting their message out, and in most contemporary democracies this message is not (or not only) "I am a trustworthy, public-spirited person" but "I care about unemployment" or "will protect old-age pensions" or "will cut

181

taxes." If policy positions are just one of several reasons why voters support one candidate or party over another, why do candidates care so much about advertising them?

One answer is that constraints may serve the broader interests of those who are constrained. Consider a home builder. A contract is constraining; it says that if he builds a defective structure, he has to fix it. Without contracts, the risks of hiring builders would be such that many fewer people would hire them, with the effect of depressing builders' earnings (see Ferejohn, 1999). Campaign messages and manifestos may for similar reasons benefit politicians. If politicians face incentives to treat campaign statements as loose contracts, as we have seen they do, then messages become commitment devices. Consider a candidate running for office for the first time in a district of strongly pro-abortion-rights voters. The candidate announces his intention to defend abortion rights. If voters know – and know that he knows – that he will be punished by constituents should he reverse himself in office, they will be more willing to vote for him than if he were unable to precommit to this position. The important point is that precommitment devices, though in a sense constraining, ultimately empower politicians.

An additional feature of mandates attractive to politicians is that they may strengthen the hand of those who can claim them against opponents who want to block politicians' favored legislation. In presidential systems, as Jones (1994) notes, politicians who come to power emitting only vague platitudes will have trouble overcoming legislative opposition. A candidate who predicts winning handily is well advised to make her policy wishes clear lest opponents block her efforts, claiming she has no mandate for some particular course of action.

In sum, even though the independence of legislators is desirable in some limited ways, and even though campaign messages will sometimes be reversed for good reasons, we should not be complacent about misleading campaigns and policy switches. Violating the expectations created in campaigns is risky for governments and potentially harmful for democracy. An unmandated policy may turn out to be superior but perhaps not enough so to overcome voters' prior opposition. When politicians repeatedly violate mandates, even if they believe they are acting in people's best interests, they threaten to debase *all* campaign messages, authentic and disingenuous alike. If citizens stop believing campaign messages, these messages lose the power to precommit politicians, and politicians' scope of action becomes narrower.

We saw that politicians who want to pursue the interests of their constituents – to represent – will sometimes signal their real beliefs about conditions and real policy intentions in campaigns, even when doing so means forfeiting the election. When a government interested in voters' welfare believes voters wrongly oppose policies that in fact are in their interest, what path other than the policy switch along the lines described in this book is open to them?

Ex Post Explanation

When politicians offer little explanation for a change of course, they run the risk of appearing dismissive of the wishes of constituents. George Bush violated his "read my lips: no new taxes" pledge in 1990. When journalists tried to interrupt him while he was jogging to ask for an explanation, he blithely invited them to "read my hips."[6] Voters have good reasons to look for evidence that governments would at least like to follow the people's preferences and that only under unusual circumstances, circumstances demanding an explanation, will leaders abandon their electoral pledges.

Perhaps the most troubling aspect of the Latin American experiences is that governments that changed course failed to provide candid explanations after the fact for why they had switched. This, it would seem, is a minimal requirement. It falls far short of the renewed authorization that historically was often demanded of representatives who changed party affiliation or policy position between elections. Fresh from elections and in a combative climate, Latin American presidents offered partisan explanations for the change of course. The canonical excuse was that it was the outgoing government's fault: it had mishandled public monies and hid this fact from the public and the opposition. Presidents, ministers, and legislative leaders might have believed that neoliberalism by surprise was good for voters: that inflation would not subside unless the deficit was seriously reduced, or that investment would never revive without a favorable international reputation for toughness in reforms. But they did not communicate these beliefs to the public. During the campaign, politicians found themselves in a bind: if they were honest, they risked losing the elections and depriving themselves of the chance to follow the policy course that was – they thought – urgently in the public interest. But once in office,

---

[6] I am grateful to Stanley Kelley for this example and interpretation.

their hold on power was more or less secure.[7] They had four, five, or six years to carry out their policies. They should have used this opportunity to offer more honest explanations. All evidence suggests that had they done so, voters would have been forgiving.

Referendums

When mandates and representation are in conflict, another device for reconciling better policy with the people's preferences is the referendum. It upholds the principle of the negative imperative, allowing "the electorate the opportunity to consider [major innovations] in an election," just not an election in which the candidate's access to power is directly at stake (Kelley, 1983). The device also resolves candidates' interest in avoiding unpopular policy stances with their interest once in office in being able to claim popular support – a mandate – for innovations. Furthermore, undistracted by other issues, the government may have greater success at persuading the public than it had in the campaign. The referendum has been widely used for this purpose (see Butler and Ranney, 1994). For example, it was used by the Spanish government of Felipe González precisely to steer delicately toward a new policy unpopular among constituents that the government nonetheless believed was the best course (see Maravall, 1999). When the Irish party Fianna Fáil, in a coalition government, changed its campaign position and endorsed joining the North Atlantic Treaty Organization (NATO)-sponsored Partnership for Peace, opinion leaders called for a referendum on the question – in particular *because* the party had changed its position (see *The Irish Times*, July 29, 1999).

Do predictive campaign messages matter for democracy? They matter greatly, even if they are not all that elections are about, and even though good governments will sometimes violate them. Citizens wish to make future-oriented electoral choices, and politicians have substantial interests in their ability to do so. Even when a link in the chain between the people's will and government's actions must be severed, governments that care about their own reputation and the legitimacy of democracy will attempt to restore to citizens the sense that their views count.

---

[7] These remarks are relevant only to policy switchers who formed majority governments or preelection coalitions.

7

Summary, Predictions, Unsettled Questions

A general characteristic of democracy is that, before elections, candidates and parties reveal their intentions regarding what policies they will pursue if they win. Since the mid-eighteenth century, they have used campaign manifestos as the vehicle for this self-revelation, as well as speeches, ads, debates, and so on, to create expectations about what their government would do and how this contrasts with what their competitors would do. Because campaign pronouncements generally serve as a blueprint for a government's actions in office, voters have a meaningful choice about the future course of public policy. Over the course of a term conditions change, and the blueprint will have to be revised or scrapped. But if campaign pronouncements reveal intentions, then, at least early in the government's term, policies will match campaign announcements.

Yet this general characteristic does not always hold. An American candidate promises "no new taxes" and then raises them. A German party promises higher old-age pensions but then leaves them unchanged. A New Zealand party manifesto promises support for state programs and then begins to cut them. A British party opposes protections for Catholics, but their new prime minister then proposes a bill to protect them. Another British party, two and a half centuries later, pledges in its campaign to protect scholarships for private-school students and then eliminates them. And a wave of Latin American candidates promise to buck pressures to liberalize their economies and then liberalize.

Each of these events is an anomaly in the broader experience of democratic government. Their wide distribution across time and place suggests that the condition for mandate violation was not being a country located in Latin America toward the turn of the twenty-first century, but some other conditions that occur from time to time in every democracy but appeared simultaneously and frequently in this part of the world in this period.[1]

A central task of this book was to identify the conditions for mandate violation by identifying the systematic differences between governments that switched and those that didn't in a region and period where switches often occurred. Another central task was to understand the normative implications of violations of mandate or, perhaps more accurately, the difficulties entailed in the fact that democracy generally induces continuity between campaign messages and government policy but doesn't – indeed shouldn't – *guarantee* such continuity. The difficulties were evinced by the British judge, mentioned in Chapter 1, who with one breath refused to find legal merit in a claim against the government that reneged on a campaign pledge and chastised the government for lying.

In this final chapter, I first summarize the results of my inquiry and then highlight some questions that remain unanswered.

What Causes Politicians to Abandon Mandates?

1. *Conflicting beliefs between politicians and voters.* When voters prefer one policy and politicians another, politicians may mislead to get into office and then switch. In many Latin American experiences, conflicting beliefs and preferences arose from peculiar historical circumstances. Voters saw efficiency-oriented policies as linked with class interests opposed to their own. Latin American political leaders in this era were under intense pressure to liberalize, and even many that had in the past been associated with worker-oriented protectionist schemes now were persuaded that a failure to liberalize would only hurt their mass constituency and hence their own political careers.

Political leaders, then, interpreted the reality they faced as involving *structural dependence* of the mass electorate on policies that would be pleasing to markets: domestic and foreign investors, foreign governments, and international financial institutions (Przeworski and Wallerstein, 1982). That is, they believed that voters would be harmed by the actions of

---

[1] This statement should be taken not as proven but as a hypothesis to be tested. For example, a cross-national statistical study (of a sort that does not yet exist) that included democracies from all the world's regions might find that, controlling for the variables predictive of switches identified in this study, a dummy variable for Latin America was significant.

markets if the government pursued policies other than those favored by markets. But they believed voters saw things differently and would not be brought around by words alone, but only by the eventual fruits that liberalization would bear. Or, to put it negatively, governments believed that if they did not implement the policies markets preferred, economic havoc would follow, their constituents would be harmed, and constituents would punish them at the polls.

It was no easy task to distinguish empirically governments that responded to the pressure of markets because they thought doing so would be best for their constituents and governments that caved in to pressure because this was easier than sticking to their campaign commitments or because they expected some private payoff from markets for switching. Both responses predict policy switches. The normative status of the two is quite distinct. I characterized the first response as an effort to *represent* constituent interest, within the real constraints markets imposed.[2] The second was an instance of *rent-seeking*, with politicians trading away benefits to constituents in favor of benefits to themselves.

2. *Competitive elections.* Given conflicting beliefs of candidates and voters, a candidate who enjoys a secure lead – a lead based, for example, on some other popular stance she has taken or some personal flaw of her opponent – is more likely to reveal her true intentions than one who is locked in a tight race. The close-race effect reflects politicians' expectation that, all things equal, if they promise one policy and adopt another, voters will punish them. Norms among voters of honesty and consistency, their desire to invest in the future predictability of campaigns, their suspicion that politicians are deriving some personal benefit for switching, and the weight they give to their initial beliefs about the effect of unmandated policies are all possible reasons why voters punish inconsistent politicians.

3. *Voter uncertainty.* Politicians are more likely to abandon mandates when voters are uncertain about the impact of policy on their welfare. If Latin American voters had been unmovably certain that economic liberalization was against their interest, they would have attributed even excellent results under liberalization to some happy circumstance having

---

[2] In Chapter 6, however, I raised questions about whether the suppression of policy intentions in campaigns, even for good reasons, might not work against voters' interest in learning to interpret conditions and evaluate policy proposals. If so, even politicians who hide their intentions for good reasons would fail to represent.

nothing to do with policies of liberalization, and governments that liberalized by surprise would have been turned out of office.

4. *Policies with uncertain effects.* Uncertainty attaches to certain kinds of policies more than others. We should expect governments to change course with greater frequency when the policy in question has complex, multiple, and uncertain effects, less when the effects are straightforward and easily predicted. I offered the example of the contrast between economic policies and abortion policies. The relatively large uncertainty of the mapping of economic policies onto outcomes, compared to the mapping of other policies, may explain why economic policies appear particularly prone to bait-and-switch tactics.

5. *Young political parties.* Governments led by young parties are more likely to renege on campaign messages than those led by old parties. Leaders of political parties of recent founding may have more power relative to rank-and-file activists than do leaders of older parties, and future candidates in young parties less capacity to influence the policies of incumbents. Whether switches are (from voters' perspective) for good or ill, they are therefore more likely when parties are young.

6. *Minority and coalition governments.* Nonmajority governments are more likely to change policies than majority governments. The reason is that they lack full control over policy and must abandon some positions in negotiations with the other parties. Are governments or their member parties acting as good representatives when they make such programmatic adjustments? The answer depends on whether their constituents benefit more from their participation in government than the constituents lose when preferred policies are abandoned. To the extent that it is harder for voters to hold minority and coalition governments accountable for their actions (see Powell, 1990), these governments will be more tempted to switch policies in pursuit of rents.

Identifying these conditions helps explain the rash of policy switches in Latin America at the same time that it reinforces our expectation that, under certain conditions, campaign messages will sometimes fail to predict policy in any democracy. Some of these conditions were more likely to hold in Latin American democracies during this period of economic upheaval than in the advanced industrial countries; others could be expected in any region at any time. Widespread in Latin America was pressure from markets on governments to adopt policies that voters feared; yet to a lesser degree, such pressure is exerted in all capitalist democracies, more so as regional economies integrate and markets globalize. Weak, young political parties are endemic in new democracies but not unique to them. In contrast, highly competitive elections are frequent events in any democracy. The uncertainty-of-effects condition leads us to expect that, in any democracy, *economic* messages and policies lend themselves to inconsistency, whereas we expect consistency in areas in which the mapping of policy on outcome is more straightforward. The association of mandate violations with minority and coalition governments means that we should expect less inconsistency in systems less prone to coalition and minority governments. Predictive campaigns should be more common, for example, in parliamentary than in presidential systems and in two-party than in multiparty systems. (This implication is consistent with the findings of the Comparative Manifestos Project; see Klingemann et al., 1994.)

The Effects of Mandate Violations

These, then, are the conditions that we expect to induce new governments to switch policies. What have we learned about the effects of switches?

1. *Punishment at the polls.* All else equal, we expect voters to punish policy switchers by reducing their share of the vote when they (or their party) stand for reelection. Another way of stating this prediction is that voters will hold incumbents who switch to a higher retrospective standard than the one applied to consistent politicians.

2. *Reelection prospects: policies versus outcomes.* In deciding whether to support the incumbent government, we expect voters to pay more attention to *outcomes* of policies under policy-switching incumbents and more attention to the *policies* themselves when incumbents acted consistently with campaign messages. This follows from the greater uncertainty of voters in settings in which policies change. Voter uncertainty is both a cause and an effect of abrupt changes of course.

3. *Outcomes: better or worse?* When office-seeking politicians change course because they think doing so will turn out to be best for voters, we expect voters' welfare to be significantly enhanced, in comparison to their lot had politicians remained constrained by campaign messages. The representation model was the better fit in the Latin American cases we studied, and indeed, economic outcomes there on average were better after policy switches. It seems unwise, however, to infer that policy switches are never carried out by rent-seeking politicians. We saw in theory that

189

they very well might be. When rent-seeking politicians carry out policy switches, we expect the outcomes of their policies on average to be worse than the outcomes that would have attained had they not switched.

Even in Latin America, where the office-seeking (representation) model explained policy switches better than the rent-seeking model, voters seemed aware that politicians might well change course for bad reasons. They believed that the pool of candidates included both office-seekers and rent-seekers, and that campaign messages did not allow them to distinguish representatives from rent-seekers. This belief was important, because it helped explain why candidates could not simply persuade voters in campaigns that the policies they feared would in fact turn out for the best.

Unsettled Questions

Voters' Views of Policy Alternatives

In the abstract model of policy switches that I considered in Chapter 3, voters had preferences regarding policies. During the campaign voters preferred one policy, a, over another, b. Their beliefs about the effects of policies were not stagnant but evolved dynamically. If they preferred policy a but the government implemented b and b performed very well, their preferences changed. In this model, the only reason for voters to pay attention to politicians' campaign pronouncements was to gauge their intentions. Politicians' messages about policies – that they would make constituents richer, or enhance the nation's position in the world, or make the air and water cleaner – no communications of these sorts would change voters' beliefs or policy preferences.

Yet we know that in real democracies, campaign messages, as well as politicians' pronouncements between elections, do influence voters. A more realistic model of mandates would relax the assumption that voters' policy preferences are influenced only by prior beliefs and observed outcomes and acknowledge a role for candidates' messages.

Students of public opinion emphasize the role of elite discourse in shaping opinion. In one influential account, people's socialization, values, and hence party affiliation lead them to take cues from their party leaders on what to think about issues (Zaller, 1992). If I am a Christian Democrat and the leader of the Christian Democratic Party says that a given bill will increase employment in my region, I support the bill. If I am a Social Democrat and a foreign policy crisis arises in some remote part of the world, I won't know what I think until I receive a cue from my party (or, if there is cross-partisan consensus, from political leaders in general) about what the appropriate response to the crisis should be.

The endogeneity of voter preferences to politicians' messages in this account is a helpful antidote to the representation model, in which voter preferences are driven by observed outcomes, unmediated by political discourse or debate. Yet one would not want to go too far in the other direction. The endogenous account perhaps concedes less than it should to people's lived experience. If, after the Christian Democratic bill passes, unemployment in my region rises, I may find my party's pronouncements less persuasive.

The endogenous account also leans heavily on the political ignorance of most people. In the United States, respondents to public opinion polls have remarkably little knowledge about politics and government. Many don't know who their vice-president is or who are the justices on the Supreme Court. Zaller (1992) notes that in a 1986 National Election Study survey, not one of the 1,500 respondents could correctly name all justices of the Supreme Court. To attribute to the masses of ill-informed and inattentive citizens opinions of or preferences about policies would seem ludicrous. Do such facts not argue against any model of politics that attributes to voters the capacity to formulate and reformulate policy preferences in light of their experiences under a policy regime?

The answer, I believe, is no. First, we should not generalize too hastily from one national context (the United States) to all democracies. In developing countries with highly volatile economies and interventionist economic policies, what the government does one day can have a drastic impact on common people's welfare the next. Fiscal adjustments, *paquetes*, which may include exchange-rate adjustments and hikes in the prices of fuels, food, and medicine, are announced publicly, often on television, often by the finance minister. Overnight these adjustments can turn working-class people into paupers, middle-class people into scroungers, and reduce the value of wealthy people's assets. One might *wish* to be inattentive in such settings in the same way one would like to wake up from a bad dream. But it's hard to escape some knowledge of politics and policy when they are so relentlessly determinant of one's day-to-day welfare. Little wonder, then, that when an Argentine survey conducted in 1992 asked people their opinion of Domingo Cavallo, the finance minister, less than 2% responded "don't know him."[3]

People's understanding of policies and their effects are undoubtedly vague and uncertain. The model I have used makes this uncertainty central. What this model lacks is a sense of how politicians' arguments shape people's opinions of policies and their beliefs about policy effects. But it would be a mistake to compensate for this shortcoming by rushing to the view that political rhetoric alone determines people's opinions and beliefs, rhetoric that is not evaluated, in part, in light of experience.

Politicians' Beliefs and Ideology

If a full understanding of the role of mandates forces us to comprehend how the persuasive rhetoric of politicians influences the preferences of citizens, then we also need some account of where politicians' beliefs come from and how they change. Beliefs may have a technical basis, but they also clearly form part of a broader ideological structure, and understanding the dynamics of belief acquisition and change among political actors would require that we understand more about the dynamics of ideology formation and change.

The representation model, useful in many of its simplifications, is silent on questions of elite belief formation and ideology. This silence leads to paradoxes within the model itself. Note that in the model, politicians competing for office had beliefs about whether policy *a* or policy *b* was better for voters. The model treated candidates' beliefs as defined by nature; they were random draws on a distribution. In one equilibrium, candidates had different beliefs, but one dissimulated and their announcements were identical. When faced with candidates with identical messages, voters choose by flipping a coin. If the coin flip comes out in favor of *A*, who has announced her true beliefs, she will then implement policy *a* and it will turn out to have been appropriate, meaning that it improves income more than *b*. But suppose that the coin flip comes out in favor of *B*. He announced *a* in the campaign to get elected and then implements *b* – and *this* policy now turns out to be the right one, even though nothing has

[3] Romer and Associates conducted the poll in the Federal Capital, greater Buenos Aires, and five other cities in May and June 1992. The sample size was 1,250. Respondents were asked "How would you say that Domingo Cavallo is managing his work as Minister of the Economy? Very well, well, fair, badly, don't know him." Two percent of respondents answered "Don't know him" or did not answer the question.

192

changed except the outcome of the flip of a coin. It appears then that politicians' beliefs *cause* outcomes. Indeed, Harrington (1993a:82–83) seems to elide politicians' beliefs with reality when he writes, for example, that "when the politician and voters are in agreement over which policy is best . . . a politician's reelection prospects are quite promising because implementation of the best policy generates high income."

This tension brings to light the need for a more satisfying account of politicians' beliefs and ideologies. Here too recent social science has made some advances. The case has been made powerfully that ideologies are how people make sense of a complex political world, and that a central function of politicians is to create, diffuse, and occasionally refurbish ideology (Hinich and Munger, 1994). Political leaders do the work of fitting issues for us into the reduced dimensions of ideologies. When new issues arise, political parties will connect them with preexisting ideological schemes. The work parties do to fashion political debate into ideological conflict, as opposed to inchoate conflict over myriad individual matters, is advantageous to voters. It reduces the room for issue cycling and agenda manipulation, so that voters can hold governments accountable, and governments may therefore be empowered to act in people's interests (see Ferejohn 1995, 1999).

But the functions of ideologies cannot explain their origins. Presumably, in forming beliefs, politicians absorb information about how various policies have worked out in their country in the past and in other countries under similar conditions; they listen to advice of experts, and so on. In the real-world experiences studied here, politicians' beliefs about the mapping of policies onto outcomes sometimes turned out to be dead wrong. In general, governments that adopted expansionary policies featuring wage and price controls overestimated the duration of economic growth with price stability. And governments that adopted austerity programs and liberalization underestimated the duration of austerity-induced recession. The first mistake was made by governments like Raúl Alfonsín's in Argentina and Alan García's in Peru; the second by a long list of governments, including Víctor Paz Estenssoro's in Bolivia, Carlos Andrés Pérez's in Venezuela, and Alberto Fujimori's in Peru.

The predictability of these mistakes suggests that the processes by which politicians formulate their beliefs falls short of a textbook version of rationality. Some mistakes, it is claimed, were technical: the magnitude of some effects was simply incorrectly estimated, such as, according to Hausmann (1995), when the IMF's technical model miscalculated the effect of exchange rate liberalization on economic activity in Venezuela. Perhaps the error was technical. Yet there is no mistaking the fact that wishful thinking was pervasive, both among technocrats and among politicians. Wishful thinking means beliefs shaped by preferences rather than by information (Elster, 1989.) Is it conceivable that the international financial institutions repeatedly made the same technical mistake, over and over, of underestimating the depth and length of postadjustment recessions? Or were their predictions not also meant to reassure government leaders, who worried about the effects of recession on their political support? Another example of nonrational belief formation came during the transition between the Belaúnde and García governments in Peru in 1985. At that time, left-leaning economists extolled features of the program like the one the APRA government would soon introduce. A key assumption of the program was that unused industrial capacity would allow economic stimulation to take place without inflation. When these economists were pressed for evidence on this point, it became clear that the existence and extent of the unused capacity was an article of faith.

Another cognitive phenomenon that seems to impinge on policy decisions is our reduced capacity to treat with cold detachment ideas that emanate from the powerful, the wealthy, the attractive. It may be in our interest to pay attention to these ideas – they may come attached with rewards, loans, prestige. Yet they may also fail, and in so doing make us fail in ways that neutralize the value of the rewards.

These considerations suggest a modification of the concept of representation I used in this book. In Chapter 1, I defined governments as representative if they pursued policies that they believed to be in the best interest of voters. If their beliefs turned out to be wrong, they were incompetent but still representative. The distinction between representation and competence makes sense if we think of competence as a trait inhering in actors, who may be more or less skilled, more or less knowledgeable, more or less farsighted. But if policy-relevant beliefs are the product of political processes, then an officeholder may hold incorrect beliefs because he can't muster the energy to assess them fully, or the psychological detachment to consider them independently of what he wishes to be right, or the ability to discount sufficiently the power of the people or institutions that promote them. It is in the interest of voters that he should consider these beliefs rationally. To the extent that he might have mustered more energy, detachment, or skepticism, such a politician no longer appears as an incompetent representative, but as a rent-seeker. He fails to represent by allowing himself to adopt irrational beliefs. We saw that, on average, governments that changed course probably did have reasonably accurate beliefs, and their about-face probably improved the economic situation of constituents. But some governments' beliefs turned out to be wrong, and they went down to defeat, or had to compensate by backtracking on their policy change or mobilizing support on some other grounds. I am suggesting that their apparent incompetence may really have been a form of rent-seeking.

Whatever the right way to think about ideologies and politicians' beliefs, it seems clear that the ideological anchors came loose in late-twentieth-century Latin America. Neoliberalism began to claim hegemonic status in the sense that it defined what could be said (believed?) and not said by opinion leaders who wanted to be taken seriously. To say that a new economic hegemony was forged in this period should not be taken as saying that there were no real, responsible policy alternatives available to leaders with distinct constituencies and priorities. There were alternatives, and one can point to successes and failures of various policy approaches. Yet certain forms of expression about the economy that had been common only a decade or two earlier now nearly disappeared. This hegemonic shift did not in any simple sense *cause* the shift to neoliberal policies; the turn to neoliberal policies, we have seen, was the result of the strategic calculations of politicians. Yet clearly one of the greatest achievements of those who pressured for such a shift was the consequent rise of a neoliberal hegemony.

To get a sense of the change, consider the following extract from a declaration written in 1986 by Peronist labor activists:

The development of the crisis at the international level and the consequent recomposition of the balance of forces at the backbone of the new transnational order has made us the chosen victims of financial interests and the World Bank – impregnable bulwarks of a transnational capitalism that has reinforced its plan of domination over three-quarters of the planet's population. (Movimiento Sindical Peronista Renovador, *Documento Final*, cited in McGuire 1997:193)

The declaration is indistinguishable from hundreds of others emitted by labor activists throughout Latin America until not very long ago. It reads now like an epistle from another epoch. This particular declaration is all the more remarkable in that it was produced by the faction of the Peronist labor movement called *renewal* (*renovador*), which was linked to the renewal movement of the Peronist Party, of which Carlos Menem was a leader. A mere three years later, Menem's government was making cabinet appointments and crafting policies with an eye toward pleasing these same "impregnable bulwarks of a transnational capitalism" bent on domination. The Menem government, only a few years removed from Peronist anti-imperialism, was now sending a signal "to . . . Morgan Guaranty, the U.S. government, the World Bank."

Certainly we know less than we would like to about how ideologies change and why hegemonic orders rise and fall – how the unthinkable becomes the commonplace, the commonplace the unthinkable (or, at least, the inexpressible). And to have a full sense of the role of mandates in an era of ideological change, we need a better understanding of hegemonic trends and cycles.

In the end, which side wins the debate about policy inconsistency and democracy? Did unkept promises make governments "authoritarian and antidemocratic," as my friend insisted? Or was it results, not promises, that mattered, as my colleagues implied? Were politicians who ignored the people's will, as expressed in elections, some other species than representatives? Or did accountability, the fact that governments would eventually face the people's judgment, force them to act in the people's interest? Both sides, it turns out, are tapping into an important dimension of democracy. We want governments to act in our interest. And we have good reason to assume, usually, that this means acting as we would have them act, in accord with current opinion. When governments don't do what we want, we worry that they are motivated by self-interest or special interests; and even if we later reelect them, this is no guarantee that we have become persuaded that they undertook unpopular measures for good reasons. When governments think our opinions misguided, they may enhance our *welfare*, for a certain period, by misleading us in campaigns and disappointing us, initially, with their policies. But baiting and switching will improve the *quality of democracy* only if governments that switch also go to some lengths to make us better judges, in the future, of the real alternatives we face.

References

Abramowitz, Alan I., David J. Lanoue, and Subha Ramesh. 1988. "Economic Conditions, Causal Attributions, and Political Evaluations in the 1984 Presidential Elections." *Journal of Politics* 50(4):848–863.

Achen, Christopher H. 1978. "Measuring Representation." *American Journal of Political Science* 22:475–510.

Aldrich, John H. 1995. *Why Parties? The Origin and Transformation of Political Parties in America.* Chicago: University of Chicago Press.

Alesina, Alberto. 1988. "Credibility and Convergence in a Two-Party System with Rational Voters." *American Economic Review* 78:796–805.

Alesina, Alberto and Allen Drazen. 1991. "Why Are Stabilizations Delayed?" *American Economic Review,* 81:1170–1188.

Alesina, Alberto and Stephen E. Speer. 1988. "An Overlapping Generations Model of Electoral Competition." *Journal of Public Economics* 37(3):359–379.

Alvarez, Angel E. 1996. "La Crisis de Hegemonía de los Partidos Políticos Venezolanos." In Angel E. Alvarez, ed., *El Sistema Político Venezolano: Crisis y Transformaciones,* Caracas: Universidad Central, pp. 131–154.

Alvarez, Michael. 1997. *Information and Elections.* Ann Arbor: University of Michigan Press.

Alvarez, Norma. 1999. "Nuevos estilos – viejas costumbres: las prácticas electorales de la UCR y el PJ en Misiones 1955–1995." Unpublished manuscript, Department of History, Universidad Nacional de Misiones, Posadas, Argentina.

American Political Science Association. 1950. *Toward a More Responsible Two-Party System.* New York: Rinehart.

Andean Commission of Jurists. 1989. *Andean Newsletter.* Lima: Andean Commission of Jurists.

Andean Group Report. 1993. No. 10 (December).

Anderson, Christopher J. 1995. "The Dynamics of Public Support for Coalition Government." *Comparative Political Studies* 28(3):350–383.

Angell, Allen and Benny Pollack. 1990. "The Chilean Elections of 1989." *Bulletin of Latin American Research* 9(1):1–24.

Ansolobehere, Stephen, R. Behr, and Shanto Iyengar. 1993. "Mass Media and Elections – An Overview." *American Politics Quarterly* 19(1):109–139.

197

Arnold, Douglas. 1993. "Can Inattentive Citizens Control their Elected Representatives?" In Lawrence C. Dodd and Bruce I. Oppenheimer, eds., *Congress Reconsidered*, 5th ed. Washington, D.C.: CQ Press, pp. 401–416.

Arriagada Herrera, Genaro, and Carol Graham. 1994. "Chile: Sustaining Adjustment during Democratic Transition." In Stephan Haggard and Steven B. Webb, eds., *Voting for Reform: Democracy, Political Liberalization, and Economic Adjustment*. Washington, D.C.: The World Bank and Oxford University Press, pp. 242–289.

Arrow, Kenneth J. 1963. *Social Choice and Individual Values*, 2nd ed. New Haven: Yale University Press.

Austen-Smith, David, and Jeffrey Banks. 1989. "Electoral Accountability and Incumbency." In Peter C. Ordeshook, ed., *Models of Strategic Choice in Politics*. Ann Arbor: University of Michigan Press, pp. 155–177.

Banco Central de Ecuador. 1992. *Ecuador: Plan macroeconómico de estabilización*. Quito: Banco Central de Ecuador.

Banks, Jeffrey S. 1990. "A Model of Electoral Competition with Incomplete Information." *Journal of Economic Theory* 50:309–325.

Banks, Jeffrey S. and Rangarajan K. Sundaram. 1993. "Adverse Selection and Moral Hazard in a Repeated Elections Model." In William A. Barnett, Melvin J. Hinich, and Norman J. Schofield, eds., *Political Economy: Institutions, Competition, and Representation*. New York: Cambridge University Press, pp. 295–312.

Barnes, William A. 1992. "Rereading the Nicaraguan Pre-Election Polls." In Vanessa Castro and Gary Prevost, eds., *The 1990 Elections in Nicaragua and Their Aftermath*. Lanham, Md.: Rowman & Littlefield, pp. 41–128.

Barreto, Wilson Jaime. 1990. *Marketing Político: Elecciones 1990*. Lima: Universidad del Pacífico.

Barry, Albert. 1997. "The Income Distribution Threat in Latin America." *Latin American Research Review* 32(2):3–40.

Barry, Brian. 1977. *Economists, Sociologists, and Democracy*. Chicago: University of Chicago Press.

Bartels, Larry M. 1991. "Constituency Opinion and Congressional Policy Making: The Reagan Defense Build-Up." *American Political Science Review* 85:457–474.

1992. "The Impact of Electioneering in the United States." In David Butler and Austin Ranney, eds., *Electioneering: A Comparative Study of Continuity and Change*. Oxford: Clarendon Press, pp. 244–277.

1993. "Messages Received: The Political Impact of Media Exposure." *The American Political Science Review* 87(2):267–285.

Bartels, Larry M. and the Task Force on Campaign Reform. 1998. *Campaign Reform: Insights and Evidence*. Princeton: Woodrow Wilson School of Public and International Affairs.

Bartolini, Stefano and Peter Mair. 1990. *Identity, Competition, and Electoral Availability: The Stabilization of European Electorates, 1885–1985*. Cambridge: Cambridge University Press.

References

Baughman, John and Susan C. Stokes. 1999. "From Policy Change to Preference Change? Neoliberalism and Public Opinion in Latin America." Chicago Center on Democracy, Working Paper No. 19.

Becker, Gary. 1958. "Competition and Democracy." *Journal of Law and Economics* 1:105–109.

Bosworth, Barry P., Rudiger Dornbusch, and Raúl Labán, eds. 1994. *The Chilean Economy: Policy Lessons and Challenges.* Washington, D.C.: Brookings Institution.

Brody, Richard A. and Benjamin I. Page. 1972. "The Assessment of Policy Voting." *American Political Science Review* 66:450–458.

Budge, Ian, David Robertson, and Derek Hearl, eds. 1987. *Ideology, Strategy, and Party Change: Spatial Analysis of Post-War Programs in Nineteen Democracies.* London: Cambridge University Press.

Buendía Laredo, Jorge. 2000. "Uncertainty, Incumbency, and Voting Behavior in Transitions to Democracy." Ph.D. dissertation, Political Science Department, University of Chicago.

Burggraaff, Winfield J. and Richard Millett. 1995. "More Than Failed Coups: The Crisis in Venezuelan Civil–Military Relations." In Louis W. Goodman, Johanna Mendelson Forman, Moisés Naím, Joseph S. Tulchin, and Gary Bland, eds., *Lessons of the Venezuelan Experience.* Washington, D.C.: Woodrow Wilson Center, pp. 54–78.

Burke, Edmund. 1949 [1774]. *Burke's Politics.* Ross J. S. Hoffman and Paul Levack, eds. New York: Knopf.

Butler, David, and Austin Ranney. 1994. *Referendums Around the World: The Growing Use of Direct Democracy.* Washington, D.C.: American Enterprise Institute.

Calvert, Randall. 1985. "Robustness of the Multidimensional Voting Model: Candidates' Motivations, Uncertainty, and Convergence." *American Journal of Political Science* 29:69–95.

Cambio '90. 1990. *Lineamientos del Plan de Gobierno 1990.* Lima: Cambio 90.

Cameron, Maxwell A. 1994. *Democracy and Authoritarianism in Peru: Political Coalitions and Social Change.* New York: St. Martin's Press.

Campbell, Angus, Philip E. Converse, Warren E. Miller, and Donald E. Stokes. 1960. *The American Voter.* New York: John Wiley and Sons.

Campbell, J. E. and K. A. Wink. 1990. "Trial-Heat Forecasts of the Presidential Vote." *American Politics Quarterly* 18(3):251–269.

Canes-Wrone, Brandice, Michael C. Herron, and Kenneth W. Shotts. 1999. "Pandering, Fake Leadership, and Even Some Real Leadership: A Theory of Executive Behavior." Unpublished manuscript, Massachusetts Institute of Technology.

Canitrot, Adolfo. 1993. "Crisis and Transformation of the Argentine State (1978–1992)." In William C. Smith, Carlos H. Acuña, and Eduardo A. Gamarra, eds., *Democracy, Markets, and Structural Reform in Latin America: Argentina, Bolivia, Brazil, Chile, and Mexico.* New Brunswick, N.J.: Transaction Books and the North-South Center, pp. 75–102.

Carey, John. 1996. *Term Limits and Legislative Representation*. New York: Cambridge University Press.

Carrión, Julio. 1996. "La Opinión Pública Bajo el Primer Gobierno de Fujimori: ¿De Identidades a Intereses?" In Fernando Tuesta Soldevilla, ed., *Los Enigmas del Poder: Fujimori, 1990–1996*. Lima: Fundación Friedrich Ebert.

Cheibub, José Antonio, and Adam Przeworski. 1999. "Democracy, Elections, and Accountability for Economic Outcomes." In Adam Przeworski, Susan C. Stokes, and Bernard Manin, eds., *Democracy, Accountability, and Representation*. New York: Cambridge University Press, pp. 222–249.

Conaghan, Catherine M. and James M. Malloy. 1994. *Unsettling Statecraft: Democracy and Neoliberalism in the Andes*. Pittsburgh: University of Pittsburgh Press.

Conover, Pamela, and Stanley Feldman. 1989. "Candidate Perception in an Ambiguous World: Campaigns, Cues and Inference Processes." *American Journal of Political Science* 33:912–940.

Conroy, Michael. 1990. "The Political Economy of the Nicaraguan Elections." *International Journal of Political Economy* 20:5–33.

Coppedge, Michael. 1994. *Strong Parties and Lame Ducks: Presidential Partyarchy and Factionalism in Venezuela*. Stanford, Calif.: Stanford University Press.

  1995. "Democratic Consolidation and Party-System Volatility in Latin America." Unpublished manuscript, Johns Hopkins University.

Cornejo Menacho, Diego. 1992. "Los 100 Días de Durán-Dahik." *Ecuador Debate* 27:9–21.

Crisp, Brian F. 1998. "Lessons from Economic Reform in the Venezuelan Democracy." *Latin American Research Review* 33(1):3–41.

Cukierman, Alex and Mariano Tommasi. 1998. "When Does It Take a Nixon to Go to China?" *American Economic Review* 88(1):180–197.

Daeschner, Jeff. 1993. *La Guerra del Fin de la Democracia: Mario Vargas Llosa versus Alberto Fujimori*. Lima: Peru Reporting.

Dahl, Robert A. 1956. *A Preface to Democratic Theory*. Chicago: University of Chicago Press.

  1989. *Democracy and Its Critics*. New Haven: Yale University Press.

Degregori, Carlos Iván, and Romeo Grompone. 1991. *Demonios y redentores en el nuevo Perú*. Lima: Instituto de Estudios Peruanos.

De Soto, Hernando. 1989. *The Other Path: The Invisible Revolution in the Third World*. New York: Harper and Row.

Dietz, Henry. 1985. "Political Participation in the Barriadas: An Extension and Reexamination." *Comparative Political Studies* 18(3):323–355.

Dietz, Henry and William E. Duggan. 1996. "Clases Sociales Urbanas y Comportamiento Electoral en Lima: Un Análisis de Datos Agregados." In Fernando Tuesta Soldevilla, ed., *Los Enigmas del Poder: Fujimori 1990–1996*. Lima: Fundación Friedrich Ebert, pp. 251–274.

Domínguez, Jorge I., ed. 1997. *Technopols: Freeing Politics and Markets in Latin America in the 1990s*. University Park: Pennsylvania State University Press.

  1998. "Free Politics and Free Markets in Latin America." *Journal of Democracy* 9(4):70–84.

References

Dornbusch, Rodiger and Sebastian Edwards. 1991. "The Macroeconomics of Populism." In R. Dornbusch and S. Edwards, eds., *The Macroeconomics of Populism in Latin America*. Chicago: University of Chicago Press, pp. 7–13.

Downs, Anthony. 1957. *An Economic Theory of Democracy*. New York: Harper and Row.

Dromi, Roberto. 1994. *Nuevo Estado, Nuevo Derecho*. Buenos Aires: Ciudad Argentina.

Echegaray, Fabian and Carlos Elordi. 2001. "Public Opinion, Presidential Popularity and Economic Reform in Argentina 1989–1996." In Susan C. Stokes, ed., *Public Support for Market Reforms in New Democracies*. New York: Cambridge University Press.

Edelman, Murray. 1964. *The Symbolic Uses of Politics*. Urbana: University of Illinois Press.

Edwards, Sebastian. 1995. *Crisis and Reform in Latin America: From Despair to Hope*. Washington, D.C.: The World Bank.

Eisenstadt, Shmuel N. and L. Roniger. 1984. *Patrons, Clients and Friends: Interpersonal Relations and the Structure of Trust in Society*. Cambridge and New York: Cambridge University Press.

Elster, Jon. 1989. *Nuts and Bolts for the Social Sciences*. Cambridge, Cambridge University Press.

1995. "The Impact of Constitutions on Economic Performance." *Proceedings of the World Bank Annual Conference on Development Economics 1994*, pp. 209–226.

1998. "Introduction." In Jon Elster, ed., *Deliberative Democracy*, Cambridge: Cambridge University Press, pp. 1–18.

Emden, Cecil S. 1956. *The People and the Constitution*, 2d ed. Oxford: Clarendon Press.

Enelow, James M., James W. Endersby, and Michael C. Munger. 1995. "A Revised Probabilistic Spatial Model of Elections: Theory and Evidence." In Bernard Grofman, ed., *Information, Participation, and Choice: An Economic Theory of Democracy in Perspective*. Ann Arbor: University of Michigan Press, pp. 125–140.

Fearon, James. 1999. "Electoral Accountability and the Control of Politicians: Selecting Good Types versus Sanctioning Poor Performance." In Adam Przeworski, Susan C. Stokes, and Bernard Manin, eds., *Democracy, Accountability, and Representation*. New York: Cambridge University Press, pp. 55–97.

Ferejohn, John. 1986. "Incumbent Performance and Electoral Control." *Public Choice* 50:5–25.

1995. "The Spatial Model and Elections." In Bernard Grofman, ed., *Information, Participation, and Choice: An Economic Theory of Democracy in Perspective*. Ann Arbor: University of Michigan Press, pp. 107–174.

1999. "Accountability and Authority: Toward a Theory of Political Accountability." In Adam Przeworski, Susan C. Stokes, and Bernard Manin, eds., *Democracy, Accountability, and Representation*. New York: Cambridge University Press, pp. 131–153.

Ferreira Rubio, Delia. Buenos. 1997. "Dinero y Partidos Políticos en Argentina."

In Ferreira Rubio, ed., *Financiamiento de Partidos Políticos*. pp. 17–79. Buenos Aires: CIEDLA.

Ferreira Rubio, Delia and Matteo Gorretti. 1998. "When the President Governs Alone: The *Decretazo* in Argentina, 1989–93." In John M. Carey and Matthew Soberg Shugart, eds., *Executive Decree Authority*. Cambridge: Cambridge University Press, pp. 33–61.

Figueroa, Adolfo. 1993. *Crisis Distributiva en el Perú*. Lima: Pontificia Universidad Católica del Perú.

Fiorina, Morris P. 1980. "The Decline of Collective Responsibility in American Politics." *Daedalus* 109:25–45.

1981. *Retrospective Voting in American National Elections*. New Haven: Yale University Press.

Fishel, Jeff. 1985. *Platforms and Promises*. Washington, D.C.: Congressional Quarterly Press.

Frente Sandinista de Liberación Nacional (FSLN). 1990. "Principios y programa político del Frente Sandinista de Liberación Nacional (FSLN)." In *Programas y principios de los partidos políticos en Nicaragua*. Managua: Consejo de Partidos Políticos.

Gay, Robert. 1998. "The Broker and the Thief: A Parable (Reflections on Popular Politics in Brazil)." Paper presented at the XXI International Congress of the Latin American Studies Association, Chicago, September.

Geddes, Barbara. 1994. *Politician's Dilemma: Building State Capacity in Latin America*. Berkeley: University of California Press.

Gelman, Andrew and Gary King. 1993. "Why Are American Presidential Election-Campaigns So Variable When Votes Are So Predictable?" *British Journal of Political Science* 23:409–451.

Gibson, Alan. 1991. "Impartial Representation and the Extended Republic: Towards a Comprehensive and Balanced Reading of the Tenth Federalist Paper." *History of Political Thought* 12(2):264–304.

Graham, Carol. 1991. *From Emergency Employment to Social Investment: Alleviating Poverty in Chile*. Brookings Occasional Papers. Washington, D.C.: Brookings Institution.

Grindle, Merilee S. and John W. Thomas. 1991. *Public Choice and Policy Change: The Political Economy of Reform in Developing Countries*. Baltimore: Johns Hopkins University Press.

Grossman, Herschel I. and Suk Jae Noh. 1990. "A Theory of Kleptocracy with Probablistic Survival and Reputation." *Economics and Politics* 2:157–171.

Gujarati, Damodar N. 1995. *Basic Econometrics*, 3rd ed. New York: McGraw-Hill Book Company.

Haggard, Stephan and Robert Kaufman. 1992. "Economic Adjustment and the Prospects for Democracy." In Stephan Haggard and Robert Kaufman, eds., *The Politics of Economic Adjustment: International Constraints, Distributive Conflicts, and the State*. Princeton: Princeton University Press, pp. 319–350.

1995. *The Political Economy of Democratic Transitions*. Princeton: Princeton University Press.

References

Harrington, Joseph E., Jr. 1993a. "The Impact of Reelection Pressures on the Fulfillment of Campaign Promises." *Games and Economic Behavior* 5:71–97.

1993b. "Economic Policy, Economic Performance, and Elections." *American Economic Review* 83:27–42.

Hausmann, Ricardo. 1990. "Venezuela." In John Williamson, ed., *Latin American Adjustment: How Much Has Happened?* Washington, D.C.: Institute for International Economics.

1995. "Quitting Populism Cold Turkey: The 'Big Bang' Approach to Macroeconomic Balance." In Louis W. Goodman et al., eds., *Lessons of the Venezuelan Experience*. Baltimore: Johns Hopkins University Press and the Woodrow Wilson Center, pp. 252–281.

Hibbs, Douglas A., Jr. 1977. "Political Parties and Macroeconomic Policies." *American Political Science Review* 71:1467–1487.

Hibbs, Douglas A., Jr. with Douglas Rivers and Nicholas Vasilatos. 1982. "On the Demand for Economic Outcomes: Macroeconomic Performance and Mass Political Support in the United States, Great Britain, and Germany." *The Journal of Politics* 44(2):426–462.

Hinich, Melvin J. and Michael C. Munger. 1994. *Ideology and the Theory of Political Choice*. Ann Arbor: University of Michigan Press.

Hirschman, Albert O. 1970. *Exit, Voice, and Loyalty*. Cambridge, Mass.: Harvard University Press.

1973. "The Changing Tolerance for Income Inequality in the Course of Economic Development." *Quarterly Journal of Economics* 87(4):544–566.

1977. *The Passions and the Interests: Arguments for Capitalism Before Its Triumph*. Princeton: Princeton University Press.

Hofstadter, Richard. 1969. *The Idea of the Party System: The Rise of Legitimate Opposition in the United States, 1780–1840*. Berkeley: University of California Press.

Hojman, David. 1990. "Chile After Pinochet: Aylwin's Christian Democrat Economic Policies for the 1990s." *Bulletin of Latin American Research* 9(1):25–47.

Holbrook, Thomas M. 1996. *Do Campaigns Matter?* Thousand Oaks, Ca: Sage.

Huber, John D. and G. Bingham Powell, Jr. 1994. "Congruence Between Citizens and Policymakers in Two Visions of Liberal Democracy." *World Politics* 46(3):291–326.

Iguíñiz, Javier. 1991. "Perú: ajuste e inflación en el Plan Fujimori." In *Elecciones y Política Económica en América Latina*. Buenos Aires: CEDES and TESIS, pp. 387–432.

Irish Times. 1999. "Government awards itself a high score at end of a stressful term." July 27, p. 12.

Iversen, Torben. 1994. "The Logics of Electoral Politics: Spatial, Directional, and Mobilizational Effects." *Comparative Political Studies* 27(2):155–189.

Jackisch, Carlota. 1998. "La representación política en cuestión." In Carlota Jackisch, ed., *Representación Política y Democracia*. Buenos Aires: CIEDLA, pp. 9–43.

Jackson, John E. and David C. King. 1989. "Public Goods, Private Interests, and Representation." *American Political Science Review* 83:1143–1164.

Jacobson, Gary. 1992. *The Politics of Congressional Elections*, 3rd ed. New York: HarperCollins.

Jamieson, Kathleen Hall and David S. Birdsell. 1988. *Presidential Debates: The Challenge of Creating an Informed Electorate*. New York: Oxford University Press.

Jones, Charles O. 1994. *The Presidency in a Separated System*. Washington, D.C.: Brookings Institution.

Karl, Terry Lynn. 1987. "Petroleum and Political Pacts: The Transition to Democracy in Venezuela." *Latin American Research Review* 22(1):63–97.

1997. *The Paradox of Plenty: Oil Booms and Petro-States*. Berkeley, Calif.: University of California Press.

Kay, Bruce. 1996. "'Fujipopulism' and the Liberal State in Peru, 1990–1995." *Journal of Interamerican Studies and World Affairs* 38(4):55–98.

Keck, Margaret E. 1992. *The Workers' Party and Democratization in Brazil*. New Haven: Yale University Press.

Keeler, John T. S. 1993. "Opening the Window for Reform: Mandates, Crises, and Extraordinary Decision-Making." *Comparative Political Studies* 25:4, 433–486.

Kelley, Stanley Jr. 1983. *Interpreting Elections*. Princeton: Princeton University Press.

Key, V. O., Jr. 1966. *The Responsible Electorate*. New York: Vintage Books.

King, Gary, and Michael Laver. 1993. "Party Platforms, Mandates, and Government Spending." *American Political Science Review* 87(3):744–747.

King, Gary, Michael Tomz, and Jason Wittenberg, 1998. "Making the Most of Statistical Analyses: Improving Interpretation and Presentation." Paper presented at the annual meetings of the American Political Science Association, Boston.

Kitschelt, Herbert. 1989. "The Internal Logics of Parties: The Law of Curvilinear Disparity Revisited." *Political Studies* 37:400–421.

Kitschelt, Herbert, Zdenka Mansfeldova, Radoslaw Markowski, and Gábor Tóka. 1999. *Post-Communist Party Systems: Competition, Representation, and Inter-Party Cooperation*. Cambridge: Cambridge University Press.

Klaiber, Jeffrey. 1990. "Fujimori: Race and Religion in Peru." *America* 15.

Klingemann, Hans-Dieter, Richard I. Hofferbert, and Ian Budge. 1994. *Parties, Policies, and Democracy*. Boulder, Colo.: Westview Press.

Kornblith, Miriam and Daniel Levine. 1995. "Venezuela: The Life and Times of a Party System." In Scott Mainwaring and Timothy R. Scully, eds., *Building Democratic Institutions: Party Systems in Latin America*. Stanford, Calif.: Stanford University Press, pp. 37–71.

Krukones, Michael G. 1984. *Promises and Performance: Presidential Campaigns as Policy Predictors*. Lanham, Md.: University Press of America.

Landé, Oscar H. 1977. "The Dyadic Basis of Clientelism." In Steffan W. Schmidt, Laura Guasti, Karl H. Landé, and James C. Scott, eds., *Friends, Followers, and Factions: A Reader in Political Clientelism*. Berkeley: University of California Press, pp. xiii–xxxvi.

Lazersfeld, Paul, Bernard Berelson, and Hazel Gaudet. 1944. *The People's Choice*. New York: Columbia University Press.

References

Levine, Daniel. 1973. *Conflict and Change in Venezuela*. Princeton: Princeton University Press.

Levitsky, Steven Robert. 1999. "From Laborism to Liberalism: Institutionalization and Labor-Based Party Adaptation in Argentina (1983–1997)." Ph.D. dissertation, Department of Political Science, University of California, Berkeley.

Lewis-Beck, Michael. 1988. *Economics and Election: The Major Western Democracies*. Ann Arbor: University of Michigan Press.

Lizano, Eduardo. 1991. *Economic Policy Making: Lessons from Costa Rica*. San Francisco: ICS Press.

Madison, James. 1982 [1787]. *The Federalist Papers*. Ed. by Gary Wills. New York: Bantam Books.

Mainwaring, Scott P. 1999. *Rethinking Party Systems in the Third Wave of Democratization: The Case of Brazil*. Stanford, Calif.: Stanford University Press.

Mainwaring, Scott P. and Timothy R. Scully. 1995. "Introduction." In Scott Mainwaring and Timothy R. Scully, eds., *Building Democratic Institutions: Party Systems in Latin America*. Stanford, Calif.: Stanford University Press, pp. 1–34.

Manin, Bernard. 1997. *Principles of Representative Government*. New York: Cambridge University Press.

Manin, Bernard, Adam Przeworski, and Susan C. Stokes. 1999. "Elections and Representation." In Adam Przeworski, Susan C. Stokes, and Bernard Manin, eds., *Democracy, Accountability, and Representation*. New York: Cambridge University Press, pp. 29–54.

Maravall, José María. 1999. "Accountability and Manipulation." In Adam Przeworski, Susan C. Stokes, and Bernard Manin, eds., *Democracy, Accountability, and Representation*. New York: Cambridge University Press, pp. 154–196.

Martinelli, Cesar and Mariano Tomassi. 1994. "Sequencing of Economic Reforms in the Presence of Political Constraints." UCLA Working Paper 701, June.

Martz, John. 1982. "Peligros de la petrificación: El sistema de los partidos venezolanos y la década de los 80." In Enrique A. Baloyra and Rafael López Pintor, eds., *Iberoamérica en los años 80: Perspectivas de cambio social y político*. Madrid: Centro de Investigaciones Sociológicas, pp. 149–187.

　1995. "Political Parties and the Democratic Crisis." In Louis W. Goodman, Johanna Mendelson Forman, Moisés Naím, Joseph S. Tulchin, and Gary Bland, eds., *Lessons of the Venezuelan Experience*. Baltimore: Johns Hopkins University Press and the Woodrow Wilson Center, pp. 31–53.

May, John D. 1973. "Opinion Structure of Political Parties: The Special Law of Curvilinear Disparity." *Political Studies* 21(2):133–151.

Mayhew, David R. 1974. *Congress: The Electoral Connection*. New Haven: Yale University Press.

McGuire, James W. 1997. *Peronism without Perón: Unions, Parties, and Democracy in Argentina*. Stanford, Calif.: Stanford University Press.

McKelvey, Richard D. 1976. "Intransitivities in Multidimensional Voting Models and some Implications for Agenda Control." *Journal of Economic Theory* 12:472–482.

McKelvey, Richard D. and Peter C. Ordeshook. 1986. "Information, Electoral Equilibria, and the Democratic Ideal." *Journal of Politics* 48:909–937.

Menem, Carlos and Eduardo Duhalde. 1989. *La Revolución Productiva*. Buenos Aires: Peña Lillo.

Mill, John Stuart. 1962 [1861]. *Considerations on Representative Government*. South Bend, Ind.: Gateway.

Miller, Warren E. and Donald E. Stokes. 1966. "Constituency Influence in Congress." In Angus Campbell, Philip E. Converse, Warren E. Miller, and Donald E. Stokes, eds., *Elections and the Political Order*. New York: Wiley, pp. 351–372.

Morgan, Robert J. 1974. "Madison's Theory of Representation in the Tenth Federalist." *The Journal of Politics* 36(4):852–885.

Nagle, J. 1996. "Social Choice in a Pluralitarian Democracy: The Politics of Market Liberalization in New Zealand." Unpublished manuscript, Department of Political Science, University of Pennsylvania.

Naím, Moisés. 1993. *Paper Tigers and Minotaurs: The Politics of Venezuela's Economic Reforms*. Washington, D.C.: Carnegie Endowment for International Peace.

Nelson, Joan M. 1990. "Introduction: The Politics of Economic Adjustment in Developing Nations." In Joan Nelson, ed., *Economic Crisis and Policy Choice: The Politics of Adjustment in the Third World*. Princeton: Princeton University Press, pp. 1–32.

  1992. "Poverty, Equity, and the Politics of Adjustment." In Stephan Haggard and Robert Kaufman, eds., *The Politics of Economic Adjustment: International Constraints, Distributive Conflicts, and the State*. Princeton: Princeton University Press, pp. 221–269.

Neuman, Russell W. 1986. *The Paradox of Mass Politics: Knowledge and Opinion in the American Electorate*. Cambridge, Mass.: Harvard University Press.

Nun, José. 1994. "Post-modern Politics? The Paradoxes of Peronism." Unpublished manuscript, School of Advanced Studies in the Social Sciences, Banco Patricios Foundation, Buenos Aires.

O'Donnell, Guillermo. 1994. "Delegative Democracy?" *Journal of Democracy* 5(1):55–69.

O'Donnell, Guillermo and Phillipe Schmitter. 1986. *Transitions from Authoritarian Rule: Tentative Conclusions*. Baltimore, Md.: Johns Hopkins University Press.

Offe, Claus. 1984. *Contradictions of the Welfare State*. Cambridge, Mass: MIT Press, pp. 179–206.

Oquist, Paul. 1992. "The Sociopolitical Dynamics of the 1990 Nicaraguan Elections." In Vanessa Castro and Gary Prevost, eds., *The 1990 Elections in Nicaragua and Their Aftermath*. Lanham, Md.: Rowman & Littlefield, pp. 1–40.

Page, Benjamin, I. and Robert Y. Shapiro, 1992. *The Rational Public: Fifty Years of Trends in American Policy Preferences*. Chicago: University of Chicago Press.

Paldam, Martin. 1991. "How Robust Is the Vote Function?: A Study of Seventeen Nations Over Four Decades." In Helmut Northop, Michael S. Lewis-Beck, and Jean-Dominique Lafay, eds., *Economics and Politics: The Calculus of Support*. Ann Arbor: University of Michigan Press, pp. 9–31.

References

Palermo, Vicente and Marcos Novaro. 1996. *Política y Poder en el Gobierno de Menem*. Buenos Aires: Grupo Editorial Norma.

Pastor, Manuel, Jr. and Carol Wise. 1992. "Peruvian Economic Policy in the 1980s: From Orthodoxy to Heterodoxy and Back." *Latin American Research Review* 27(2):83–117.

Petras, James F. and Fernando Ignacio Leiva. 1994. *Democracy and Poverty in Chile: The Limits to Electoral Politics*. Boulder, Colo.: Westview Press.

Pitkin, Hanna Fenichel. 1967. *The Concept of Representation*. Berkeley: University of California Press.

Planas, Pedro. 1996. "Existe un Sistema de Partidos en el Perú?" In Fernando Tuesta Soldevilla, ed., *Los Enigmas del Poder: Fujimori 1990–1996*. Lima: Friedrich Ebert, pp. 169–201.

Pole, J. R. 1983. *The Gift of Government: Political Responsibility from the English Restoration to American Independence*. Athens: University of Georgia Press.

Popkin, Samuel. 1991. *The Reasoning Voter*. Chicago: University of Chicago Press.

Powell, G. Bingham, Jr. 1990. "Holding Governments Accountable: How Constitutional Arrangements and Party Systems Affect Clarity of Responsibility for Policy in Contemporary Democracies." Paper presented at the meetings of the American Political Science Association, San Francisco.

Przeworski, Adam. 1993. "Economic Reform, Public Opinion, and Political Institutions: Poland in the Eastern European Perspective." In Luis Carlos Bresser Pereira, José María Maravall, and Adam Przeworski, *Economic Reforms in New Democracies: A Social-Democratic Perspective*. New York: Cambridge University Press, pp. 132–198.

Przeworski, Adam and John Sprague. 1986. *Paper Stones: A History of Electoral Socialism*. Chicago: University of Chicago Press.

Przeworski, Adam and Michael Wallerstein. 1982. "The Structure of Class Conflict in Democratic Capitalist Societies." *American Political Science Review* 76:215–238.

Rabinowitz, George and Stewart McDonald. 1989. "A Directional Theory of Issue Voting." *American Political Science Review* 83:93–121.

Ranney, Austin. 1975. *Curing the Mischief of Faction: Party Reform in America*. Berkeley: University of California Press.

Rehfeld, Andrew. 2000. "Silence of the Land: An Historical and Normative Analysis of Territorial Political Representation in the United States." Ph.D. dissertation, Department of Political Science, University of Chicago.

Remmer, Karen L. 1990. "Democracy and Economic Crisis: The Latin American Experience." *World Politics* 52(3):315–355.

    1991. "The Political Impact of the Economic Crisis in Latin America in the 1980s." *American Political Science Review* 85(3):777–800.

Riker, William H. 1980. "Implications from the Disequilibrium of Majority Rule for the Study of Institutions." *American Political Science Review* 74(2):432–446.

Roberts, Kenneth M. and Moisés Arce. 1998. "Neoliberalism and Lower-Class Voting Behavior in Peru." *Comparative Political Studies* 31(2):217–246.

Roberts, Kenneth M. and Erik Wibbels. 1999. "Party Systems and Electoral Volatility in Latin America: A Test of Economic, Institutional, and Structural Explanations." *American Political Science Review* 93(3):575–590.

Rosenstone, Steven J. 1983. *Forecasting Presidential Elections*. New Haven: Yale University Press.

Saborío, Sylvia. 1990. "Central America." In John Williamson, ed., *Latin American Adjustment: How Much Has Happened?* Washington, D.C.: Institute for International Economics.

Salmon Jordan, Jorge. 1993. *Entre la Vanidad y el Poder: Memoria y Testimonio*. Lima: Editorial Apoyo.

Salmore, Barbara and Stephen Salmore. 1989. *Candidates, Parties, and Campaigns*. 2nd edition. Washington, D.C.: CQ Press.

Sartori, Giovanni. 1976. *Parties and Party Systems: A Framework for Analysis*, vol. 1. New York: Cambridge University Press.

Schady, Norbert. 2000. "The Political Economy of Expenditures by the Peruvian Social Fund (FONCODES), 1991–1995." *American Political Science Review* 94(2):289–304.

Schattschneider, E. E. 1942. *Party Government*. New York: Rinehart and Company.

Schemo, Diana Jean. 1997. "Ecuadoreans Rally in Drive to Oust President." *New York Times*, February 2.

Schmidt, Gregory D. 1996. "Fujimori's 1990 Upset Victory in Peru: Electoral Rules, Contingencies, and Adaptive Strategies." *Comparative Politics* 28(3):321–354.

Schuler, Mary. 1994. "An Inquiry into the Logic Behind President Carlos Menem's Policy Shift." Unpublished manuscript, University of Chicago.

Scott, James C. 1969. "Corruption, Machine Politics, and Political Change." *American Political Science Review* 63(4):1142–1158.

Shugart, Matthew and John Carey. 1992. *Presidents and Assemblies*. Cambridge: Cambridge University Press.

Silva, Eduardo. 1996. "From Dictatorship to Democracy: The Business–State Nexus in Chile's Economic Transformation, 1975–1994." *Comparative Politics* 28(3):299–320.

Smith, William C. 1991. "State, Market, and Neoliberalism in Post-Transition Argentina." *Journal of Interamerican Studies and World Affairs* 33(4):45–82.

Smith, William C., Carlos H. Acuña, and Eduardo A. Gamarra, eds. 1993. *Democracy, Markets, and Structural Reforms in Latin America: Argentina, Bolivia, Brazil, Chile, and Mexico*. New Brunswick, N.J.: Transaction Books and the North-South Center.

Sniderman, Paul, Richard A. Brody, and Philip A. Tetlock. 1991. *Reasoning and Choice: Explorations in Political Psychology*. Cambridge: Cambridge University Press.

Sniderman, Paul, J. James M. Glaser, and Robert Griffin. 1990. "Information and Electoral Choice." In John Ferejohn and J. Kuklinski, eds., *Information and Democratic Processes*. Urbana: University of Illinois Press, pp. 117–135.

References

Southern Cone Report. 1995, No. 6 (August).

Stahler-Sholk, Richard. 1990. "Stabilization, Destabilization, and the Popular Classes in Nicaragua, 1979–1988." *Latin American Research Review* 25(3):55–88.

1995. "The Dog That Didn't Bark: Labor Autonomy and Economic Adjustment in Nicaragua under the Sandinista and UNO Governments." *Comparative Politics* 28:77–102.

Stigler, George J. 1975. *The Citizen and the State: Essays on Regulation*. Chicago: University of Chicago Press.

Stimson, James A. 1999. "Party Government and Responsiveness." In Adam Przeworski, Susan C. Stokes, and Bernard Manin, eds., *Democracy, Accountability, and Representation*. New York: Cambridge University Press, pp. 197–221.

Stimson, James A., Michael B. Mackuen, and Robert S. Erikson. 1995. "Dynamic Representation." *American Political Science Review* 89:543–565.

Stokes, Donald E. 1966. "Spatial Models of Party Competition." In Angus Campbell, Philip E. Converse, Warren E. Miller, and Donald E. Stokes, eds., *Elections and the Political Order*. New York: Wiley, pp. 161–179.

Stokes, Susan C. 1995. *Cultures in Conflict: Social Movements and the State in Peru*. Berkeley: University of California Press.

1999. "Political Parties and Democracy." In Nelson Polsby, ed., *Annual Review of Political Science*, vol 2. Palo Alto, Calif.: Annual Reviews, pp. 243–267.

2001a. "Public Opinion of Market Reforms: A Framework." In Susan C. Stokes, ed., *Public Support for Market Reforms in New Democracies*. New York: Cambridge University Press.

2001b. "Economic Reform and Public Opinion in Fujimori's Peru." In Susan C. Stokes, ed., *Public Support for Market Reforms in New Democracies*. New York: Cambridge University Press.

Templeton, Andrew. 1995. "The Evolution of Popular Opinion." In Louis W. Goodman, Johanna Mendelson Forman, Moisés Naím, Joseph S. Tulchin, and Gary Bland, eds., *Lessons of the Venezuelan Experience*. Baltimore: Johns Hopkins University Press and the Woodrow Wilson Center, pp. 79–114.

Thompson, Dennis F. 1976. *John Stuart Mill and Representative Government*. Princeton: Princeton University Press.

Tommasi, Mariano and Andrés Velasco. 1995. "Where Are We in the Political Economy of Reform?" Unpublished manuscript, Harvard–MIT RTG in Positive Political Economy.

Tuesta Soldevilla, Fernando. 1996. "El Impacto del Sistema Electoral sobre el Sistma Político Peruano." In Fernando Tuesta Soldevilla, ed., *Los Enigmas del Poder: Fujimori 1990–1996*. pp. 129–168.

Tullock, Gordon. 1988. "Rents and Rent-Seeking." In Charles K. Rowley, Robert Tollison, and Gordon Tullock, eds., *The Political Economy of Rent-Seeking*. Boston: Kluwer Academic Publishing, pp. 51–66.

Valenzuela, Arturo. 1978. *The Breakdown of Democratic Regimes: Chile*. Baltimore: Johns Hopkins University Press.

1994. "Party Politics and the Crisis of Presidentialism in Chile: A Proposal for a Parliamentary Form of Government." In Juan J. Linz and Arturo

Valenzuela, eds., *The Failure of Presidential Democracy: The Case of Latin America*, vol 2. Baltimore: Johns Hopkins University Press, pp. 91–150.

Vargas Llosa, Mario. 1993. *El Pez en el Agua: Memorias*. Barcelona: Seix Barral.

Verbitsky, Horacio. 1991. *Robo para la Corona: Los Frutos Prohibidos del Arbol de la Corrupción*. Buenos Aires: Planeta.

1993. *Hacer La Corte: La Construcción de un Poder Absoluto sin Justicia ni Control*. Buenos Aires: Planeta.

Vowles, Jack. 1995. "The Politics of Electoral Reform in New Zealand." *International Political Science Review* 16(1):95–115.

Weffort, Francisco. 1992. "New Democracies, Which Democracies?" Working Paper, Woodrow Wilson Center for Scholars.

Wills, Garry. 1981. *Explaining America: The Federalist*. New York: Doubleday.

Wilson, Bruce M. 1999. "Leftist Parties, Neoliberal Policies, and Reelection Strategies: The Case of the PLN in Costa Rica." *Comparative Political Studies* 32(6):752–779.

Wilson, James Q. and Edward Banfield. 1963. *City Politics*. Cambridge, Mass: Harvard University Press.

Wittman, Donald A. 1977. "Candidates with Policy Preferences: A Dynamic Model." *Journal of Economic Theory* 14:180–189.

Yashar, Deborah J. 1995. "Civil War and Social Welfare: The Origins of Costa Rica's Competitive Party System." In Scott Mainwaring and Timothy R. Scully, eds., *Building Democratic Institutions: Parties and Party Systems in Latin America*. Stanford, Calif.: Stanford University Press.

Zaller, John R. 1992. *The Nature and Origins of Mass Opinion*. New York: Cambridge University Press.

Zielinsky, Jacob. 1997. "Dynamic Agency and Overlapping Generations." Unpublished manuscript, University of Chicago.

Author Index

Abramowitz, Alan, 175
Achen, Chris, 31n
Acuña, Carlos, 77
Aldrich, John, 66, 103
Alesina, Alberto, 10, 27, 83, 106–107
Alvarez, Angel, 134
Alvarez, Michael, 151
Alvarez, Norma, 105
Anderson, Christopher, 176
Angell, Allen, 32, 34
APSA, 103
Arce, Moisés, 145
Arnold, Douglas, 11
Arriagada Herrera, Genaro, 32, 33
Arrow, Kenneth, 124
Austen-Smith, David, 9, 167

Banco Central de Ecuador, 45
Banfield, Edward, 105
Banks, Jeffrey, 8, 10, 82, 167
Barnes, William, 37
Barreto, Wilson, 81
Barry, Albert, 32
Barry, Brian, 9
Bartels, Larry, 31n, 151, 167, 175, 180
Bartolini, Stefano, 119
Becker, Gary, 10, 81
Berelson, Bernard, 174
Birdsell, David, 175
Bosworth, Barry, 34
Brody, Richard, 175
Budge, Ian, 9

Buendía Laredo, Jorge, 151
Burggraaff, Winfield, 55n
Burke, Edmund, 6, 104, 156–158, 161, 168, 169, 172, 176, 177
Butler, David, 184

Calvert, Randall, 10, 106
Cameron, Maxwell, 52, 57
Campbell, Angus, 174
Campbell, J. E., 175
Canes-Wrone, Brandice, 10
Canitrot, Adolfo, 77
Carey, John, 42, 91
Cheibub, José Antonio, 167
Conaghan, Catherine, 57, 111
Conover, Pamela, 175
Conroy, Michael, 35
Converse, Philip, 174
Coppedge, Michael, 39, 105, 112, 114, 119
Cornejo Menacho, Diego, 44, 111
Crisp, Brian, 134
Cukierman, Alex, 84

Daeschner, Jeff, 73
Dahl, Robert, 18, 160
Datos, S. A., 134n
Degregori, Carlos Iván, 52
Dietz, Henry, 52
Domínguez, Jorge, 5, 9–10, 28, 67, 122–123, 125, 153
Dornbusch, Rodiger, 27, 34

211

Downs, Anthony, 7–8, 88, 108, 174
Drazen, Allen, 27
Duhalde, Eduardo, 45

Echegaray, Fabián, 77, 137, 138
Edelman, Murray, 16
Edwards, Sebastian, 27
Eisenstadt, Shmuel, 105
Elordi, Carlos, 77, 137, 138
Elster, Jon, 2, 68, 157, 194
Emden, Cecil, 168, 169n
Endersby, James, 16
Enelow, James, 16
Erickson, Robert, 31n

Fearon, James, 16
Feldman, Stanley, 175
Ferejohn, John, 10, 11, 12, 22, 82,
    108, 174, 182, 193
Ferreira Rubio, Delia, 81, 91
Fiorina, Morris, 103, 151n, 167, 174
Fischel, Jeff, 8

Gamarra, Eduardo, 77
Gaudet, Hazel, 174
Gay, Robert, 105
Geddes, Barbara, 27
Gelman, Andrew, 175
Gibson, Alan, 160
Glaser, James, 175
Gorreti, Matteo, 91
Graham, Carol, 32, 33
Greenberg, Stanley, 37n
Griffin, Robert, 175
Grindle, Merilee, 27
Grompone, Romeo, 52
Grossman, Herschel, 11
Gujarati, Damodar, 95

Haggard, Stephan, 27
Harrington, Joseph, 10n, 60n, 62ff,
    107n, 193
Hartington, Marquess of, 154, 168
Hausmann, Ricardo, 39, 54, 55, 80n,
    193
Hearl, Derek, 9

Herron, Michael, 10
Hibbs, Douglas, 175
Hinich, Melvin, 8, 193
Hirschman, Albert, 67, 86, 108, 109, 143
Hofferbert, Richard, 9
Hofstadter, Richard, 104
Hojman, David, 34
Holbrook, Thomas, 175
Huber, John, 90

Iguíñiz, Javier, 49, 53
Iversen, Torbin, 108

Jackisch, Carlota, 5
Jackson, John, 31n
Jacobson, Gary, 103
Jamieson, Kathleen Hall, 175
Jones, Charles, 182

Karl, Terry Lynn, 39
Kaufman, Robert, 27
Kay, Bruce, 145
Keck, Margaret, 31
Keeler, John, 8
Kelley, Stanley, 171, 172, 183, 184
Key, V. O., 151n, 167, 174
King, David, 31n
King, Gary, 9, 117n, 175
Kitschelt, Herbert, 105, 108
Klaiber, Jeffrey, 52
Klingemann, Hans-Dieter, 9, 90, 104,
    174, 188
Kornblith, Miriam, 39
Krukones, Michael, 8

Labán, Raúl, 34
Landé, Oscar, 105
Latin American Weekly Reports, 43
Laver, Michael, 9
Lazersfeld, Paul, 174
Leiva, Fernando Ignacio, 34
Levine, Daniel, 39
Levitsky, Steven, 105, 114
Lewis-Beck, Michael, 167
Lizano, Eduardo, 42
Luxembourg, Rosa, 104

MacKuen, Michael, 31n
Madison, James, 104, 158ff, 172–173,
 176, 177
Mainwaring, Scott, 103, 105
Mair, Peter, 119
Malloy, James, 57, 111
Manin, Bernard, 10, 12, 161ff, 177,
 178
Mansfeldova, Zdenka, 105
Maravall, José María, 184
Markowski, Radoslaw, 105
Martinelli, Cesar, 55
Martz, John, 39, 68
May, John, 108
Mayhew, David, 8
McDonald, Stewart, 175
McGuire, James, 46, 114, 195
McKelvey, Richard, 124, 175
Michels, Robert, 104
Mill, John Stuart, 163–164, 169–172,
 173, 176ff
Miller, Warren, 31n, 174
Millett, Richard, 55n
Morgan, Robert, 160
Munger, Michael, 8, 16, 193

Nagle, Jack, 165
Naim, Moisés, 54, 69, 114
Nelson, Joan, 27
Neuman, Russell, 175
Noh, Suk Jae, 11
Novaro, Marcos, 71n, 72, 91
Nun, José, 72

O'Donnell, Guillermo, 5, 9, 18ff, 59,
 122, 153, 154
Offe, Claus, 104
Oquist, Paul, 35, 36
Ordeshook, Peter, 175

Page, Benjamin, 31n, 175
Paldam, Martin, 107
Palermo, Vicente, 71n, 72, 91
Pastor, Miguel, 40, 41
Petras, James, 34
Pitkin, Hanna F., 18, 163

Pole, J. R., 168
Pollack, Benny, 32, 34
Popkin, Samuel, 175
Powell, G. Bingham, 11, 90, 101n,
 167, 188
Przeworski, Adam, 10, 31, 105, 138,
 167, 186

Rabinowitz, George, 175
Ranney, Austin, 103, 104, 184
Rehfeld, Andrew, 159
Remmer, Karen, 125
Riker, William, 124
Roberts, Kenneth, 56, 145
Robertson, David, 9
Roniger, L., 105
Rosenstone, Steven, 175

Saborío, Sylvia, 42
Salmon Jordan, Jorge, 73
Salmore, Barbara, 175
Salmore, Stephen, 175
Sartori, Giovanni, 104
Schady, Norbert, 145
Schattschneider, E. E., 103
Schemo, Diana Jean, 112
Schmidt, Gregory, 48n, 50n, 51n
Schmitter, Phillipe, 59
Schuler, Mary, 46
Scott, James, 105
Scully, Timothy, 103
Shapiro, Robert, 31n, 175
Shotts, Kenneth, 10
Shugart, Matthew, 91
Silva, Eduardo, 33, 34
Smith, William, 46, 47, 77
Sniderman, Paul, 175
Speer, Stephen, 10, 83, 106–107
Sprague, John, 31, 105
Stahler-Sholk, Richard, 35, 37
Stigler, George, 10, 11, 81
Stimson, James, 31n, 176
Stokes, Donald, 31n, 132, 174
Stokes, Susan, 10, 52, 107n, 138, 143,
 146
Sundaram, Rangarajan, 10, 82

Tanaka, Martín, 51n
Templeton, Andrew, 135
Tetlock, Philip, 175
Thomas, John, 27
Thompson, Dennis, 170
Tóka, Gábor, 105
Tommasi, Mariano, 27, 55, 84
Tomz, Michael, 117n
Tullock, Gordon, 10

Valenzuela, Arturo, 105
Velasco, Andrés, 27
Verbitsky, Horacio, 80
Vowles, Jack, 165

Wallerstein, Michael, 186
Weffort, Francisco, 4
Wibbels, Erik, 56
Wills, Gary, 160
Wilson, Bruce, 42, 125
Wilson, James, 105
Wink, K. A., 174
Wise, Carol, 40, 41
Wittenberg, Jason, 117
Wittman, Donald, 10, 106

Yashar, Deborah, 42

Zaller, John, 190–191
Zielinsky, Jacob, 107

Subject Index

abortion, 86, 182
Acción Popular (AP, Peru), 111
accountability, 5–6, 153, 165
AD, *see* Democratic Action
Aerolíneas Argentinas (Argentina
  Airlines), 72, 75
Alfonsín, Raúl, 38, 45, 46, 77, 193
Alsogaray, Alvaro, 47, 127
Alva Castro, Luís, 51n
Andean Commission of Jurists, 55n
Andean Report, 148
Angeloz, Eduardo, 45, 72, 127
anti-shock (*see also* fiscal adjustment), 2,
  50
Apoyo, 48, 74, 130, 143, 146
APRA (Peru), 40, 47–48, 51, 111
ARENA (El Salvador), 119
Argentina, 30, 38, 45, 71–72, 74,
  80–81, 89, 114
  inflation, 46–47, 75–77, 126, 137,
    138, 152
  and mass neoliberalism, 136ff
  reelection of policy switcher, 5,
    126–129, 138–139
Arias, Oscar, 38, 55n
Armijos, Ana Lucía, 113
Australia, 2
Aylwin, Patricio, 32, 33–34, 41, 58, 73

Balaguer, Joaquín, 38, 42
Banzer, Hugo, 42–43, 113
Bárbaro, Julio, 71, 82n

Barco, Virgilio, 38
Barrantes, Alfonso, 40, 48, 51n, 52
Batle, Jorge, 31
Bayes's rule, 14–15, 180, 181
  and policy switches, 60
Belaúnde Terry, Fernando, 39–40, 52,
  194
Belgium, 90
beliefs
  of politicians, 24, 56, 65, 67, 68–78,
    186–187
  of voters, 24, 60–63, 186–187,
    192–194
Betancur, Belisario, 118
Blair, Tony, 3
Blanco, Carlos, 68, 77
Blancos (Uruguay), 30
Bolivia, 30, 84, 92, 114
  1985 presidential campaign, 113,
    116
  1989 presidential campaign, 42
Bordón, José, 136
Borja, Rodrigo, 43–44, 84, 111
Brazil, 30, 67, 79, 80, 120
Bridas (Argentina), 71
Bristol, 156
Bucaram, Abdalá, 1, 111
Büchi, Hernán, 34
Bulgheroni, Carlos, 71
Bunge y Born, 46, 71, 81, 82n
Bunge y Born plan, 47
Bush, George H. W., 2, 69, 165, 183

Cafiero, Antonio, 72
Caldera, Rafael, 39, 148
Calderón, Rafael, 55n, 83, 84
Cambio90 (Change90, Perú), 48, 51, 130
Camdessus, Michel, 70
Canitrot, Adolfo, 77
Cardoso, Fernando Henrique, 67n
Cardozo, Rubén, 71
Carriaga, Juan, 113–114
Cavallo, Domingo, 47, 137, 192
Cavallo plan (see also convertibility plan), 138
Chamorro, Violeta, 26n, 35–38, 43, 84
changing calculus of support, 124, 126ff, 132, 135–136
Chávez Frías, Hugo, 59n, 134
Chile, 58, 59, 120
  under Allende, 105
  1988 plebiscite, 34
  1989 presidential campaign, 32–35, 41
China, 84
Chirac, Jacques, 42n
Christian Democratic Party (Partido Demócrata Cristiano, Chile), 32, 33
Clarín, 46, 77
CODESA (Costa Rica), 42
Cole, Jonathan, 114
Collor, Fernando, 30, 79, 80
Colombia, 38, 116, 188–189
Colorados (Uruguay), 30–31
Comparative Manifestos Project, 8, 90, 104, 188
Conable, Barber, 70
Concertación (Chile), 32–34, 38, 41, 73
Confederación General de Trabajadores (CGT, Argentina), 46, 114
Confederación General de Trabajadores del Perú (CGTP), 49
Conservative Party (Partido Conservador, Colombia), 119

Consultores, 21, 135n, 149n
convertibility plan, 47, 137
COPEI (Venezuela), 38, 54, 59n, 74
Corzo, Julio, 71
Costa Rica, 38, 55n, 83, 84, 114, 117, 119, 120
credibility of campaigns, 26, 31–32
Cristiani, Alfredo, 119
cycling majorities (see also changing calculus of support), 124, 129

Dahik, Alberto, 79–80
Danish voters, 176
debt, 51, 83
  in campaign debates, 2, 39, 46, 47, 51
  crisis, 21–22, 93
delegative democracy, 4, 154
Democracia y Progreso (Democracy and Progress, Chile), 34
democracy, quality of, 21, 172, 196
Democratic Action (Acción Democrática, Venezuela), 38–39, 53, 59n, 84, 114–115, 118
Democratic Left (Izquierda Democrática, Ecuador), 43, 84, 111
Democratic Party (United States), 177
De Soto, Alvaro, 70
De Soto, Hernando, 69, 111
Díaz, Rodolfo, 76
distinction requirement, 164
Dominican Republic, 38, 43, 84
  next election after a switch, 5
Dominican Revolutionary Party (PRD), 84
Dromi, Roberto, 71, 75, 80–81
Duarte, Napoleón, 38
Durán Ballen, Sixto, 44, 79–80, 83, 84, 111, 112, 116

economic crisis, and policy switches, 29–30
Ecuador, 1, 43–45, 79, 83, 84, 111, 112, 114, 116
efficiency-oriented policies, 2, 13–15,

19, 25ff, 43, 50, 55n, 56, 58, 59, 62, 68, 71, 75, 80, 87, 89, 92, 186
elections
as selection of types, 16–17
aristocratic theory of (*see also* Manin, Bernard), 161ff
campaigns as educational, 179ff
close, 35, 58–59
competitiveness of, 26, 58, 187
as involving retrospective judgments, 167–168, 174–175
volatility of outcomes, 112, 115–116, 119
El Salvador, 38, 119
Erman González, Antonio, 47
Errázuriz, Francisco Javier, 34n
exchange rate policies, 53, 54, 86
in campaign debates, 54

Febres Cordero, León, 84, 111
Federalist Papers, 158–160
Fernández, Eduardo, 54
Fianna Fáil (Ireland), 184
Figueres, José María, 84
Figueroa, Adolfo, 50, 69, 70
fiscal adjustment, 53, 54, 75
in campaign debates, 47, 49, 50, 72
Foxley, Alejandro, 33
FREDEMO (Peru), 110, 130
Frepaso (Argentina), 136
Fujimori, Alberto, 45, 48, 57, 83, 193
1990 presidential campaign, 2, 12, 50–52, 81, 110, 116
during 1990 transition, 69–72, 77, 82, 111
1995 reelection, 145–148
background, 48, 52–53
majority status, 91
policies in first term, 53
and public opinion, 124, 129–133, 142–148
and term limits, 67n

García, Alan, 26–27n, 38, 39–41, 48, 51n, 52, 58, 69, 70, 194
and term limits, 67n

Gladstone, William, 154, 168
Godoy, Virgilio, 36
González, Felipe, 184
Gran Virage (*see* Great Turnaround)
Great Britain, 3–4, 46, 72, 154, 157, 162, 185
Great Turnaround, 54, 55, 78, 82, 85, 114–115, 133, 135, 148–149
Guatemala, 119

Heckman selection model, 95, 98
Herrera Campins, Luís, 39
Honduras, 38, 119
Hurtado Miller, Juan Carlos, 111

ideology, 56, 62, 83–85, 107, 192–194
IESA (Institute for Advanced Study of Administration, Venezuela), 114
Iglesias, Enrique, 70
imperative mandates, 165
independence of representatives, 155ff, 178–182
Independent Liberal Party (PLI, Nicaragua), 36
inflation (*see also under* Argentina, Peru, and Venezuela), 117, 124
as a campaign issue, 46, 48–51, 126, 129, 134–135, 137–139, 152
and policy switches, 29–31, 75, 88, 97
and voter information, 88, 138, 178
Interamerican Development Bank (IDB), 55n, 70
International Monetary Fund (IMF), 37, 39, 41, 51, 54, 70, 82, 83, 111, 193
intertemporal framing, 138

Japan, 70
Jorge Blanco, Salvador, 84

Kohan, Alberto, 71

Labor Party (New Zealand), 165
Lacalle, Ernesto, 30–31, 116
Lacayo, Antonio, 37
Lepage, Octavio, 53

Liberal Unionist Party (Great Britain), 168
Lula, Luiz Ignacio da Silva, 30–31
Lusinchi, Jaime, 38, 39, 53, 68, 78, 134n

Machiavelli, Nicolo, 75
majority status of governments, 65, 90–92, 101, 188
Malvinas/Falkland Islands, 46
mandates
  definitions of, 4, 168
  as informal contracts, 109, 182
  legality of (*see also* imperative mandates), 12
  and representation, 5–6, 19
markets, and pressure to switch policies, 26, 75–76
Martínez Móntola, Ricardo, 69
mass neoliberalism (*see also* beliefs, of voters), 123, 136ff, 153
Mayorga, Francisco, 36, 37
Menem, Carlos
  in 1989 campaign, 2, 12, 45–47, 71–72, 74, 76, 77, 81–82, 114
  corruption, 80
  first term, 89, 91
  and labor unions, 46
  and public opinion, 124, 126–129, 136ff
  and term limits, 67n
Mexico, 139
MNR, *see* Movimiento Nacionalista Revolucionario
Monge, Luis Alberto, 42, 43, 125
Movimiento Libertad (Peru), 110
Movimiento Nacionalista Revolucionario (MNR, Bolivia), 57, 113–114, 118
Movement of the Revolutionary Left (MIR, Bolivia), 84, 92

National Democratic Action (ADN, Bolivia), 92
National Liberation Party (PLN, Costa Rica), 42, 55n, 84, 118, 125

National Opposition Union (Unión Nacional Opositor, UNO, Nicaragua), 35, 37, 38
Nebot, Jaime, 44, 111
neoliberalism (*see also* efficiency-oriented policies), 23, 27, 29, 31, 52, 55, 64, 71, 73, 74, 79, 84, 92, 138, 153, 195
Netherlands, 90
New Economic Program (Nuevo Programa Económico, Bolivia), 92, 113–114
New Route, 44–45, 83, 112
New Zealand, 2, 165, 185
Nicaragua, 30, 32
  1990 presidential elections, 35–38
Nixon, Richard, 84
North Atlantic Treaty Organization (NATO), 184
Norwegian voters, 176
NPE (*see also* New Economic Program [Nuevo Programa Económico]), 57, 113–114
Nuevo Rumbo, *see* New Route

opinions of constituents (*see also* beliefs), 155
Ortega, Daniel, 35–37, 58, 59

Paredes, Pablo Lucio, 83, 112
Partido Popular Cristiano (Peru), 110
patronage, 105
Paz Estenssoro, Víctor, 56, 57, 113, 193
Paz Zamora, Jaime, 84, 91
Peel, Sir Robert, 169n
Pérez, Carlos Andrés, 45, 53–55, 56, 58, 77, 82, 83, 84, 114, 193
  in 1988 campaign, 2, 53–55, 68–69, 74
  impeachment, 80
  and public opinion, 124, 135, 148–150
Pérez de Cuellar, Javier, 70, 111
Peronist Party (also Partido Justicialista, Argentina), 45, 76,

84, 129, 136, 139
Peru, 30, 38, 45, 47–53, 69–71, 110,
112, 114, 116, 119
1992 coup, 120n, 132
inflation, 41, 48–51, 129, 143
and mass neoliberalism, 142ff
reelection of policy switcher, 5,
129–133, 146, 148
Peruvian Social Fund (FONCODES),
145, 146n
petitions, 168
Pinochet, Augusto, 32, 33, 34, 73
plural voting, 169
political parties, 22
age of, 115–119, 188
and clientelism, 108, 120–121
and law of curvilinear disparity,
107–110, 121
overlapping generations models of,
106–110, 121
and representation, 106 passim
policy switches
number in Latin America, 12
and rent-seeking, 11
and subsequent reelection, 5, 125
privatization, 37, 53, 75, 80
in campaign debates, 47, 54, 72, 75

Ramos, Julio, 71
Rapanelli, Nestor, 46
referendums, 184
Reform Bill of 1832, 169n
Reina, Carlos Roberto, 38
reliability, 8, 18, 88
rent-seeking, 180
models of democracy, 6
and policy switches, 9–11, 20, 64–
65
and representation, 18
representation
definitions, 18, 155
and democracy, 4–5, 155
descriptive, 163
model of violation of mandates,
18–20, 60–64, 88, 123, 130
Republican Party (U.S.), 165

responsiveness, 7
definition of, 9
and representation, 155, 178
and unresponsiveness, 18
revolución productiva, 45, 77
Ribadeneira, Mario, 112
Roca, Santiago, 50, 69, 70
Rodríguez, Miguel, 69
Roig, Miguel, 46
Romer and Associates, 126n, 127, 192

Sachs, Jeffrey, 113
salariazo, 46, 47, 77
Samper, Ernesto, 38
Sánchez de Lozada, Gonzálo, 114
Sandinista Front for National
Liberation (FSLN), 35–38
Sandinista National Workers' Front
(FNT), 37
Sanguinetti, Julio, 38
School of Higher Studies in
Administration (ESAN, Peru), 50
security-oriented policies, 2, 12–14,
25–26, 28–31, 38–39, 43, 45, 53,
56, 58, 59, 62, 68, 71, 75, 80, 83,
87, 89, 92, 95, 97, 125n, 132
Shining Path (Sendero Luminoso,
Peru), 40, 77, 132
Smith, Roberto, 114
Social Christian Party (Partido Social
Cristiano, Ecuador), 44, 111,
112
Socialist Party (Partido Socialista,
Chile), 32, 33
Sourrouille, Juan, 45
spatial models of party competition, 6,
7–9, 123, 130

Tamworth Manifesto, 169n
term limits, 21, 65–66, 67n, 89, 92,
99–100
Tinoco, Pedro, 114
Tories (Britain), 169n
Torres, Herbert, 115
trade liberalization, 53
in campaign debates, 54

transition to democracy, 59
  years elapsing since, 30n, 33, 115,
  120
Triaca, Jorge, 46

Ubaldini, Saúl, 46, 114
Uchuraccay, 48n
Ugarteche, Oscar, 69
uncertainty, 58, 60–63, 65, 86–87, 95,
  187–188
unemployment, 19, 30, 32, 39, 42, 47,
  49, 139, 143
  as a campaign issue, 31, 46, 49, 127,
  134n, 138–139, 152
  and voter information, 86, 138, 178,
  181, 191
Unified Republican Party (Partido
  Unidad Republicana, Ecuador),
  44, 112
Unión Cívica Radical (Radical Party,
  Argentina), 46, 47, 127
Unión del Centro Democrático
  (UCD, Argentina), 45, 46, 47,
  127
United Left Coalition (Izquierda
  Unida, Peru), 40, 48, 111
United Nations (UN), 70, 111
United Social Christian Party (Costa

Rica), 55n
United States, 165, 171, 174, 176,
  180, 185
Uruguay, 30, 31, 38, 116
utilitarianism, 168

vague campaigns, 28, 41–43
valence issues, 132, 134, 176
Vargas Llosa, Mario, 48, 55n, 57, 74,
  91
  1990 presidential campaign, 49–50,
  51, 52, 56, 58, 73, 110, 129–131
Venezuela, 38–39, 45, 68–69, 114–
  115
  1989 election campaign, 53–55, 84,
  118, 134
  corruption, 134, 135
  coup attempts, 134, 148
  impeachment, 80, 149
  inflation, 68, 134–135, 148
  next election after a switch, 5
  public opinion, 148–149
  under second Pérez administration,
  1, 133–134
Villarán, Fernando, 72, 77

West Germany, 2, 185
World Bank, 54, 70, 75

Continuation of other books in the series

Torben Iversen, Jonas Pontusson, David Soskice, eds., *Unions, Employers, and Central Banks: Macroeconomic Coordination and Institutional Change in Social Market Economies*

Thomas Janoski and Alexander M. Hicks, eds., *The Comparative Political Economy of the Welfare State*

Robert O. Keohane and Helen B. Milner, eds., *Internationalization and Domestic Politics*

Herbert Kitschelt, *The Transformation of European Social Democracy*

Herbert Kitschelt, Peter Lange, Gary Marks, and John D. Stephens, eds., *Continuity and Change in Contemporary Capitalism*

Herbert Kitschelt, Zdenka Mansfeldova, Radek Markowski, and Gabor Toka, *Post-Communist Party Systems*

David Knoke, Franz Urban Pappi, Jeffrey Broadbent, and Yutaka Tsujinaka, eds., *Comparing Policy Networks*

Allan Kornberg and Harold D. Clarke, *Citizens and Community: Political Support in a Representative Democracy*

David D. Laitin, *Language Repertories and State Construction in Africa*

Mark Irving Lichbach and Alan S. Zuckerman, eds., *Comparative Politics: Rationality, Culture, and Structure*

Doug McAdam, John McCarthy, and Mayer Zald, eds., *Comparative Perspectives on Social Movements*

Scott Mainwaring and Matthew Soberg Shugart, eds., *Presidentialism and Democracy in Latin America*

Anthony W. Marx, *Making Race, Making Nations: A Comparison of South Africa, the United States and Brazil*

Joel S. Migdal, Atul Kohli, and Vivienne Shue, eds., *State Power and Social Forces: Domination and Transformation in the Third World*

Ton Notermans, *Money, Markets, and the State: Social Democratic Economic Policies since 1918*

Paul Pierson, *Dismantling the Welfare State? Reagan, Thatcher and the Politics of Retrenchment*

Marino Regini, *Uncertain Boundaries: The Social and Political Construction of European Economies*

Yossi Shain and Juan Linz, eds., *Interim Governments and Democratic Transitions*

Theda Skocpol, *Social Revolutions in the Modern World*

David Stark and László Bruszt, *Postsocialist Pathways: Transforming Politics and Property in East Central Europe*

Sven Steinmo, Kathleen Thelan, and Frank Longstreth, eds., *Structuring Politics: Historical Institutionalism in Comparative Analysis*

Sidney Tarrow, *Power in Movement: Social Movements and Contentious Politics*

Ashutosh Varshney, *Democracy, Development, and the Countryside*